The Popular Wobbly

The Popular Wobbly

Selected Writings of T-Bone Slim

T-Bone Slim

Edited by Owen Clayton and Iain McIntyre

Foreword by David R. Roediger

MINNESOTA

University of Minnesota Press
Minneapolis
London

Franklin Rosemont, "Homage to T-Bone Slim," from *Morning of a Machine Gun* (Chicago: Surrealist Editions, 1968) is published with permission from Penelope Rosemont. "A Man Called America" from Ville-Juhani Sutinen, *Hobon elämän mysteerit: T-Bone Slimin jalanjäljillä* (The mysteries of a hobo's life: In the footsteps of T-Bone Slim) (Palladium Books, 2018) is translated from the Finnish by and reprinted with permission from the author.

Published by the University of Minnesota Press
111 Third Avenue South, Suite 290
Minneapolis, MN 55401–2520
http://www.upress.umn.edu

ISBN 978-1-5179-1495-0 (hc)
ISBN 978-1-5179-1496-7 (pb)

Library of Congress record available at https://lccn.loc.gov/2024061926

Printed in the United States of America on acid-free paper

34 33 32 31 30 29 28 27 26 25 10 9 8 7 6 5 4 3 2 1

For Franklin,
for keeping the flame alive

Contents

1923

1924

1925

1926

1927

1928–1929

1930

1931–1932

1933–1936

1937–1939

1940–1942

Responses to T-Bone Slim

Foreword

David R. Roediger

Allen Ginsberg's beat poetry classic "America" includes lots of things at a rapid-fire pace, not unlike T-Bone Slim's relentless language. Among them is a plea for the appreciation of a left-wing past. We might balk at the poem's asking of America: "When will you be *worthy* of your million *Trotskyites*?" Both the wishful math—if the United States had ever had a million Trotskyists, they would have sorted their own memorialization(s)—and the supposition that the United States could be summoned to make good the memory of radicals are questionable. But Ginsberg's confession that "I feel sentimental about the Wobblies" will seem irresistible to many readers of this collection. "America" shares the great historian E. P. Thompson's desire to spare those who struggled for a new world from the "enormous condescension of posterity." I do, too, on balance.

I thought a lot about condescension, its opposites, and what it means to remember ancestors in digesting this glorious collection. The book's editors aptly encourage readers to sample the book in small chunks, as Slim's gems came to his editors at the newspapers published by the Industrial Workers of the World (IWW or Wobblies). They converted his words from careful penmanship to type, parceled out to readers in small bites. I had a deadline to write this foreword and did read all of the book in one sitting, just as I read Franklin Rosemont's first collection of T-Bone Slim's work, *Juice Is Stranger Than Friction,* when that volume was in production thirty-three years ago. Rosemont and I both worked then to sustain the world's oldest radical labor publisher, the Charles H. Kerr Company, which bears some discussion below.

Much as I now look forward to rereading the book's selections over a period of months (three jokes and a song at a throw), the overconsumption of T-Bone has its own advantages. It takes us into his astonishingly creative world, one so wide and wonderful that we begin to think it is possible to write and think like Slim, seeing the endless variations on the same joke at the parasitic boss's expense at every turn, even if it remains impossible to reproduce Slim's matchless wordplay and invention of language. In such quantity we begin to credit his tongue-in-cheek bravado in pegging himself as a giant of literature and philosophy. We believe his madcap humor and sober truths because his brilliance hews so close to our everyday experiences even as his creative impulse remains beyond us.

All of Slim's inspired bragging betrays not a bit of condescension toward lesser souls among fellow workers. Even jokes about clueless, boss-believing workers are clearly directed at a system and allow the probability that those it robs will see through that which victimizes them. The Charles H. Kerr translation of labor's anthem, "The Internationale," rendered a key line as "We want no condescending saviors." Slim wanted no part of being such an on-high deliverer from evil. He instead cherished the great ambition "to be a party to all current heartaches, want and oppression—we desire no special privilege." He got his share of such misery partly while incarcerated, spending time in jails where, as a later tribute poem by Rosemont puts it, the "crocodiles slept in unopened envelopes."

Nor did Slim condescend to his readers, many of whom, like himself, came from childhood homes where languages other than English thrived and lacked any but rudimentary formal education. So much of our recent left newspaper press dumbs down from even the grade six or so reading level for which the commercial newspapers long strove, especially the left papers produced by those with elite educations. Wobbly publications are thus a revelation, offering much in the way of allusions to high literature and, in Slim's case, intricate and constant playfulness with language, while also taking care to be clear. The trust was not that everyone would understand every reference or word but that they would do their best to comprehend the meaning.

Hard knocks proved to be part of what made Slim the most popular Wobbly writing for the *Industrial Worker.* Above all, he shared hunger as a frequent reality and took food as an arena for desire, redress, renewal, and liberation. The Marxist–humanist thinker Raya Dunayevskaya once noted that the abolitionist and feminist fighter Sojourner Truth's very name defined a surpassing social location and philosophy. So surely did T-Bone Slim's moniker.

The editors underline how perilously close we came to losing T-Bone Slim's history and artistry. I was there as it was rescued. The Kerr Company had long reproduced classic, even canonical, work in the Marxist tradition, from Marx's *Capital* in its initial English translation to Paul Lafargue's extraordinary *The Right to Be Lazy.* Founded in 1886, the company faltered by the 1980s as militants from the Proletarian Party, who had heroically kept the press afloat for decades, died. The older activists who agreed to take Kerr forward (especially Fred Thompson, Theo Waldinger, Virgil Vogel, Carlos Cortez, and Joe Giganti) brought on then-young people like Penelope Rosemont, Franklin Rosemont, and myself. We all revered the Kerr Company as a treasure.

Thompson, the great Wobbly organizer and historian—sometimes in younger days he had been the IWW editor bringing Slim's columns to press in the *Industrial Worker*—spoke at first of providing a "decent burial" for the company. We ended up reviving it, first with reprints from Marx, Eugene V. Debs, and the labor organizer Mary "Mother" Jones. Soon we preserved not only the words of relatively well known radicals but also the out-of-print and uncollected works of writers such as Lucy Parsons, Voltairine de Cleyre, Covington Hall (who is present in this volume as Covami, interviewing Slim), Ben Fletcher, Clarence Darrow, Mary Marcy, and, for all his reluctance, Thompson himself.

Franklin's pitch (the company stayed perpetually broke and agonized over what to print) for Kerr to publish *Juice Is Stranger Than Friction* was the easiest sell possible. Older board members loved Slim. Many of the younger editors and volunteers (young on the left often means forty or fifty) doubled as members of the Chicago Surrealist Group. As such, we embraced the idea of featuring someone exemplifying the power of the imagination and of dreams, a writer showing studied disrespect and disregard for the state, and one seeming to illustrate Sigmund Freud's insistence and ours that humor is rebellious.

Even so, the way in which the Kerr Company continued to be committed to the recovery and recirculation of revolutionary voices generally (and Slim's in particular) ought not be taken for granted. Even as we brought these books to fruition, many of us would have agreed with Marx that the "social revolution . . . cannot draw its poetry from the past, but only from the future." We had inherited a world capable of producing revulsion and despair, and at times the New Leftists among us understandably suspected that we would find little in the long-ago words of even revolutionary ancestors. There were new social struggles and new surrealist projects that commanded our attention.

Perhaps the history of the Kerr Company kept us remembering. Maybe it was the surrealist movement's habit of not only recalling its own history but also searching for "precursors" to surrealist views. In any event, we decided that we wanted our radical ancestors recognized as bards, thinkers, dreamers, and fighters. Especially in the case of Slim, I am delighted that we did, and that others—in a still more terrible planetary crisis—have brought more of his brilliant and challenging words to new readers.

Introduction

Mysteries of a Hobo's Life

Owen Clayton and Iain McIntyre

T-Bone Slim is an enigma. A man of many names, he was largely unknown even to the people who knew him best. A hobo and transient worker in the early twentieth-century United States, he led a peripatetic lifestyle, never truly revealing himself to anyone. To some he was T-Bone Slim, a comic philosopher, a musician, and the best prose writer that the radical union the Industrial Workers of the World (IWW, also known as the Wobblies) ever produced, referred to by fellow worker Harvey O'Connor as the "Laureate of the Logging Camps."[1] To others he was Matti Valentinpoika Huhta, the name he was given when he was born in Ashtabula, Ohio, the son of Priita Johanna Anderssdotter Huhtaketo (also known in the United States as Brita Johanna Huhta) and Matt Mattsson Leppihuhta (known as Matt Huhta), immigrants from Finland who had arrived in the United States in 1879.[2] He was born on 14 February 1882, and his middle name means "Son of Valentine," a poetic epithet that may speak to the creativity of his family lineage but also anticipated his future as a columnist, poet, and songwriter. He sometimes used the names Matt Arlund and its anglicized version, Matt Arnold. At other times he was known as Matt Houghton, an anglicized version of Huhta that several of his family members adopted, though Slim seems to have used this name only in his youth and on rare occasions afterward. And on yet further occasions he became Joseph Hilger, a name with which he sometimes signed letters to his family and which, upon his arrest in New York City in 1939, he gave to the authorities.[3] This final name was an homage to Joe Hill, the famous IWW martyr and musician, with whom Slim clearly identified.[4]

Along with these shifting identities, T-Bone Slim presents many mysteries to those trying to understand his life and work. Indeed, it has become something of an in-joke that anyone studying T-Bone Slim will inevitably encounter weird coincidences, paradoxical occurrences, and suggestive but inconclusive puzzles. One such is the fact that as a nineteen-year-old, Slim was among a group of hoisters on the Hanna Docks in Erie, Pennsylvania, who saw the body of his father, Matti Huhta Sr., a gang boss on the docks, floating in the water. The local newspapers portrayed the death as a suicide, citing a note that blamed Slim's mother for running off with "a festive boarder."[5] The death took place during a fractious strike, and so there is some suspicion that there may be more to this story than meets the eye. In any case, as you will see in this collection, drowning is a topic that Slim returned to frequently in his work, sometimes writing from the perspective of a person watching someone in the water, as if reenacting the trauma of his father's death, and sometimes imagining himself drowning. To this we must add the fact that at age sixty, in May 1942, Slim died under similarly mysterious circumstances, his lifeless body found in New York City's East River. Was his death accidental, did he kill himself, or was he a victim of political or mob violence aimed at silencing his antiwar voice?[6] We don't know. His death may have been the inspiration for the novel *The Savage Streets* (1956), written by Floyd Miller, a Communist double agent who worked on the New York City waterfront at the same time as Slim, spied on Trotskyites (and even on Trotsky himself) for Joseph Stalin, and collaborated with the FBI. In Miller's novel (one of the worst pieces of fiction ever written, by the way), a "philosophical Wobbly" is murdered and his death passed off as accidental drowning after he discovers a drug-smuggling operation run by the mob.[7] Was the novel based on Slim? We don't know.[8] It seems appropriate that one of Slim's most famous songs is "Mysteries of a Hobo's Life."[9]

Another mystery is why Slim was forgotten so soon after his death. Although he had been a prominent writer for the IWW and well known on the left more generally, memory of Slim and his work vanished without a trace for three-quarters of a century. As the surrealist poet Franklin Rosemont put it, "T-Bone Slim won for himself a total exclusion from academic histories and textbooks of American literature, a distinction legions of lesser writers, before or since, have found it nearly impossible to obtain."[10] Rosemont played a crucial role in keeping Slim's flickering memory alive during the latter half of the twentieth century by pursuing research independently for decades without the resources of a university behind him, work for which he deserves a great deal of praise. The end result was, until now, the only published collection of Slim's work: *Juice Is Stranger Than Friction: Selected Writings of T-Bone Slim,* produced in 1992 by the Charles H. Kerr Company. Unfortunately, copies of *Juice* are now extremely difficult to find, in part because of a recent surge of interest in Slim, which is one reason we believe that this is the right moment for a new volume of selected works. Another reason is that in the years since *Juice,* and following Rosemont's own death in 2009, many new facts about and works by T-Bone Slim have been unearthed, including an archive in the possession of Slim's living descendants. Although one of Rosemont's interviewees had hyperbolically claimed, "I don't think he [Slim] ever had a family. I don't think he was ever even born—he just growed," we now know much more about Slim's family background and his early influences.[11] A two-year KONE-funded research project led by Kirsti Salmi-Niklander has also provided a great deal of new information about Slim, much of which we gratefully cite in this Introduction.[12] This project has produced an online database and corpus of all of Slim's known writings, so those of you who would like more Slim after reading this book now have a wonderful resource available.[13]

Matti Huhta's Early Life

Among the facts recently uncovered thanks to research led by Salmi-Niklander, ably assisted by Lotta Leiwo, is that Slim knew Finnish not only well enough to speak it but to write in it fluently as well.[14] This has significant implications for thinking about the development of his literary style, as we will discuss later. Salmi-Niklander and Leiwo also discovered that as a young man in Erie, Slim, along with other family members, was a member of the Lutheran Tyyni Temperance Society, for which he worked as a "literary agent," which most likely means that he handled the society's correspondence.[15] Given his frequent comments about alcohol and later accusations about drunkenness that were made against him by his wife, it is possible that as a man who drank, at least until Prohibition, Slim was rebelling against the enforced sobriety of his youth. It is also important to think of him as a person who seems to have lost his religious faith at some point. In their research, Salmi-Niklander and Leiwo uncovered his earliest known publication, a letter written in Finnish under the name Mathew Houghton. Published on 1 January 1903 in the Ashtabula paper *Amerikan Sanomat,* this letter was aimed at correcting earlier correspondence that the newspaper had received claiming that the temperance society had held a Christmas party above a saloon. Mathew Houghton's reply states that this was not the case, that the party was actually held in the upstairs of a butcher shop, and then goes on to depict the program of the event. In addition to the very fact that it is in Finnish, this letter is notable for being the earliest known example of Slim (as Houghton) correcting an inaccurate newspaper story. This is a theme that would continue throughout his writing career.[16]

During his childhood in Ashtabula, Slim would have attended (though for how many years is unknown) the Ashtabula Harbor School system, which provided both primary and secondary education. Research by local Ashtabula historian May Colling reveals that the Harbor schools, built originally to accommodate the children of settlers from New England, were soon populated mostly by Finnish immigrants.[17] The education that was provided to Anglicized immigrants included what F. R. Leavis would famously call the "The Great Tradition": a canon of traditional British and Anglophone U.S. American literature, as well as a smattering of Greco-Roman classics.[18] This literary background would influence Slim enormously, as can be seen in his frequent references to figures from this "Great Tradition," such as William Shakespeare, Thomas Gray, Charles Dickens, Henry Wadsworth Longfellow, and Seneca the Younger. His frequent use of trochaic tetrameter, which is often and somewhat misleadingly known as "*Kalevala* meter," after the famous

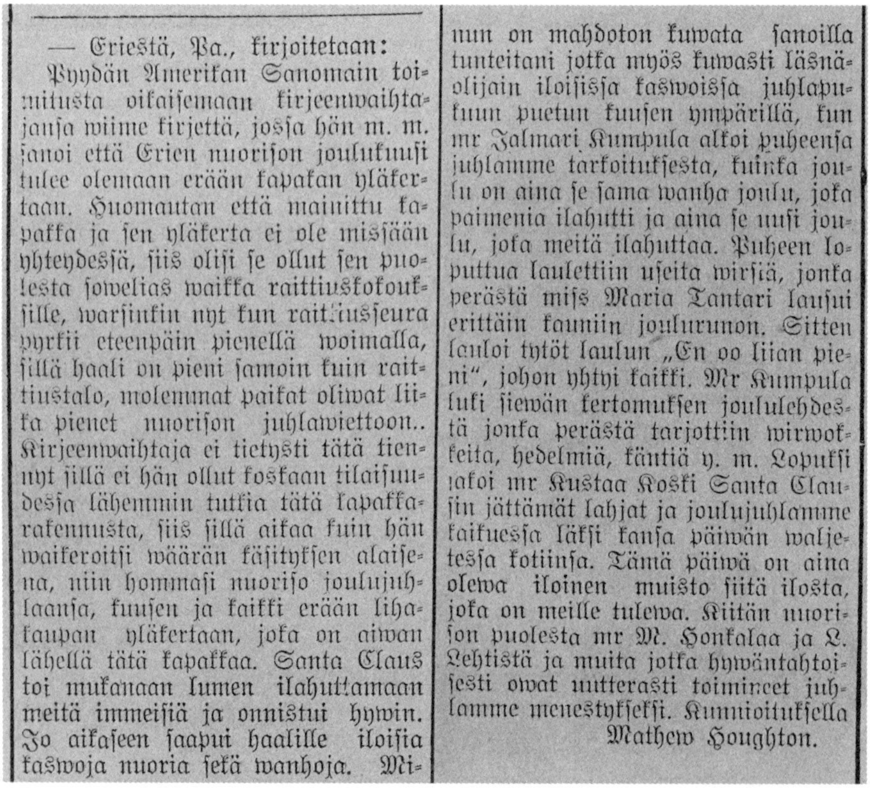

— Eriestä, Pa., kirjoitetaan:

Pyydän Amerikan Sanomain toimitusta oikaisemaan kirjeenwaihtajansa wiime kirjettä, jossa hän m. m. sanoi että Erien nuorison joulukuusi tulee olemaan erään kapakan yläkertaan. Huomautan että mainittu kapakka ja sen yläkerta ei ole missään yhteydessä, siis olisi se ollut sen puolesta sowelias waikka raittiuskokouksille, warsinkin nyt kun raittiusseura pyrkii eteenpäin pienellä woimalla, sillä haali on pieni samoin kuin raittiustalo, molemmat paikat oliwat liika pienet nuorison juhlawiettoon.. Kirjeenwaihtaja ei tietysti tätä tiennyt sillä ei hän ollut koskaan tilaisuudessa lähemmin tutkia tätä kapakkarakennusta, siis sillä aikaa kuin hän waikeroitsi wäärän käsityksen alaisena, niin hommasi nuoriso joulujuhlaansa, kuusen ja kaikki erään lihakaupan yläkertaan, joka on aiwan lähellä tätä kapakkaa. Santa Claus toi mukanaan lumen ilahuttamaan meitä immeisiä ja onnistui hywin. Jo aikaseen saapui haalille iloisia kaswoja nuoria sekä wanhoja. Minun on mahdoton kuwata sanoilla tunteitani jotka myös kuwasti läsnäolijain iloisissa kaswoissa juhlapukuun puetun kuusen ympärillä, kun mr Jalmari Kumpula alkoi puheensa juhlamme tarkoituksesta, kuinka joulu on aina se sama wanha joulu, joka paimenia ilahutti ja aina se uusi joulu, joka meitä ilahuttaa. Puheen loputtua laulettiin useita wirsiä, jonka perästä miss Maria Tantari lausui erittäin kauniin jouluruunon. Sitten lauloi tytöt laulun „En oo liian pieni", johon yhtyi kaikki. Mr Kumpula luki siewän kertomuksen joululehdestä jonka perästä tarjottiin wirwokkeita, hedelmiä, käntiä y. m. Lopuksi jakoi mr Kustaa Koski Santa Clausin jättämät lahjat ja joulujuhlamme kaikuessa läksi kansa päiwän waljetessa kotiinsa. Tämä päiwä on aina olewa iloinen muisto siitä ilosta, joka on meille tulewa. Kiitän nuorison puolesta mr M. Honkalaa ja L. Lehtistä ja muita jotka hywäntahtoisesti owat uutterasti toimineet juhlamme menestykseksi. Kunnioituksella

Mathew Houghton.

Scan of a letter to the editor by Mathew Houghton, *Amerikan Sanomat,* 1 January 1903.

Karelian epic poem of the same name, suggests an indirect Finnish influence as well.[19] Slim's knowledge of *Kalevala* meter is not proof that he had read the *Kalevala,* though it is likely that a copy of this text would have been held by the library of the temperance society.[20] If he had in fact read this epic poem, then the fact that he does not, to our knowledge, ever reference it directly in his writings may indicate a desire to "Americanize" himself by leaning more toward Anglophone influences. This admittedly speculative hypothesis finds tentative evidence in the fact that the overwhelming majority of Slim's writings are in English, even though the IWW published a popular Finnish-language paper, *Industrialisti,* in which articles by Slim appeared, sometimes in English and sometimes in translation.[21]

It is likely that Slim worked as a hoister on the docks in Ashtabula from a young age, work that we know he definitely undertook once the family moved to Erie, Pennsylvania, at the end of the nineteenth century. When the Huhtas moved, they opened up a boardinghouse, but this does not seem to have been a very happy time for the family. In January 1901 Slim's father was found

Slim in his early twenties. Newberry Library, Rosemont–T-Bone Slim Research Collection.

drowned in Lake Erie, allegedly having killed himself after Priita Johanna had eloped with a lover. Whether or not she actually did this, Slim's mother was once again running the boardinghouse, where Slim also resided, in 1903 when the house was the scene of a knife attack between two drunken boarders.[22] By this time Slim was recently married, and he and his new wife were living at the boardinghouse, presumably because of a lack of money. Between his family's situation and the hard manual labor required as a hoister at the Hanna Docks, it is fair to say that Slim's early years, like those of many young people from immigrant and working-class backgrounds, were tough.

On 25 May 1902, in Buffalo, New York, Huhta had married Rosa Mathilda Kotila, who, according to Salmi-Niklander and Leiwo, would have been unable to speak English very well, if at all, having immigrated to the United States only in August 1901.[23] We can assume, then, that the language the couple

Matt and Rosa Huhta. Newberry Library, Rosemont–T-Bone Slim Research Collection.

spoke at home was Finnish. By 1906 at the latest, but probably sometime earlier, they moved out of the Huhta boardinghouse.[24] It is unclear whether their early life together was happy or not, but by 1910, and presumably sometime before, the couple were in conflict. As John Westmoreland, a musician and T-Bone Slim researcher who is also Slim's great-grandnephew, has uncovered, on 7 December 1910 Rosa had Matt arrested on charges of nonsupport.[25] Slim

Matt and Rosa Huhta with their young son Paul. Newberry Library, Rosemont–T-Bone Slim Research Collection.

could not afford bail, so presumably he spent some time in jail, perhaps for the first but certainly not for the last time.[26] In addition to low pay, drink may have been a factor in Slim's failure to support his wife financially. Seemingly finding his family burdensome, he abandoned Rosa and their four children in 1912, taking to the road as a hobo. For a variety of legal and practical reasons, this was a form of escapism that at the time was far more open to men than to women.[27] Though we admire Slim as a writer, it is hard not to be critical of him for this action. Indeed, it was his abandonment of his family that caused him to be largely forgotten by his ancestors until John Westmoreland decided to investigate his hidden family heritage. In 1915 Rosa sued for divorce, citing her husband's "habitual drunkenness," "willful absence," and "gross neglect of duty," which included failing to provide the family with "the common necessities of life." The divorce was granted in January 1916.[28]

Becoming T-Bone Slim

The court's divorce records indicate that Slim's whereabouts were by this time unknown. Nor can we shed much light on the subject, though it seems probable that he was living the life of a transient worker, moving in seasonal patterns from harvest work to lumber camps to railroading, and spending the winter in the "main stem" of a city such as Duluth or Chicago. In one of his articles, he claims to have been introduced to the concept of industrial unionism in 1916. Though with Slim we can never be certain that his biographical references are true (and many are obviously not intended to be taken seriously), if this statement is accurate, then 1916 may have been the year in which he first became a Wobbly. We do not think he served in World War I, a war to which, like the IWW generally, he was opposed. He was drafted, and his draft card shows him as an unemployed millwright living in a hotel in Minneapolis, Minnesota, in 1918, using the name Matt Arlund, a slightly Anglicized version of a family surname.[29] Having multiple names may have made it easier to evade the call-up. By 1919, he seems to have switched to using Matt Arnold, perhaps simply as an even more Anglicized form of the family name, or possibly as an homage to the famous English poet Matthew Arnold. Either way, as John Westmoreland also discovered, "Matt Arnold" was arrested and jailed for illegally riding a freight train in July 1919 near Aberdeen, South Dakota—he was one of a group of thirteen harvest hands whom the local paper claimed were all IWW members.[30] Having pled guilty and then spent more than two months in jail awaiting sentencing, Slim wrote a poem titled "Only a Mouse in Jail" (seemingly a nod to Robert Burns's famous poem "To a Mouse"), which would be published in the *Aberdeen American* on 7 September 1919. If "Only a Mouse in Jail" is by Slim (and we think it is), then, at least until other material comes to light, it stands as his first published poem.[31]

His first publication in the IWW press, in April 1920, would be what is today his best-known song, "The Popular Wobbly." The song explores the experiences of men like those pulled off the train in Aberdeen, punished for their political beliefs by the railroad police, judges, and many others. This theme of political persecution, carried off with trademark Wobbly humor, would be a persistent thread throughout his work. At the time of the song's publication, he had not yet adopted the name T-Bone Slim, and so the enigmatic "???" was credited as the author of "The Popular Wobbly." By the time he came to write his first prose piece for the Wobbly press, an article titled "An Earfull," published on 2 April 1921, he had hit upon the moniker by which he would become best known.

The IWW provided the milieu in which Slim would write and publish for the rest of his life, and the organization's basic precepts and analysis of society furnished the political and social framework for his work. He also drew on the caustic and often black humor of the union, which was most typically found in its songs and cartoons. Although he was not alone in doing so, one of Slim's impacts was to extend and entrench stoic humor within the organization's press, adding a measure of spice and satire alongside more didactic and serious accounts of union beliefs and activities. As his columns proved highly popular and became key features within IWW newspapers, Slim was lauded by the union's members, and he in turn thanked them for treating him as a "favored child."[32]

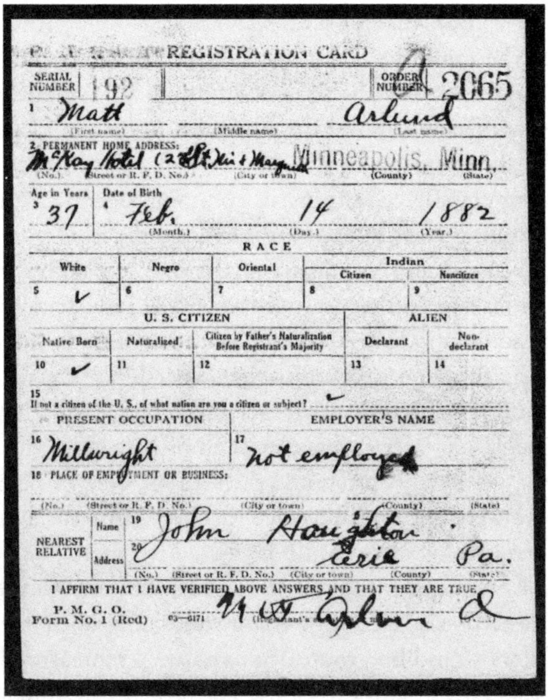

REGISTRATION CARD

SERIAL NUMBER 192 | ORDER NUMBER A 2065

1 Matt (First name) (Middle name) Arlund (Last name)

2 PERMANENT HOME ADDRESS: McKay Hotel (2nd St. Nic & Marquette) Minneapolis, Minn.
(No.) (Street or R. F. D. No.) (City or town) (County) (State)

Age in Years	Date of Birth			
3 37	4 Feb. (Month.)		14 (Day.)	1882 (Year.)

RACE

White	Negro	Oriental	Indian	
			Citizen	Noncitizen
5 ✓	6	7	8	9

U. S. CITIZEN			ALIEN	
Native Born	Naturalized	Citizen by Father's Naturalization Before Registrant's Majority	Declarant	Non-declarant
10 ✓	11	12	13	14

15 If not a citizen of the U. S., of what nation are you a citizen or subject? —

PRESENT OCCUPATION	EMPLOYER'S NAME
16 Millwright	17 not employed

18 PLACE OF EMPLOYMENT OR BUSINESS:
(No.) (Street or R. F. D. No.) (City or town) (County) (State)

NEAREST RELATIVE — Name: 19 John Haughton. Address: 20 Erie Pa.
(No.) (Street or R. F. D. No.) (City or town) (County) (State)

I AFFIRM THAT I HAVE VERIFIED ABOVE ANSWERS AND THAT THEY ARE TRUE.

P. M. G. O. Form No. 1 (Red) 63—6171 (Registrant's signature or mark)

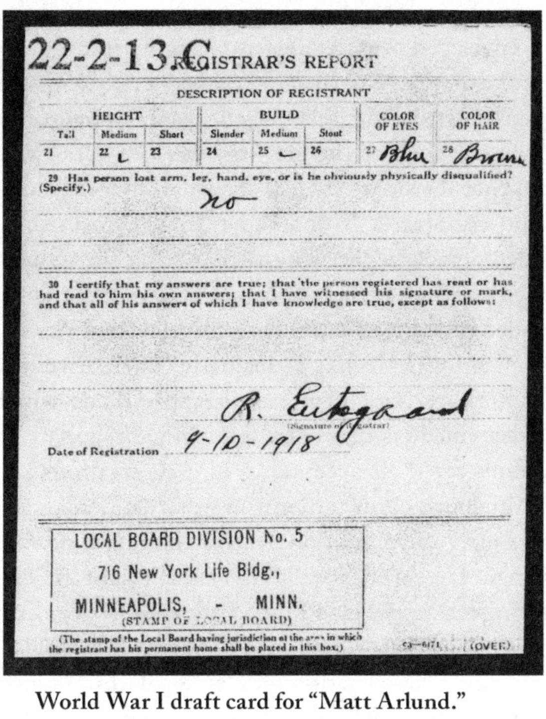

22-2-13 C REGISTRAR'S REPORT

DESCRIPTION OF REGISTRANT

HEIGHT			BUILD			COLOR OF EYES	COLOR OF HAIR
Tall	Medium	Short	Slender	Medium	Stout		
21	22 ✓	23	24	25 ✓	26	27 Blue	28 Brown

29 Has person lost arm, leg, hand, eye, or is he obviously physically disqualified? (Specify.)
no

30 I certify that my answers are true; that the person registered has read or has had read to him his own answers; that I have witnessed his signature or mark, and that all of his answers of which I have knowledge are true, except as follows:

R. Eirkegaard (Signature of Registrar)

Date of Registration 9-10-1918

LOCAL BOARD DIVISION No. 5
716 New York Life Bldg.,
MINNEAPOLIS, - MINN.
(STAMP OF LOCAL BOARD)

(The stamp of the Local Board having jurisdiction of the area in which the registrant has his permanent home shall be placed in this box.)

63—6171 (OVER)

World War I draft card for "Matt Arlund."

History and Philosophy of the IWW

Formed in 1905 when militants from the Western Federation of Miners joined with socialists and other radicals, the IWW combined American and overseas labor traditions with new innovations.[33] In the Preamble to its constitution, the IWW implacably condemned the class system, holding that "working class and the employing class have nothing in common" and that it is "the historic mission of the working class to do away with capitalism."[34]

In response to the changing nature of the U.S. economy and the greater entwining of various types of workers within single industries and workplaces, the Wobblies prescribed industrial unionism as the solution to poverty and exploitation. Echoing the concentration of the ownership of the means of production into fewer and fewer hands via trusts and monopolies, the IWW sought to counter the increased unity and power of employers through increased unity and power among workers. It promoted the idea of "One Big Union," an organization of all workers within industries that would be so large that when it took action the employing class would be forced to listen.[35]

This philosophy was the antithesis of the hierarchy and vanguardism of the socialist, and later Marxist-Leninist, traditions, being bottom-up rather than top-down. Workers would be grouped into clusters represented by individual "Industrial Unions" covering, for instance, all those involved in construction or maritime labor. Employing the strategy of "education, organization, emancipation," the IWW envisaged these bodies as engaging in militant action, building confidence and experience until they reached a point of such strength that a society-wide general strike could be called. Having prefiguratively built "the new society within the shell of the old," the working class would be so thoroughly organized that it would "abolish the wage system," take over the reins of production, and establish a "Cooperative Commonwealth." The Wobblies advocated total democracy in the workplace, noting the absurdity that in so-called democratic countries citizens spend a large proportion of their waking hours at work under what are effectively dictatorial conditions.[36]

Industrial unionism was posited as a superior alternative to what was then the main form of working-class organization, craft unions, which were divided by individual trades, much as many "trade unions" are today. The IWW condemned craft unions for their acceptance of class relations under capitalism and engagement in "pork chop" unionism—that is, demanding incremental improvements in wages and conditions, rather than fighting for bold demands and systemic change. However, Slim (as his name might indicate) emphasized the importance of meeting people's immediate needs, including his own. The IWW also characterized craft unions as outdated, weak, and counterproductive. Catering to specific classifications of workers within industries, they were by their nature exclusionary. Many used high membership dues and lengthy apprenticeship processes to control the pool of specialized and skilled tradespeople. They often refused membership to women, recent immigrants, and people of color. Workers involved in seasonal labor and other tasks for which unskilled workers could easily be hired were commonly dismissed as too difficult or unprofitable to organize.[37]

The Wobblies rejected sectional interests as unethical and oppressive, and so opened their union to workers performing any kind of paid labor and from any background or gender. In doing so they emphasized the efficacy of mass unionism, forging unity and putting pressure on employers. In offering a solution for the marginalized, and actively recruiting them, much of the IWW's core constituency drew on people like Slim, who was both a migratory worker and a second-generation immigrant.[38]

Initially, the IWW's constitution allowed for some form of what was deemed "political action," that is, involvement in parliamentary and state politics. After a major split at the union's 1908 convention, however, references to these tactics and strategies were removed. While individual members could, and did, remain active in political parties, the IWW's approach as an organization became one of "direct action." This involved activities carried out and guided by rank-and-file workers to confront opponents and solve problems without recourse to mediators, government, or entrenched leadership.[39] Slim personally signed on to the idea that traditional politics was a waste of time—another point of difference between him and socialists and communists.

If Slim did join the IWW in 1916, then this was both an auspicious and a tumultuous time for him to do so. Although it represented only a fraction of the U.S. working population, and was much smaller than its craft union rival the American Federation of Labor (AFL), the IWW punched far above its weight both industrially and culturally, capturing the radical zeitgeist of the time. Having gained strongholds among workers in the lumber industry of the Pacific Northwest, maritime workers in various eastern ports, and agricultural harvesters in the Midwest, the IWW rapidly improved wages and conditions through militant action during the 1910s, with some spectacular successes on the picket line and in so-called free speech fights.[40] In 1916 the Wobblies led Minnesota iron ore workers in the Mesabi Iron Range strike, one of the largest labor conflicts in that state's history. The strike ended with mixed results, including a crackdown against activists that led to the action being called off. Yet shortly afterward many of the changes the workers had demanded, such as pay increases, a shortened workday, and reforms to the contract labor system, were implemented.[41] We don't know exactly where Slim was or what work he was doing at this time, but it is possible that he was involved in this strike or that he read about it and was attracted by the Wobblies' high-profile action.

The IWW's concentration in key industries, and its ability to disrupt them, made the organization a target of massive federal repression after the United

States entered World War I. Officially the government's actions against the union rested on claims that it operated as a fifth column for Germany and the other Central Powers. The union did not hold an official position on the war and conscription, but statements in its press and by many members prior to and during the hostilities were used to allege that it had engaged in illegal antimilitarist activity. In addition, amid a sensationalistic media campaign, it was falsely claimed that IWW members had carried out widespread acts of mayhem and violence in pursuit of revolutionary change.[42]

Using recently enacted espionage laws, federal agents raided and trashed dozens of union halls and personal homes on 5 September 1917, seizing records and equipment. These attacks were followed by others from local and state police, right-wing vigilantes, and soldiers. Key IWW newspapers were shut down. Mass trials saw prominent Wobblies jailed, given sentences of up to twenty years. Another federal offensive in 1919, combined with the passing of state criminal syndicalism laws that made IWW membership a jailable offense, led to the arrests of thousands of Wobblies, hundreds of whom were subsequently imprisoned.[43]

Slim's earliest years in the IWW were therefore during a time when the union was forced to swing into defensive work focused on asserting its right to exist while getting members out of jail. In this context, it is unsurprising that his first work published by the IWW was "The Popular Wobbly," a song parodying state repression. After its appearance in the April 1920 edition of the journal *One Big Union Monthly,* "The Popular Wobbly" was anthologized with other Slim songs in the seventeenth edition of the union's famous Little Red Songbook. In 1921 he began publishing columns in both the IWW's primary East Coast newspaper, *Industrial Solidarity,* and its West Coast equivalent, the *Industrial Worker.*

Bone-Mots: Slim as a Writer

In its formation the IWW had taken advantage of, and contributed to, a subculture that emerged among transient workers in the early twentieth-century United States. Known as "hobohemia" for its alternative outlook and values, this was arguably the first American counterculture. As one of us has argued elsewhere, hobohemia was a literary subculture not only because many of its members could read and write well but also because it privileged the art of storytelling.[44] The hobo turned sociologist Nels Anderson noted that "the art of telling a story is diligently cultivated by the 'bos' in the assemblies about the fire. . . . Many of them develop into fascinating *raconteurs* in the literal as well as the literary sense of the term."[45] Indeed, the spinning of tall tales around hobo campfires was so common and such an important element of creating the hobo community that it was part of the appeal of transiency and became

T-Bone Slim cartoon that was printed at the head of many of his *Industrial Worker* columns. This example comes from *Industrial Worker*, 13 February 1926.

the stuff of legend. Jack London famously claimed that being a hobo, and specifically learning how to lie convincingly, taught him how to be an author.[46] As London knew, there was a popular market for stories of the road. Nor was he the only one to recognize this fact. Hobohemians produced approximately eighty books of memoir, fiction, and poetry during the first half of the twentieth century, prompting popular novelist and ex-hobo Louis L'Amour to comment, "During the knockabout years the hobo acquired a literature of his own."[47] In entering hobohemia in or around 1916, then, Slim also entered a countercultural space in which working-class writings were welcomed and encouraged, not least in the pages of IWW papers.

In the early years Slim's IWW publications were prolific, appearing in almost every issue of the *Industrial Worker* even though it was produced twice a week at this point, as well as in *Industrial Solidarity* and *One Big Union Monthly*. For a time Slim's work also appeared in the communist-aligned *Truth*, which was published by Duluth's West End Labor Association, until that paper was shut down following government repression.[48] His writings were also featured, generally as reprints, in other IWW newspapers, including the Finnish-language *Industrialisti*. In later periods his columns would disappear for months, even years, on end. Occasionally a brief explanation was given, usually relating to work or health, but often no comment was made at all. By the time of his death Slim had written more than a thousand columns for the IWW, as well as a large number of pieces that were never published.

A one-off cartoon utilizing Slim's trademark image. From *Industrial Worker,* 28 April 1923. By "Retlaw."

Slim's core audience was made up of fellow Wobblies and those in the associated radical and hobohemian milieu. In addition to being sold to the public via street sales, single copies of IWW newspapers and publications circulated beyond individual purchasers, who passed them on and shared them in IWW halls, left-wing libraries, work camps, and hobo jungles. Through these networks Slim's columns would have reached tens of thousands of people per week during the early to mid-1920s. His songs and poems extended much further through being communally sung and recited by generations of radicals and hoboes as well as being reprinted as cards and appearing in multiple editions of the Little Red Songbook. The nature of this audience, and the quality and distinctiveness of Slim's writing, ensured that his aphorisms and observations were repeated and dissected in IWW halls and around campfires, as well as sketched on walls and boxcars. Rosemont notes that Slim's work was admired by "many radicals otherwise critical of the IWW," including writers such as "Jack Conroy, Harvey O'Connor, Upton Sinclair and Meridel LeSueur," and that it occasionally drew the attention of mainstream figures such as H. L. Mencken.[49]

In his early and most prolific years as a writer, Slim came to the attention of the radical editor L. S. (Leland Stanford) Chumley, who wanted Slim to write a booklet for him. This recent finding comes from the research of Marija Dalbello, who discovered a 1922 letter from Slim to Chumley in which Slim politely turned down Chumley's offer, though he kept the possibility open for the future: "Just at present am 'indisposed' (not in high spirits) but I hope to be able to send you material from time to time."[50] Slim did produce two pamphlets for the Wobblies, *Starving amidst Too Much* and *The Power of These Two Hands,* though it is unclear whether Chumley was involved in either of these publications.

Slim's writing mostly consists of nonfiction articles, both reportage of his life as a transient worker and opinion pieces giving his views on a range of subjects. Interspersed among and within these are poems, songs, and other formal experiments such as short works of fiction and even the occasional one-page play. Though his tone tends toward the humorous and at times the absurd, some of the articles and poems are, variously, angry and melancholic. The earlier writings contain more first-person reportage because this was a period during which Slim was, with some exceptions, living a transient life, moving between jobs in different states during the spring, summer, and fall, followed by a winter period spent in a large town or city. His articles from the mid-1930s onward are more opinion based, since by this time he was settled into his work in the New York docklands and therefore less able to report from what he would have seen as the hobo front line. Whenever they were written, Slim's articles are typically fragmentary, comprising unconnected observations made over a series of days or weeks and then sent on to his editor for publication. Slim had several different editors over the years. One of them, the well-known IWW activist and historian Fred Thompson, claimed to have instigated a practice of rearranging Slim's fragments into what he considered coherent articles without changing the words themselves, a practice of which he said Slim approved. Thompson also noted that whenever Slim spotted a typo in the final publication of one of his pieces he would be much aggrieved, since he had spent a great deal of time and effort getting his words just right.[51] This makes sense—along with his wit and gallows humor, precise wordplay is one of the most distinctive features of Slim's work.

Generally speaking, Slim's writing is characterized by a combination of an accessible and direct style, dark humor, and literary experimentation. The directness of his style, which he himself described as "a little blunt," was in part a result of his background, but we believe it was also a choice he made as he attempted to create a literature for and of the working class. Slim criticized authors who were overly verbose and praised those, such as Oscar Wilde, who could say a great deal in a short space. In a sense his view was similar to that of communist author Mike Gold, who called on "proletarian literature" to use "as few words as possible."[52] The reasons for this were fairly straightforward: working-class people have less time and energy than the wealthy for pursuits such as reading, as well as less formal education. But the use of a direct style was not simply due to lack. It was also part of a hermeneutics of suspicion, a stripping back of the bourgeois obfuscations typically found in language, such as legalese or political economy, that working-class people were not trained to understand, and that they often saw as deliberately deployed to conceal the reality of their exploitation. Such an attitude and approach was also in keeping with Wobbly, and more broadly syndicalist, sensibilities. While many IWW members were well-read, the theory and observations they produced were typically framed as direct expressions of practical "truths," emphasizing grassroots knowledge from below. Wobbly works were intended to foster workers' capacities, but they also served as a contrast to the more densely philosophical writings propagated by mainstream economists and academics as well as, Gold's injunction notwithstanding, the IWW's communist rivals.[53] The task still remains for literary scholars to identify the qualities of a working-class literary aesthetic, and in our view such scholars could do worse than beginning their studies with Slim.

Above all, though, it was humor that made Slim's work popular. Hard-bitten observation laced with levity and satire, given in response to depredation and prejudice, was common among hoboes and Wobblies, in song, oral storytelling, and written form.[54] These qualities also formed part of the hobohemian subculture that influenced Slim's approach to writing and use of slang. Hobohemia privileged stoic humor in the face of adversity, and Slim's articles certainly contributed to creating that culture. Slim understood that humor often works best through incongruence. Sometimes this might involve using deliberately overblown language to recount mundane events, as when he calls applying for a job as a dishwasher an offer to "emancipate" his future boss "from the drudgery of the sink," or when he describes a safe falling out of a skyscraper window and landing on a "good citizen" who "tries to retreat in four different directions—in this he is only partially successful." At other times Slim's humor operates through a rhetoric of disgust, as when he describes the snot rolling down a lumber camp cook's nose and being rolled into the piecrust meant for lunch, and the cook telling Slim he cannot understand why men keep quitting the job: "That's the way they are, I consoled him, they quit for no reason at all, at all." And sometimes his humor is so serious it makes us want to cry, as when he describes conditions as being so bad that it is too expensive to commit suicide: "Even the lowly rope is beyond the means of an average citizen." For Slim, as for the best comedians, humor was often serious and the serious business of life was often funny, or, as he put it: "I am on the verge of hysterics because of my seriousness."

For those who are new to Slim's work, perhaps the most surprising aspect of it is that, despite his commitment to writing accessibly, Slim often experimented with literary form and played with language in a manner at times reminiscent of literary modernists. Franklin Rosemont saw in Slim a proto-surrealist forebear and inspiration, a writer who privileged play above all else. A good example of this is that Slim loved to create neologisms by combining words, a technique that may have been inspired by his bilingualism, since Finnish is a compound language in which creating composite words is much more common than it is in English. Speaking two languages also gave him an understanding that the concordance of sound and meaning, signifier and signified, is arbitrary. As a result he would play with language until the sounds of words became more important than their meanings, as with his phrase "Muzuma is the rutabaga of boll-weavil," a rephrasing of the biblical "Money is the root of all evil," which, as the Finnish rap artist Paleface (Karri Miettinen) has noted, approaches language in a way reminiscent of contemporary hip-hop.[55] Slim also relentlessly experimented with literary styles, especially in the first decade or so of his publishing career, with his columns changing from straightforward reportage to parodic novels to poetry to newspaper puzzles, and back again.

A common focus of Slim's writing is the struggle for the necessities of life, such as wages and decent food. He concentrated on these everyday features because they were what most concerned him and, as he knew, his audience. "Labor," he writes, "has a bad habit of getting hungry," while "meal time," he says in another article, "is an epoch in the history of today." Focusing on these quotidian elements allowed him to point out their absurdity, frequently finding humor in otherwise grim situations, such as encountering lice in his cheap flophouse bed, or finding four and three-quarters flies in his meat pie (one-quarter of the fifth fly having been cut through by his knife), or spending an entire night fending off Michigan mosquitoes while sleeping on the streets of Detroit. He rejected the notion that labor has inherent dignity, noting wryly that the people who popularize such ideas are never the people actually doing the work. He observed that the capitalist system does not provide equity for those who make its products, pointing out that workers are typically fed cheap, processed foods while the rich enjoy the highest-quality ingredients.

His obsession with food may be explained in part by the fact that he was an excellent cook, sometimes serving in this capacity on worksites. Indeed, the author and musician James Stevens, best known for writing the song "The Frozen Logger," describes encountering Slim's cooking while he was constructing railroad lines at a work camp near Eugene, Oregon:

> They had a cook who was just as good [as the previous cook], a team hand called T Bone Slim. I did like the way he cooked T bone steaks—always tender steer meat here. Slim fried them to a rich brown outside, but he left the fat slices a warm, juicy red inside. He peppered his steaks good; and I did like to sit with my eyes shut, chewing slowly, the hot juice of the meat just oozing down my throat, and the pepper making it tingle along just right. Then, to put in a big forkful of mashed potatoes rich with butter, and a little bite of pickle one time, and a little bite of cheese the next time, for flavoring, and to chew it all around what was left of the steak, and to follow about every three mouthfuls down with a draft of creamy, steaming coffee—this was living, I can tell you. Then, after a couple of big T bones

> and the trimmings, to tackle a quarter of an apple pie, sirupy and cinnamon-flavored, and to finish it; and to tackle a chocolate layer cake a foot high, and to finish three whacking big pieces of that; and to wash all this down with another fine cup of coffee—this was living some more. Then, to go out puffing on a mellow, old-fashioned long-stemmed corn-cob, enjoying such a splendid warm, stuffed feeling inside, to stretch out on my bunk and watch the smoke curl up and listen to the drone of talk in the tent, if this wasn't good living, then there never was such a thing.[56]

There is obviously hyperbole here, but if this description is anything to go by, then Slim knew his way around a kitchen (indeed this, along with his slender frame, seems the most likely explanation for his hobo name), and so we can better understand his frustration at the nasty, synthetic foodstuffs that were increasingly being pushed on the working class, often to the detriment of their health.

Slim's work only rarely touched on issues of gender. When it did, he could at times be extremely progressive, as when arguing that women ought to be paid the same as men, a position that was vanishingly rare in the early twentieth century, especially among male authors. At other times he disappointingly fell back on the gender stereotypes and expectations of his day. When he discussed marriage he was particularly cutting, and we can easily speculate that he was letting personal frustration about his own failed relationship with Rosa spill out and negatively affect his ability to think clearly about patriarchy. More positively, Slim rarely engaged in the kind of macho idealization of working-class men that was common in Wobbly publications, both in writing and (perhaps especially) in imagery, as well as in proletarian literature more widely.[57] Indeed, Slim was more likely to portray his own male body as weedy, sick, and old than as a shining paragon of brawny, working-class masculinity.

For the most part, Slim's work is also praiseworthy for its antiracist elements.[58] Drawing on his immigrant family's experiences, he exposed the opportunism, slipperiness, and exploitation at the heart of supposedly immutable categories of "whiteness." He is known to have been close friends with the Black Wobbly organizer Ben Fletcher, and his columns lampooned xenophobic immigration policies and racist organizations such as the Ku Klux Klan. Indeed, Slim's antiracism was on display in one of the only accounts we have of him performing music, at a rally organized by the communist Al Lannon. According to Lannon, the audience wanted Slim to sing his famous song "The Popular Wobbly," but instead he launched into a tirade against "those fuckin' bastards down in Alabama" who had framed the Scottsboro Boys, a well-known racially motivated miscarriage of justice; his outburst was apparently so violent that the "living legend" had to be ushered offstage.[59]

It is also true that in a small number of his articles Slim made use of racial stereotypes and caricatured language, especially in regard to people from East Asia, though this seems to have been something that mostly plagued his earlier work. It must also be added that, as with the early IWW in general, much of his understanding and characterization of exploitation and discrimination came through a lens and set of experiences that prioritized class and the workplace over other forms and locations of oppression.

The IWW and Slim's Later Years

The period during which Slim began writing for the IWW saw the union weather the initial impacts of repression only to find itself facing further challenges from within and without. These developments had a major influence on Slim's work and the methods he advocated, and also caused the IWW to shift its orientation and approach. In its formative years, the union had experimented with a range of direct-action tactics in a variety of settings. Although the IWW retained some variation in its practices, by the late 1910s it had largely abandoned community-oriented civil disobedience, as exemplified by its famous free speech fights, to focus primarily on tactics in the workplace such as strikes and slowdowns. The IWW had previously referred to the latter as "sabotage," but opponents' use of this term to smear the Wobblies as "vandals" and "wreckers" had seen it disappear from the organization's publications.[60] In keeping with this change, Slim had only negative things to say about sabotage and property damage in his columns. Other than in the early to mid-1920s, when the union was trying to pressure California businesses as a means of freeing prisoners, Slim also rarely discussed boycotts. Instead his favored means were "job action" and workplace "organization," accompanied by calls to join the IWW.

Following a difficult period of government repression, the union's formal membership bounced back to reach an estimated peak of more than 58,000 from late 1922 through 1923. In the immediate postwar years it continued to have political and industrial impacts beyond the core of those who directly paid financial dues to the organization.[61]

This situation changed following a brutal split in 1924. The direct causes of the split were many and varied. Some centered on long-running ideological and practical differences, others on more recent disputes over how to best free imprisoned members and move forward industrially. One section of the union continued to favor cautious, yet by most standards still radical, action. Others launched major but ultimately failed gambits, such as an April 1923 general strike aimed at forcing elites to release class war prisoners. Enmeshed with these were divisions over the degree to which the union should support or reject the Bolshevik Revolution and join or work with emerging national and international communist organizations. Another set of disagreements concerned

T-Bone Slim, circa 1930s. Westmoreland Collection; reprinted, with thanks, by permission of Cherie and John Westmoreland.

whether imprisoned members should accept individual government clemency offers that required implicit admissions of guilt, and the fallout that occurred when some did.[62]

These questions, and others regarding leadership and centralization, went to the heart of what kind of union the IWW would be in the future. Personality clashes and rivalries between the largest industrial unions were exacerbated by repression and subsequent rapid turnovers in organizers and leaders. Out of the 1924 convention emerged two IWWs, both with offices in Chicago. The consequences of the split were dire, as membership and influence rapidly declined.[63]

It does not appear that Slim was ever an organizer or held an administrative role in the IWW. He does not appear to have attended a convention or

T-Bone Slim, circa 1930s. Westmoreland Collection; reprinted, with thanks, by permission of Cherie and John Westmoreland.

served as a workplace delegate.[64] In his role as one of the union's most prolific writers, he interrogated many topics regarding working-class life but generally steered clear of describing IWW methods and tactics in detail. Nor did he offer much commentary on internal union matters. He made occasional remarks about the 1924 split, but these did not seem to favor one faction over another. Nevertheless, he stuck with the majority form of the organization, which continued to produce the publications to which he contributed, and which remains in operation today. Many did not join him. In addition to those who split and those who joined the communists, numerous others, tired of the squabbling, simply let their membership lapse.

This loss of support, and the resulting inability to generate resources and mobilize numbers for campaigns, largely incapacitated the union for the rest of Slim's life. While it did not provoke a public loss of Slim's belief in industrial unionism, it did cause obvious shifts in his tenor and outlook. His writings increasingly read as if his belief in the IWW and its principles represented more of an article of faith than a reflection of lived experience. The ebullience of Slim's early years was largely lost, and his predictions of change became more distant.

This pessimistic mood changed on occasion, for instance with the advent

Lithograph of T-Bone Slim by Cherie Westmoreland. The original photograph on which this image was based would likely have been taken in the 1930s and unfortunately has not survived. Reprinted, with thanks, by permission of Cherie Westmoreland.

of the Great Depression, which offered new opportunities for growth within what appeared to be capitalism's long-predicted death spiral. However, outside some pockets of activity, the solutions advocated by Slim and the IWW failed to resonate. Instead, other currents rode the new wave of radicalization. The pro-Soviet outlook, state socialism, hierarchical discipline, and at times Machiavellian approach of the Communist Party dominated the far left, drawing militant workers, intellectuals, and artists into its orbit. At the same time, the Roosevelt administration's New Deal reforms and investment in public works and welfare eventually ameliorated some of the worst depredations of the economic crisis and restored faith in representative democracy among liberals and others.[65]

The 1930s saw a major uptick in the popularity of industrial unionism, but in a form that was different from that espoused by Slim and the IWW. Unions associated with the Congress of Industrial Organizations (CIO) brought together many types of workers within single industries and became the key bodies associated with militant means. Although IWW members in some cases pioneered tactics such as sit-down strikes and did the initial groundwork to help set up major campaigns, it was the CIO that took them forward and reaped the benefits. In compromising on practices that the IWW rejected—such as signing contracts, having employers subtract dues directly from members' wages, building up large strike and organizational funds, and engaging in "political action"—the CIO was able to bed down and institutionalize victories. Formally eschewing a revolutionary anticapitalist approach by joining Roosevelt's New Deal coalition, the CIO gained valuable allies and successfully navigated employer repression, becoming a key rival to the AFL in the process. Although it would take a conservative turn, carrying out a purge of communists and others in the late 1940s and merging with the AFL in 1955, during the Depression years the CIO drew on the fervor and commitment of many radicals.[66] With these organizations dominating the scene, Slim found himself cast further into the role of critic rather than advocate. In his articles over the course of the 1930s, the idea of the One Big Union as a shining light with practical answers in the present was joined by downbeat descriptions of it as the last-hope-yet-untried amid the debris of failed revolutions and looming war.

The IWW's 1924 split and subsequent decline not only shaped what Slim wrote about but also had a major impact on his potential audience and opportunities for posterity. In 1925 a four-year biweekly run of the *Industrial Worker* came to an end, and in 1927 the English-language press of the IWW stopped publishing its monthly journal, although a Finnish publication, *Tie Vapauteen,* continued for about another ten years. With union membership and readership continuing to decline, a long-debated merging of the union's West Coast and East Coast mastheads occurred in 1931. The *Industrial Worker* lived on, but with *Industrial Solidarity* shut down, it was now produced out of the IWW's main offices in Chicago. Despite its being the primary IWW paper and now published only once a week, the *Industrial Worker* dropped in circulation from approximately twelve thousand per issue in the early 1920s to three thousand per issue by 1938.[67]

Slim's own life also underwent several changes during this period. In January 1925, having lived as a hobo for about thirteen years, Slim was working in a logging camp in Michigan, where he had a workplace accident in which his leg was "doubled up under" and his ankle was "sprained."[68] He became ill with fever a month later, though whether this was related to his accident is unclear.[69] Either way, he also seems to have become hard of hearing in one ear and developed a limp around this time. In a 1926 article he describes pain shooting up from the "cord" of his big toe, and he would later claim that he had sprained his ribs doing heavy lifting sometime in the mid-1920s.[70] In 1929 he wrote that he had been diagnosed with locomotor ataxia, which, if true, would mean that he was suffering from syphilis, a common disease among hoboes.[71]

As a result of some or all of these problems, in the mid- to late 1920s Slim gave up the transient life and moved to New York to work on the waterfront. Unfortunately, the Great Depression seems to have forced him back on the road again in 1930, something that must have been extremely difficult for him, given his age (forty-eight), his health problems, and the physical nature of the only work he could get. He moved back to New York after a few years, finally settling down to work as a deck scow captain, a type of maintenance worker who stayed at night aboard unpowered coal boats. Singer and ex-mariner Ben Bright claimed to have "camped with T-Bone in a barge in New York," so it appears that Slim would sometimes entertain aboard his scow.[72] When not spending the night on board, he stayed at a union hall or, as he had often done in the past, slept on the streets. His various personal difficulties contributed to a decline in the regularity of his written output, something his editors commented on occasionally.

Having edited *Solidarity* from 1913 to 1917, the songwriter, cartoonist, and poet Ralph Chaplin, one of the union's longest-running propagandists, took the helm of the *Industrial Worker* in 1932. Favoring a more news-oriented, propagandist style and advocacy of an idiosyncratic form of technocracy, he disliked Slim's work and seems to have wanted him to take a more didactic, preachy approach. The exact details of the conflict between the two men are unclear, but Slim, along with others who clashed with Chaplin over politics and style, stopped writing for the newspaper in 1933.

Chaplin left the union in 1936 under acrimonious circumstances, and within weeks Slim returned to the pages of the *Industrial Worker.* Apparently lacking an alternative outlet, his writings had, at least to our current knowledge, not appeared anywhere in the intervening years. Nevertheless he had not been idle, chronicling his work in a series of notebooks, which, after his return, IWW editors would draw upon occasionally to create columns. Slim continued to make erudite and insightful observations in these and new works. Yet while displaying sparks of brilliance, these later pieces were much less playful, experimental, and innovative than his earlier output. From the mid-1930s onward, Slim was relatively settled and so had less opportunity to observe life from the point of view of the transient worker. He did not write in any detail about his job as a scow captain, perhaps because this would have made him identifiable to readers and the authorities. His articles became more removed, abstract, and, ironically given his earlier falling-out with Chaplin, preachy. Each of these aspects tended to diminish his writing quality, although there were still notable exceptions.

During the late 1930s, Slim's work took an increasingly repetitive and jaundiced turn.[73] U.S. involvement in looming and then actual war became his bête noire. While hostile to fascism and mocking its leading figures, he was dismissive of those who upheld representative democracy. In doing so he partially drew on the IWW's long-held opposition to "political action" and harsh experiences at the hands of bosses and the state. In some columns he argued that the "industrial autocracy" exercised by employers in workplaces, and the misery and unemployment to which millions were subject, made life in America little or no better than that experienced under dictatorships abroad. After World War II began, he supplemented these positions with desperate and often contradictory arguments that increasingly drew on mainstream isolationist language and sentiment. Slim often appeared to be casting about freely, adopting any argument that echoed his own long-held opposition to war. Jingoistic tirades against Britain alternated with anticapitalist critiques of imperialism. His use of the word "our," in characterizing the ownership and use of American military and economic resources, increasingly took a nationalist bent rather than one emphasizing class.

Although opinions varied across the IWW, Slim was not alone in advocating antiwar positions at this time. The *Industrial Worker* ran a number of original pieces and reprinted articles from left-leaning sources that criticized the provision of aid to the Allies, the buildup of the U.S. military, and pro-war and interventionist arguments. As during World War I, the union did not take a formal position of opposition to U.S. involvement. That had not spared it in 1917, but this time around the union did not suffer repression, perhaps simply because it was too weak to cause much trouble. The IWW continued to publish its newspaper and to organize in the small number of workplaces where it still exerted influence.

Slim's contributions to the *Industrial Worker* dropped off during 1941, and he produced only two columns in 1942. The reasons behind this are unknown, although it is tempting to speculate that it reflected frustration or depression stemming from the continuing turn of global events, or possibly a falling-out with those in the union who did not appreciate the direction of his later work. Whatever the truth of the matter, it was a sad and obscure end for one of the IWW's most prolific contributors, and someone who was once the Wobblies' best-loved prose writer.

Resurrection: Slim's Legacy and the Purpose of This Collection

His body having been identified only unofficially (and by whom we do not know—yet another mystery), Slim was buried as an "unknown white man" on New York City's Hart Island (plot 161, section 1, grave 24) on 5 June 1942.[74] Hart Island is the location of the largest mass grave in the United States. It is where the poor and the despised are buried, being both a potter's field and the place where the earliest victims of both AIDS and Covid-19 were interred, evidence of the city's prejudice and paranoia.[75] Slim would have been buried by prisoners from a nearby workhouse, exactly the kind of people he had dedicated his life to writing for and about. This was a fate that he seemed to anticipate in a 1925 article:

> After capitalism is fully developed and civilization has reached its dizziest pinnacle, and when the whole land, all the ponds, and part of Lake Michigan is dotted with tombstones—and all the prairies are graveyards—all the valleys are cemeteries—and all the mountains are mausoleums, I mean—when there is left no place in which to tuck the dead, this will be a good world to live in.
>
> The graves should be dug deeper. Plant the dead two and three deep—sort of "stack 'em up." Square the tops of the tombstones—all of equal height—so that we can build our HOUSE on the remains of the dead.

In a case of death imitating art, Slim was buried in a pit with coffins stacked on top of each other, three to five deep. But this is not the end of the story. Although the Manhattan waterfront on which he worked has now become gentrified and, in many ways, unrecognizable from Slim's time, the past, as Utah Phillips once put it, didn't go anywhere. Erosion and bad weather have worn away Hart Island, loosening the bodies held within. Long-buried bones have washed up near New York's splendid and expensive skyscrapers, a deeply disturbing event for the neoliberal city that was the first to reinvent itself as a commercial product. In a sense, the dead have come back to New York, walking again like the agents of the zombie movies with which contemporary society is so obsessed, presaging perhaps the end of the world that will take place, as Slim suggested, "after capitalism is fully developed and civilization has reached its dizziest pinnacle."

His bones possibly being among those returning to New York, as a writer Slim is also going through a resurrection of sorts. He has recently been the subject of two international conferences and has been featured in podcasts, in contemporary graffiti and art exhibitions, and in academic journals and books. And, of course, he now has this brand spanking new scholarly edition to bring his words to those whom he might call the "rising generation." Resurrection is also, appropriately enough, the title chosen by John Westmoreland for his album of his great-granduncle's music, taken from the title of a Slim song in which a drunken man rises from the grave like one of the blessed, asking in confusion: "Don't other corpses deign to rise / But mine alone, alone?" Though in his unpublished manuscript notes Slim wrote, with a dark, maniacal chortle, that "I'll soon be forgotten, heh, heh, heh," we believe that it is in fact high time for him to be remembered.

We hope you find this collection to be as valuable as we find Slim's work to be. We hope that those who love words will find much to enjoy here. We hope that artists and musicians may find further inspiration in the form and content of Slim's writing, and that political activists will see in him a precursor and fellow traveler, someone who would be marching in the streets and camping on the picket lines for a better world in the twenty-first century, just as he did in the twentieth.

Notes

1. Harvey O'Connor, *Revolution in Seattle: A Memoir* (1964; repr., Chicago: Haymarket Books, 2009), 67.

2. Excellent research by Marko Leppänen has traced Slim's family heritage to Kokkola and the small village of Kälviä, where Slim's parents were tenant farmers. The name Huhta literally means "cleared woodland."

3. Docket 1115, 24 February 1939, Manhattan District 1 (Tombs), New York City Municipal Archives.

4. Franklin Rosemont argues that Slim also wrote under the IWW card number 198308. Though a handful of articles published in *Industrial Solidarity* in the late 1920s under this name do bear a resemblance to Slim's style, we are not convinced that they are in fact his work; therefore, in our view the claim that this was Slim's Wobbly card number also remains unproven. See Franklin Rosemont, ed., *Juice Is Stranger Than Friction* (Chicago: Charles H. Kerr, 1992), 22n46.

5. "Huhta Lost Wife's Love: Better Half Disappeared with Another Man," *Ashtabula Star Beacon,* 19 August 1901. For another report, see "Took His Own Life," *Erie Daily Times,* 17 August 1901.

6. The U.S. government and the mob worked together to root out maritime antiwar saboteurs in a collaboration known as Operation Underworld.

7. Floyd Miller, *The Savage Streets* (New York: Popular Library, 1956).

8. In yet another frustrating mystery, Miller's archive contains material from all of his novels except *The Savage Streets.* Why is this the case? We don't know. Floyd Miller Collection, Howard Gotlieb Archival Research Center, Boston University.

9. We would like to acknowledge the use of this song title by both Franklin Rosemont and Ville-Juhani Sutinen in their books about Slim. We thought this was such a good idea that we stole it.

10. Rosemont, *Juice,* 7.

11. Art Nurse, interview by Franklin Rosemont, 10 May 1987, Rosemont Collection, Newberry Library, Chicago.

12. KONE Foundation Award, 2022–23, "T-Bone Slim and the Transnational

Poetics of the Migrant Left in North America," Kirsti Salmi-Niklander (University of Helsinki), principal investigator; Marija Dalbello (Rutgers University) and Saku Pinta (University of Manitoba), researchers; John Westmoreland, researcher/artist; Saijaleena Rantanen (Arts University–Sibelius Academy) and Samira Saramo (Migration Institute of Finland), other researchers; Lotta Leiwo (University of Helsinki), research assistant; Owen Clayton (University of Lincoln) and Iain McIntyre (University of Melbourne), other collaborators. See "The Project" and "Team," *T-Bone Slim and the Transnational Poetics of the Migrant Left in North America* (blog), accessed 30 October 2023, https://blogs.helsinki.fi/tboneslim. Preliminary work from this project was presented at a 2021 online seminar hosted by the University of Helsinki, followed by an in-person symposium in Kälviä, Finland, 18–19 August 2023. The final research will shortly be published in book format by the Finnish Literature Society's Studia Fennica Litteraria series: Kirsti Salmi-Niklander, Marija Dalbello, and Saku Pinta, eds., *T-Bone Slim and the Transnational Poetics of the Migrant Left in North America* (Helsinki: Finnish Literature Society, forthcoming).

13. Kirsti Salmi-Niklander, Lotta Leiwo, Owen Clayton, Iain McIntyre, John Westmoreland, Saku Pinta, Marija Dalbello, Samira Saramo, and Saijaleena Rantanen, *T-Bone Slim Corpus, Source* (2024), available for download in Kielipankki–The Language Bank of Finland, http://urn.fi/urn:nbn:fi:lb-2022111621.

14. This information stands in contrast to assumptions previously made by Rosemont following his interviews with Fred Thompson.

15. The Tyyni Temperance Society also published a monthly handwritten newspaper, which was common practice in Finnish American communities of the period. This information comes from Kirsti Salmi-Niklander and Lotta Leiwo, "Family Histories from Kälviä, Central Ostrobothnia to Ashtabula, Ohio," paper presented at the symposium "T-Bone Slim and the Transnational Poetics of the Migrant Left in North America," Kälviä, Finland, 18 August 2023. It is possible that Slim contributed to this paper, though it is unclear if any issues survive.

16. For example, in an article that did not make the cut for inclusion in this volume, Slim states: "I don't believe there is necessity for a news censor. Editors have been very careful not to let any news get into the papers." See Rosemont, *Juice,* 153. The article was originally published as "Workers Can Learn Art of Better Living," *Industrial Worker,* 15 March 1941.

17. We are very grateful to May Colling, who has since passed away at age ninety-eight, for providing this information. As well as being a local Ashtabula historian, May knew Slim's former wife, Rosa, having been her neighbor and landlady in the years after the couple's divorce.

18. Slim was and was not an autodidact. He was an autodidact in the sense that many working-class people were and are, in that he did not attend college but instead pursued his own course of reading, somewhat more haphazard and unstructured than a higher education course but often undertaken with as much depth and rigor as would be expected of the best student. He also was not an autodidact in that, unlike many working-class writers, he actually did receive a solid grounding in a liberal education at school. As an adult he also seems to have attended Work People's College, the IWW's labor college in Duluth, Minnesota, although precisely when he did this is another mystery to be resolved.

19. The Finnish connection is indirect because Slim's smoothed-out trochaic meter

seems to have been influenced by Longfellow's verse, which was inspired by English and German translations of the *Kalevala,* rather than by the epic directly. It is fair to say that in both Longfellow's and Slim's cases, the verse suffered as a result of being simplified.

20. Our thanks again to Kirsti Salmi-Niklander for providing further information on this topic.

21. Though most of Slim's Finnish-language *Industrialisti* articles seem to have been translated from English by other people, Saku Pinta has discovered that Slim wrote at least two of these articles originally in Finnish. For more information, see Saku Pinta, "T-Bone Slim's Forgotten Finnish-Language Writings in the IWW Press," *T-Bone Slim and the Transnational Poetics of the Migrant Left in North America* (blog), 20 October 2022, https://blogs.helsinki.fi/tboneslim.

22. See "Slash with Razor: August Sulstrom, a Finlander, Received Severe Injuries in a Mysterious Affair Early This Morning," *Erie Daily Times,* 30 July 1903. Johanna Huhta married again, to a Matti Kosola, in February 1904, at which time it appears that Slim and Rosa were still living with her. Our thanks to John Westmoreland, Slim's great-grandnephew, whose family research, including uncovering the facts just mentioned, has been invaluable for this volume.

23. Salmi-Niklander and Leiwo, "Family Histories." Rosa also seems to have been a Tyyni correspondent, at least for a time.

24. *Erie City Directory,* 1906.

25. *Erie Daily Times,* 7 December 1910.

26. The folk singer Aunt Molly Jackson claimed to have based her song "Cross Bones Scully," about a man who goes to jail for violent robbery, on Slim, though whether the song is based on Slim's biography or on a story told by him is unclear. Aunt Molly Jackson, interview by Archie Green, circa 1957–58, Box 2, Folder 28, Rosemont–T-Bone Slim Research Collection, Newberry Library, Chicago.

27. See Owen Clayton, *Vagabonds, Tramps, and Hobos: The Literature and Culture of U.S. Transiency, 1890–1940* (Cambridge: Cambridge University Press, 2023), 107–14.

28. Ashtabula Clerk of Court Records, 1916.

29. Slim's Swedish paternal grandfather's surname was Ahrlund.

30. See "Nab 13 Wobblies at C & N. W Depot: Thirteen Transients Refuse to Pay Fare—Are Taken into Custody Here," *Aberdeen Daily News,* 24 July 1919. Only one of the men had a red IWW card, but that does not mean the others were not members.

31. We think the poem is Slim's partly because of its style and partly because Robert Burns was someone he admired, but mostly our opinion rests on the fact that in a 1923 article (not included in this volume) Slim describes seeing a mouse while he was in jail—a sighting that seems to be more than a coincidence. See T-Bone Slim, "Gila Monster," *Industrial Worker,* 1 December 1923. As John Westmoreland has pointed out, there are also similarities between some of the lines in "Only a Mouse in Jail" and other writings by Slim. "Matt Arnold" was released from jail on 23 September 1919, pending his sentencing, but in November the charges against him were dropped. See "Municipal Court," *Aberdeen Daily News,* 23 September 1919; "Proceedings of Municipal Court," *Aberdeen American,* 16 November 1919.

32. This phrase appears in a column not published in this collection: "Great Crime Wave Exposed by T-Bone May Save the Country," *Industrial Worker,* 10 October 1936.

33. Ralph Darlington, *Syndicalism and the Transition to Communism* (Farnham: Ashgate, 2013), 19–56.

34. IWW, "Preamble to the IWW Constitution," 1908.

35. IWW, "Preamble."

36. IWW, "Preamble"; William L. Niemi and David J. Plante, "Democratic Movements, Self-Education, and Economic Democracy: Chartists, Populists, and Wobblies," *Radical History Review,* no. 102 (2008): 185–200.

37. IWW, "Preamble"; Aleksi Huhta, *Toward a Red Melting Pot* (Helsinki: Työväen Historian ja Perinteen Tutkimuksen Seura, 2021), 175–76; Melvyn Dubofsky, *We Shall Be All: A History of the Industrial Workers of the World* (Chicago: University of Illinois Press, 2000), 8–9.

38. Peter Cole, *Wobblies on the Waterfront: Interracial Unionism in Progressive-Era Philadelphia* (Urbana: University of Illinois Press, 2010), 51–54; Darlington, *Syndicalism and the Transition to Communism,* 107–14; Heather Mayer, *Beyond the Rebel Girl: Women and the Industrial Workers of the World in the Pacific Northwest, 1905–1924* (Corvallis: Oregon State University Press, 2018), 3–9.

39. Dubofsky, *We Shall Be All,* 136–66.

40. Franklin Rosemont, *Joe Hill: The IWW and the Making of a Revolutionary Workingclass Counterculture* (Oakland, Calif.: PM Press, 2015), 19–33; Matthew S. May, *Soapbox Rebellion: The Hobo Orator Union and the Free Speech Fights of the Industrial Workers of the World, 1909–1916* (Tuscaloosa: University of Alabama Press, 2013), 34–46; Dubofsky, *We Shall Be All,* 173–346.

41. Dubofsky, *We Shall Be All,* 319–31.

42. Eric Chester, *The Wobblies in Their Heyday: The Rise and Destruction of the IWW during the World War I Era* (Santa Barbara, Calif.: Bloomsbury, 2014), 117–202.

43. Chester, *Wobblies in Their Heyday,* 117–202.

44. Clayton, *Vagabonds, Tramps, and Hobos,* 16–18.

45. Nels Anderson, *The Hobo: The Sociology of the Homeless Man* (1923; repr., Chicago: University of Chicago Press, 1961), 19.

46. Jack London, *The Road* [1907], in *Novels and Social Writings,* ed. Donald Pizer (New York: Library of America, 1982), 193.

47. Louis L'Amour, *Education of a Wandering Man* (New York: Bantam Books, 1989), 11.

48. This fact suggests that Slim was less anticommunist in the early 1920s than he would soon become.

49. Rosemont, *Joe Hill,* 552–54.

50. This information is based on two blog posts and a conference presentation by Dalbello. See Marija Dalbello, "From My Archival 'Digs': Part I: Finding Slim!," *T-Bone Slim and the Transnational Poetics of the Migrant Left in North America* (blog), 12 December 2022, https://blogs.helsinki.fi/tboneslim; Marija Dalbello, "From My Archival 'Digs': Part II: Envelopes," *T-Bone Slim and the Transnational Poetics of the Migrant Left in North America* (blog), 30 January 2023, https://blogs.helsinki.fi/tboneslim; Marija Dalbello, "Fluid Media of Proletarian Protest and Creativity in the Late 1910s and Early 1920s," paper presented at the symposium "T-Bone Slim and the Transnational Poetics of the Migrant Left in North America," Kälviä, Finland, 18 August 2023. In these publications, Dalbello references the letter that she discovered at Columbia University. See T-Bone Slim to L. S. Chumley, 13 February 1922, Box 1, Folder 47, Industrial Work-

ers of the World Collection, 1916–1922, Rare Book & Manuscript Library, Columbia University.

51. Fred Thompson, *Fellow Worker: The Life of Fred Thompson* (Chicago: Charles H. Kerr, 1993), 63.

52. Mike Gold, "Proletarian Realism" (1930), in *Mike Gold: A Literary Anthology,* ed. Michael Folsom (New York: International, 1972), 207.

53. Darlington, *Syndicalism and the Transition to Communism,* 18–20; Dubofsky, *We Shall Be All,* 147–57.

54. See Iain McIntyre, *On the Fly! Hobo Literature and Songs, 1879–1941* (Oakland, Calif.: PM Press, 2018).

55. Our thanks to Karri for pointing this out.

56. James Stevens, *Brawny Man* (New York: Alfred A. Knopf, 1926), 146. It is possible that Stevens is describing another T-Bone Slim, since, as was quite common on the road, more than one hobo used the same moniker. However, from the contents of Slim's articles it does seem that he was at times a camp cook.

57. Francis Shor, "'Virile Syndicalism' in Comparative Perspective: A Gender Analysis of the IWW in the United States and Australia," *International Labor and Working-Class History* 56 (1999): 73–74.

58. This is the case although it is also true that Slim's parents arrived in the United States as part of a wave of European immigrants dedicated to settler colonialism, based on the recent dispossession and ongoing genocide of Indigenous peoples.

59. Albert Vetere Lannon, *Second String Red: The Life of Al Lannon, American Communist* (Lanham, Md.: Lexington Books, 1999), 45–46.

60. Fred W. Thompson and Jon Bekken, *Industrial Workers of the World: Its First One Hundred Years* (Cincinnati: IWW, 2006); IWW, "Constructive Program of the IWW," *Solidarity,* 28 November 1914, 2; Ahmed White, *Under the Iron Heel: The Wobblies and the Capitalist War on Radical Workers* (Berkeley: University of California Press, 2022), 86–87, 133, 136.

61. Fred Thompson, "They Didn't Suppress the Wobblies," *Radical America* 1, no. 2 (September/October 1967): 1–5.

62. Other than the factors discussed below, this came in the context of the crushing of a broader 1919–22 American strike wave and a series of successful employer offensives. The split also occurred amid a postwar rise in racism and xenophobia. Thompson and Bekken, *Industrial Workers of the World*; Mayer, *Beyond the Rebel Girl,* 160–66; John Gamb, *Decline of the IWW* (New York: Columbia University Press, 1934), 99–125.

63. Thompson and Bekken, *Industrial Workers of the World*; Mayer, *Beyond the Rebel Girl,* 160–66; Gamb, *Decline of the IWW,* 99–125.

64. Thompson, *Fellow Worker,* 64.

65. Thompson and Bekken, *Industrial Workers of the World*; Darlington, *Syndicalism and the Transition to Communism,* 168–69.

66. Nigel Anthony Sellars, *Oil, Wheat, and Wobblies: The Industrial Workers of the World in Oklahoma, 1905–1930* (Norman: University of Oklahoma Press, 1998), 189–90; Judith Stepan-Norris and Maurice Zeitlin, *Left Out: Reds and America's Industrial Unions* (Cambridge: Cambridge University Press, 2003), 1–18.

67. Anderson, *The Hobo,* 191; Minutes of the Twenty-Third Constitutional General Convention of the Industrial Workers of the World, Sept. 12–17, 1938, Labadie Collection, University of Michigan.

68. T-Bone Slim, "T-Bone Slim Discusses: Not What They Seem," *Industrial Solidarity,* 21 January 1925.

69. T-Bone Slim, "Colds and Sweats," *Industrial Worker,* 7 February 1925; T-Bone Slim, "More of Colds," *Industrial Worker,* 11 February 1925.

70. See later in this volume for the reference to his toe. For the reference to his fractured ribs, see T-Bone Slim, "It's Like This," *Industrial Solidarity,* 29 July 1930.

71. T-Bone Slim, "Nothing Is Finished but There Is Hope," *Industrialisti,* 3 August 1929. On venereal disease and transiency, see Tim Cresswell, *The Tramp in America* (London: Reaktion Books, 2001), 129; Kristin O'Brassill-Kulfan, *Vagrants and Vagabonds: Poverty and Mobility in the Early American Republic* (New York: New York University Press, 2019), 134–55. Our thanks to Dr. Robert Jay for providing invaluable information about locomotor ataxia.

72. Ben Bright, *Reminiscences of Ben Bright, Mariner,* ed. Ewan MacColl and Peggy Seeger, History Workshop Pamphlets, First Series (London: Expression Printers, n.d. [circa 1980]), 22. Slim's scow was moored at Pier 9.

73. Slim may have been the recipient of this same criticism during his lifetime, since in 1937 he wrote an article in which he justified the repetitive nature of his current work, arguing that his writing was repetitive because the problems of capitalism had remained the same. T-Bone Slim, "It's the Same Old Fuss Until Slavery Ends," *Industrial Worker,* 25 September 1937.

74. Hart Island Burial Records, New York City Municipal Archives. His remains were never formally identified because that required a family member to be present. An informal identification must have been made, because the medical examiner's report reads: "Possible name of Matt Valentine Huhta." Report M42-2690, New York City Medical Examiner.

75. For more on the history of Hart Island, see Owen Clayton, "Hart Island: New York City's Dark Shadow," OpenDemocracy, 9 June 2020, https://www.opendemocracy.net.

Editors' Note

Reading through the more than one thousand published articles and hundreds of other materials by T-Bone Slim has been a genuine pleasure.

We have already stated in the Introduction what we believe are the characteristics of Slim's best work. His writings are somewhat inconsistent in quality, which is perhaps unsurprising, given the amount that he produced. His worst pieces tend to be the most abstract and propagandistic articles, which in his later years, as noted in the Introduction, become repetitive and even somewhat boring. That said, Slim wrote many excellent pieces that we would have liked to include here but could not because of space constraints. We had to make often difficult decisions, and as editors we did not always agree with each other about the merits or demerits of individual articles. Given that Slim's time and context are now quite removed from our own, one additional measure we used was how relatable (to use a word popular among today's undergraduates) particular articles are to the concerns of the twenty-first century; examples include Slim's discussion of the invention of what today we would call drone warfare, as well as his discussion of food miles. We also chose pieces based on their historical significance. Our selection process was driven primarily, however, by a desire to include Slim's best writings—"best" here meaning the funniest, most interesting, and most profound work.

Some articles are of such high quality throughout that we include them here in their entirety, but this is not always the case. As in Franklin Rosemont's earlier Slim collection, *Juice Is Stranger Than Friction,* many of the pieces in this volume are extracts. We feel justified in taking this approach because, as Slim's sometime *Industrial Worker* editor Fred Thompson makes clear in his autobiography, *Fellow Worker* (1993), the original articles were often, though certainly not always, cobbled together for publication from disparate notes—this is why many of the original articles shift subjects abruptly.

Thompson also states that Slim was frustrated by the many spelling and other errors that were introduced to his articles during their original publication. We have therefore attempted to correct obvious mistakes, while taking care not to interfere with any of Slim's deliberate wordplay. We have corrected glaring grammatical errors, standardized the placement of punctuation in relation to quotation marks, and, on rare occasions, added missing punctuation. We take full responsibility for any mistakes that we have made in making these calls, and indeed also for any errors we have introduced.

Readers will notice that this book contains only a few articles from the end of Slim's career. We want to clarify that this is not because he did not publish a large number of pieces during the late 1930s and early 1940s (although there is a large publication gap toward the end of his life); rather, we have limited our selections from this period because in our judgment the articles he wrote during this time are substantially weaker than his earlier work.

In addition to the fact that our access to the breadth of Slim's work was (understandably) far greater than Rosemont's, another advantage of this volume over *Juice Is Stranger Than Friction* is our provision of extensive footnotes to give historical context. Without this context, many of Slim's historical and political references are likely to be obscure to most readers in the twenty-first century.

Slim's uses of grammar, punctuation, and typography were innovative but also resulted in unclear meanings at times. We have made the editorial decision to remove the use of bold type in cases where it is not clear why a particular word or phrase is being emphasized. We have maintained the emphasis in those cases where it seems to serve a purpose. For clarity we have added italics to book titles and, on occasion, to in-text quotations as well.

Slim's use of quotation marks was sometimes erratic, with the purpose of the marks unclear in some cases. We have occasionally eliminated these where they seemed unnecessary to convey the intended meaning.

Slim's articles often carried his name as a tagline, but as this becomes repetitive we have deleted the name from most of these examples, except where it seems to become part of the main body of the article. We have also removed the versions of his name or initials that appeared as sign-offs at the ends of some of his pieces.

Finally, we would like to make a tentative reading suggestion. Slim's pieces were written as separate newspaper articles and typically published days or often a week apart. This publication history affected the style and content of Slim's work. In our opinion, his writing benefits from being read in a way that reproduces, at least to some extent, the original conditions of publication—that is, we suggest that you dip into his work at intervals, reading only a small number of pieces at a time and coming back for more later. In our view, Slim's work is more difficult to appreciate if read in long sittings as if it were a novel. Obviously, what you do with this book is entirely your decision, and, no matter how you approach it, we would like to thank you for choosing to learn more about this forgotten writer.

Selected Writings of T-Bone Slim

1919–1921

Only a Mouse in Jail

Letters to Editor

Brown County Jail September 4—*Aberdeen American* editor—Am enclosing you several effusions which seem so ridiculous (here in jail) that I am in hopes they will create a smile on ye face of constant reader and lighten their load of daily care. Also with view of touching your crusted heart to such effect that you will donate a copy of your esteemed paper for jail consumption. Beggin your pardon.

Matt Arnold (model prisoner), L Box 124 Aberdeen[1]

Only a Mouse in Jail

A place is vacant in our home
　　Which never can be filled
Remorseless fate in cruel hate
　　Its squeak forever stilled.

It may have been a mother love
　　A heart by sorrow wrung
That heard the call and gave its all
　　To save its starving young.

We would not let it live in strife
　　Not let it die in peace
On went the chase from place to place
　　Oh when shall murder cease.

It had no show of any kind
　　It vainly ran about
With one faint squeal, beneath a heel
　　Its tiny light went out.

Thus on life's doubtful honor roll
　　Our names we (humans) carve
What do we care how rodents fare
　　Or if their young shall starve.

Ah prisoners mark this rule
　　'Tis life you have begrudged—
And even as that mouse, alas—
　　So you too shall be judged.

The judge will play the game with you
　　You'll tremble in suspense
You'll find out too when he is thru—
　　Your hide is on the fence.

Aberdeen American, 7 September 1919

1 This letter and poem were written while Slim (who seems to have not yet taken that name) was in jail for illegally hopping a freight train. The poem was discovered by John Westmoreland.

The Popular Wobbly

(Air—They go wild over me)[1]

I'm as mild mannered a man as can be
And I've never done them harm that I can see.
Still, on me they placed a ban and they threw me
in the can
They go wild, simply wild over me.

Oh the "Bull"[2] he went wild over me
And he held his gun where everyone could see.
He was breathing rather hard when he saw my
union card
He went wild, simply wild over me.

Then the judge he went wild over me
And I plainly saw we never would agree
So I let the man obey what his conscience had
to say
He went wild, simply wild over me.

Oh, the jailer went wild over me
And he locked me up and threw away the key
It seems to be the rage so they keep me in a cage
They go wild, simply wild over me.

They go wild, simply wild over me
I'm referring to the bedbug and the flea
They disturb my slumber deep
And I murmur in my sleep
They go wild, simply wild over me.

Even God, he went wild over me
This I found out as I knelt upon my knee
Did he hear my humble yell?
No, he told me to go to hell
He went wild, simply wild over me.

---

1 This song was to be sung to the tune of the 1917 music hall hit song "They Go Wild, Simply Wild over Me," by Joseph McCarthy and Fred Fisher. Like Joe Hill and other IWW songsmiths, Slim often used familiar tunes for his songs.

2 Hobo slang for the railroad police.

Will the roses grow wild over me
When I'm gone to the land that is to be
When my soul and body part in the stillness of my
heart

Will the roses grow wild over me?

One Big Union Monthly, 1 April 1920

An Earfull

(Jewelry of His Mind)

A groan means Hallelujah—in the language of the poor! **What**, you can't see it? Well, keep on looking until all of the people exhale that one big groan.

*

You may wonder at my "awefull" intelligence—wonder no longer, I will explain; I went through confirmation school in a cord wood camp.[1]

*

If I ever marry, I'm going to raise pool tables. Pool tables earn 40 cents per hour. Moral—what's the use of raising pool "sharks" to work an hour for two bits?

*

They call the Jews, "Christ Killers." But—allow me to inform you, the Jews didn't drag him behind an automobile (like Frank Little was dragged) with a rope around his neck.[2] Lest we forget!

*

I've always wanted to be president, (since the good old schooldays when the teacher told me "I had a chance") unsuccessfully thus far, but, I am progressing. By my own diligent effort, I have raised myself to the position of a swamper in the woods.[3] This shows what would happen, were I, the noble T. Bone Slim, to enter the political "corral," either as a bull moose, demojackass, or an

---

1 That is, a lumber camp.

2 Frank Little was a leading member of the IWW who was murdered during a strike in Butte, Montana, on 1 August 1917. Six vigilantes wearing masks removed him from the rooming house where he was staying and, after tying him to a car, dragged him through the streets before hanging him. A note reading "First and last warning" was pinned to his thigh. Thousands of people lined the route of his funeral procession, with more following the cortege. Little was one of more than two hundred IWW members who died either directly at the hands of opponents or from illness or injury sustained during time spent in prison. For more information, see Jane Little Bodkin's excellent *Frank Little and the IWW: The Blood That Stained an American Family* (Norman: University of Oklahoma Press, 2019).

3 The cleaners or removal workers known as swampers held the lowest-status position in a lumber camp. They cleared debris, moved timber to places where it could be picked up for transport, and performed maintenance work.

elephant[4]—or any other animal of the political herd—All this, in spite of the fact that a fortune teller once told me I was too honest to succeed.

*

Grammar is not taught (teached) in these lumber camps (this accounts for my flowing style) in fact: only the teamsters are trusted with the use of it—and they do use it—and good grammar—with terrible effect and efficiency (when they become exasperated with the horses).

*

Our "punctuation exercises" consist of drawing a black mark (with a piece of burnt wood) on the end of a log—we count the logs.

*

Our spelling may be "overly-done" in places, but no question of its veracity must be raised—140 of the brightest lumberjacks aided me in assembling these letters into their proper stalls—This puts it up to the editor—will he have the nerve to get up and say that he knows more than 140 lumberjacks, or, even, 100 lumberjacks? If he has, and does say so—well, all I've "got" to say—He knows something!

Your Humble T bone Slim
(plainer slim during war.)

P.S.—During these times of unemployment I am reaching out for a more suitable name.

Industrial Solidarity, 2 April 1921

[4] These are references to the Progressive Party, Democratic Party, and Republican Party, respectively.

Just before the Panic, Mother!

Goodbye, master, I must leave you—
Something tells me I must go.
For—you know, I can't deceive you—
Going-wage is too darn low.
Yes—you say that you will feed me
If I split a (hardwood) cord.
Do not to temptation lead me—
I'm not toiling for my board.

Tho my trials have been sundry
I must e'er disdain to moan,
And altho I'm "good and hungry"
I would leave your work "alone."
Plans of men and lice miscarry
And I know just how you feel,
But, you see, if I'm to marry
I must earn a double meal.

If I work for bread and lodging
While the sun is high and warm,
It would cause me sundry dodging
Thru the winter's cold and storm.
I must have the "All that's in it,"
In the labor that I sell—
For one cannot tell what minute
It may start—to rain like hell.

One more question, boss, one only,
As you count your wealth, untold:
Would you have me save "bologna"
'Gainst the day when I am old?
Now, we understand each other—
And we'll play the "game of grab."
But—please do—recall my brother;
I'm too old to be a scab.

Direction: Do not try to recite this.
It must be sung. Tune: Jest, before the battle, mother![1]
My grammar may at first seem too "deep."
It's entirely unintentional.

Industrial Solidarity, 11 June 1921

[1] "Just before the Battle, Mother" was a popular Civil War song, written by George F. Root.

Twenty Years

Who knows this tune?—[1]

Sing me a song of the "trial" of life—
  Long, weary years, weary years.

Tell me the tale of a heartbroken wife—
  Long, weary years, weary years.

Show me around to the graves in the fen—
  Take me again to the hovels of men—

Let me "regale" with the slave in the "pen"—
  Long, weary years, weary years.

Sing me a song of the torments of Hell—
  Long, weary years, weary years.

Tell me the things that no tongue cares to tell—
  Long, weary years, weary years.

Show me the cell where the silences swell;
  Down where 'tis always—too late to rebel;

Let me commune with the "numbers"—and dwell—
  Long, weary years, weary years.

Sing me a song of a "kingdom of fear"—
  Long, weary years, weary years.

Tell me the tale of these men "in the clear"—
  Long, weary years, weary years.

Picture the pallor no smile comes to cheer;
  Show me indeed our most damnable gear;

Say then the word which these men wait to hear.
  Long, weary years, weary years.

Industrial Worker, 11 June 1921

---

1 This song seems to be referencing the many Wobblies who had been imprisoned during a sustained period of government repression from 1917 and then following World War I.

My Respects—Apology

Introducing:

The disappearing Hips: Few workers know the cause of this phenomena . . . Phenomena is the name masters have given it—grease, or fat, is the proper pronunciamento among workers.

The "technical" disease is intelligence . . . One afflicted with this malady or sickness, acquires a distaste for manual labor.

The Boss is an example in point . . . embonpoint. One of the symptoms of intelligence is a 48 inch waist . . . made to order.

*

The victim broadens, physically, until double doors become an absolute necessity.

*

He narrows, mentally, and becomes sharp. This is called shrewdness . . . ability . . . Ability to live without working.

*

Between me and my master, the struggle must go on until I'm heavier and he is lighter.

(P.S.—I have retained the image of God in my person.) (Except: hump on my back.)

*

The master is not humpbacked, because of his habit of straightening himself in his endeavors to see over his stomach. (Dust, please note.)

*

The coupon-clipper is forever telling us about work—how fine it is . . . how elevating . . . how noble, honest, healthy . . . where did he ever come to know so much about it?

We know what work is . . . That is how we make our . . . and his living.

Ah, come on fellers, be sports; let the master have some . . . some work.

*

Let him get a better idea of work. There is no reason he be denied that which, he says, he simply loves.

*

Finlanders, at one time, were about to be classed Mongolians.[1] They were to be forbidden free entrance into this land of the brave.

But, thereupon, it was shown to the learned professors that among other things the Finns were able to pick up a shovel full of iron-ore.

Well, says the learned professors, if that's the case . . . that settles it.

Finns have, ever since, in their humble, unassuming way been Caucasians. Necessity is the mama of invention.

*

The suffering will be great next winter. The master (tenderhearted rascal) will not be able to bear sight of it. Oh, no. He will be on his private yacht—on the way to Bermuda and Cuba.

Either place is healthy during season when people holler for bread.

*

Now is the time to start thinking about that snow shoveling job.

Industrial Solidarity, 23 July 1921

---

1 This was indeed the case. A Finnish American, Slim here seems aware of the slipperiness of racial categories. For more, see David R. Roediger, *Working toward Whiteness: How America's Immigrants Became White: The Strange Journey from Ellis Island to the Suburbs* (New York: Basic Books, 2005), as well as Roediger's classic *The Wages of Whiteness: Race and the Making of the American Working Class,* rev. ed. (London: Verso, 1999).

Soup Lines

Last night I got an idea. I found it running around in my head. Funny thing, about ideas: They always get into a fellow worker's head and interfere with his brain when it is resting.

*

Well, this idea was looking for an exit—so I reached over and got hold of my pencil and chewed on it a while. Then I decided to pass it on to posterity. (The idea, not the pencil.)

*

We, the working people of the United States of America and of the world, have made up our minds we have no special hankering to take part in any panic[1] . . . And that we can get along very well without a panic . . . And, that we will not accept a panic, if offered to us . . . And, if the masters do not like our way of doing business they are free to go to some other country . . .

*

The masters in this our country have been holding a carnival of selfishness. They have lined their pockets with our cash until their pants are ripping down the sides. They have had one Hallelujah of a time. They have blowed in our loose change on magnetoes and self-starters until their backyards are full of scrapped limousines.[2] They have laid in bed until their kidneys got sore, and now they have made arrangements for our funeral procession. Just think of it, after toughing it out for 30 or 40 years on liver and ham (burger) . . . we are scheduled to die by starvation next winter. It's tough . . . tough! It brings tears to my eyes to think of all the work I will miss next summer. The wages, too, may be higher by that time. It's tough!

*

Who knows but we will become a nation of soup-eaters? And win fame!

Locomotive boilers would make wonderful pots in which to cook the water. The soup can be mixed in the "tender." It will go through the injector, certainly.

*

Soup-lines! Oh. America! No country can compare with you in munificence.

Industrial Solidarity, 10 September 1921

---

[1] That is, a financial panic.

[2] Magnetos were ignition systems used in early automobile spark-ignition engines. It is not clear whether Slim has misspelled the plural or is making a pun, so we have left his spelling alone. "Self-starter" is also a reference to an automobile.

Mysteries of a Hobo's Life

Air: "The Girl I Left Behind Me"[1]

I.

I took a job on an extra gang,[2]
Way up in the mountain,

I paid my fee and the shark shipped me
And the ties I soon was countin'.

The boss he put me driving spikes
And the sweat was enough to blind me,

He didn't seem to like my pace,
So I left the job behind me.

II.

I grabbed a hold of an old freight train
And around the country traveled,

The mysteries of a hobo's life
To me were soon unraveled.

I traveled east and I traveled west
And the shacks could never find me,

Next morning I was miles away
From the job I left behind me.

---

1 This was an Anglo-Irish folk song whose melody was first written down in 1810 but which may date back to Elizabethan times. It was a popular tune in Slim's day, used in the U.S. military as well as in traditional and commercial music.

2 That is, a railroad construction and maintenance work crew.

III.

I ran across a bunch of "stiffs"
Who were known as Industrial Workers.

They taught me how to be a man
And how to fight the shirkers.

I kicked right in and joined the bunch
And now in the ranks you'll find me,

Hurrah for the cause—To hell with the boss!
And the job I left behind me.

From *I.W.W. Songs to Fan the Flames of Discontent*
(also known as the Little Red Songbook), 17th ed.
(Spokane, Wash.: Industrial Workers of the World, 1921)

Half-and-Half

Some of our prominent laborers are in the habit of getting drunk—because they are ashamed of themselves for supporting a bunch of worthless parasites.[1]

*

Have heart, fellow workers! Somebody's got to support them. If we don't, they will starve and die by the thousand.

*

Then, if we leave them "lay" (out in the sun) they might begin to rot—and cause "bucolic plague."

*

Karl Marx, one of our rising young authors, makes a statement that "Capitalism contains within itself the germs (?) of its own destruction." Karl, Karl! What did the I. W. W. ever do to you? Why should you call them germs—or seeds?

*

The Industrial Workers of the World (and elsewhere) have stood much, but if they withstand this latest character assassination, it will go a long way to prove Charlie Darwin's theory on the "survival of the fittest."

*

Some misguided men have been trying to coax the world's other great writer into this country. I'm referring to George Bernard Shaw.[2] This country ain't big enough (nor broad enough) for both of us.

*

Were G. B. S. in this country, ducking around like T-B. S., trying to keep out of jail, someone would surely run across one of us. This is intended as a compliment to George. I'm naturally modest, I am!

Industrial Worker, 10 September 1921

---

1 That is, members of the employing class.

2 Irish playwright, polemicist, novelist, satirist, critic, and activist George Bernard Shaw was born in 1856. Most famous for the play *Pygmalion,* he was a prolific writer until his death in 1950, winning the Nobel Prize in Literature in 1925. Having established himself in London in 1876, he developed an interest in Marxism and socialism, joining the Fabian Society in 1884 and becoming one of its leading figures.

Headin' In

We should get acquainted with our business people. A good way to start up conversation is to ask him what he is doing to combat the high cost of living.

*

Ask him if his sole function is to dish out your cash to these profiteers?

*

Your business man is not elected to office—he is self appointed. He is doing business with your money—your life. If he is not putting up a fight to protect your interests, then he is an unfaithful steward and belongs to a class which is trying to enslave you. To enslave you to the very end that they—the rich—may enjoy liberty, license, and all.

*

Pursuit of happiness? What a merry chase. . . . And we have an inalienable "right" to keep it up until we drop. Did they ever "run the gauntlet"? No. Well, happiness is there. It is at the other end of the gauntlet of swinging shillelaghs. Pursuit of happiness! Just a little of something for us to chase.

*

Slaves! The humor in the above is very delicate. To appreciate it—skip a couple of meals before reading it.

Industrial Worker, 26 November 1921

Headin' In

When the workers begin to starve in droves business will pick up in the undertakers' establishments.

*

A "boom" will be started. Funeral directors will wax wealthy and will be in position to hand a feller a piece of change—and thus again will the working class be saved to answer the country's call.

*

Labor has a bad habit of getting hungry. And just when the warehouses are full too.

*

There is to be no reprimand for the marine who, while guarding the mails, killed a hobo. "He will be backed up to the limit," said Col. E. H. Shaughnessy, second assistant postmaster general.

*

It is a good thing that the Col., however, is not guarding our mails. If he were, our hoboes would soon be crippled and they would not be able to tamp up ties or lay steel or take up the low joints.[1] Why, some of the bullets may wound them seriously.

*

Hoboes are not riding mail trains. But no doubt that many of them will avail themselves of the opportunity to commit suicide. They have no jobs, they have nothing to eat, and no money.

*

The shooting of hoboes will not discourage train robbers. It will only serve as a means to wipe out the claim that these men are holding against society.

*

If you want to put an end to robbery, hire the robbers to guard the mails. Give them light work to do; pay them well. In other words, make it unnecessary for them to rob.

*

1 "Tamping up ties" refers to laying railroad sleepers, also known as crossties.

Then it will not be necessary to shoot hoboes to scare robbers. I must be getting very sentimental in my old age. I do not like to see a hobo disappointed. I do not like for him to get a bullet when he is looking for something to eat.

Industrial Worker, 17 December 1921

1922

The Lumberjack's Prayer

I pray dear Lord for Jesus' sake,
Give us this day a T-Bone Steak,
Hallowed be thy Holy name,
But don't forget to send the same.

Oh, hear my humble cry, Oh Lord,
And send us down some decent board,
Brown gravy and some German fried,
With sliced tomatoes on the side.

Observe me on my bended legs,
I'm asking you for Ham and Eggs
And if thou havest custard pies,
I like, dear Lord, the largest size.

Oh, hear my cry, All Mighty Host,
I quite forgot the Quail on Toast,
—Let your kindly heart be Stirred,
And stuff some oysters in that bird.

Dear Lord, we know your Holy wish,
On Friday we must have a fish,
Our flesh is weak and spirit stale,
You better make that fish a whale.

Oh, hear me Lord, remove these
"Dogs,"
These sausages of powder'd logs,
Your bull beef hash and bearded
Snouts,
Take them to hell or there-abouts.

With Alum bread and Pressed-Beef
butts,[1]
Dear Lord you damn near ruin'd
my guts,
Your white-wash milk and Oleorine,[2]
I wish to Christ I'd never seen.

Oh, hear me Lord, I am praying still,
But if you won't our union will,
Put pork shops on the bill of fare,
And starve no workers anywhere.

Answer to the Prayer

I am happy to say this prayer has been answered—by the "old man" himself. He tells me He has furnished—plenty for all—and that if I am not getting mine it's because I am not organized SUFFICIENTLY strong to force the master to loosen up.

He tells me he has no knowledge on Dogs, Pressed Beef Butts, etc., and that they probably are products of the Devil. He further informs me the

1 Alum is an aluminum-based compound that was used to adulterate bread to make it feel more substantial. As well as lacking any nutritional value, its use could lead to digestive and bowel problems.

2 Patented by Hippolyte Mège-Mouriès in 1869 in France, the butter substitute Oleorine was banned in the 1880s in New York State, Iowa, and other areas of the United States with large dairy industries. It remained cheaper than butter despite being targeted by extra federal taxes. Now known in most places simply as margarine and made with vegetable oil, it was then a primarily animal fat–based product.

Capitalists are children of Hisn—and that He absolutely refuses to participate in any children's squabbles. He believes in letting us fight it out along the lines of Industrial Unionism.

Yours in faith

T-BONE SLIM.

NOTE—What you give goes in the jail-box relief fund No. 310 951 W. Madison St.[3]

Truth, 6 January 1922

---

[3] The IWW printed "The Lumberjack's Prayer" on cards and sold them to raise funds.

Lots of Sympathy but No Help

The masters' press palpitates that a practiced bum can beg $29.30 in one hour—If this is so—(and I have no reason to doubt the editors' experience) this explains the big fortunes of today (also the boneheaded editors).

Who would have believed that our hard working millionaires have been leading a double life? That they had amassed their wealth by begging?

If this be so, what is use of a practiced bum like an editor frittering away his time on a mere paltry 10 dollars a week, editing a prostitute paper, when he could step out any afternoon and beg $87.90 in 3 hours?

I cannot but believe that this is true—and by the looks of some of the editorials lately, I'm convinced the editor is out on the stem reaping the golden harvest while the janitor is doubling for him in the sanctum_ _ _[1]

*

I am easily misled, and being of a very jealous disposition, a thought penetrated my skull and I resolved to gather in a few of those golden sheckles—I had consulted my rating in Dunns and Brad-streets and found they had failed to give me a rating[2]—so, I starts out with a handicap of a double zero, in both pockets.

Well sir, even if I do say it myself, my eloquence was not entirely without results—I started a half a dozen of the finest crying matches ever seen anywhere and at times I, myself, could not restrain my tears, which would burst out in a spasm of self pity as I depicted, brokenly, the horrors of starvation in my particular case.

*

I would stop a Bourgeois on the street and soon our mutual tears would comingle and splash down to freeze on the pavement. So much wasted sentimentality.

I was out four hours and quarter—spilled about a gallon of tears—strained my voice—and collected eleven cents.

I received six hundred dollars worth of sympathy. Plenty of advice. Ninety

1 The "main stem" was a slang term for the main thoroughfare of a large city. These areas were also known as "hobohemia," most famously in Chicago, as they were where transient workers would seek accommodation, pleasure, and employment. For more information on hobohemia, see Todd DePastino, *Citizen Hobo: How a Century of Homelessness Shaped America* (Chicago: University of Chicago Press, 2003), 59–126.

2 At the time this was written, Dun and Bradstreet were separate companies that provided credit ratings and analysis to businesses. They merged in the 1930s.

three addresses (where to go to) including the address of Jesus Christ (formerly at Jerusalem) in seven different Gospel Missions. Not a Hotel or Restaurant address in the whole bunch.

I was "bummed" for all my snuff and another bum, probably a practiced editor, got the dime away from me.

I hung on to the penny for fear a dog would bite me if it should find me broke. I have resolved to bum no more—Quite clearly do the advantages of fasting present themselves to me.

Truth, 6 January 1922

An Experience

When I was a kid "our teacher" used to take great pleasure in "correcting" errors of judgment, on *our* part—on our *parts.*

*

She had a very ceremonious habit of sending one of the boys out to cut whips whenever she felt like "timbering up" on us.

*

This necessitated a jack-knife. The teacher invariably failed to specify how to cut—where to cut, with the result that whips arrived into her itching hands cut half through in several places.

*

Of course, you must remember, we were children—you would not expect that much solidarity in grown-ups.

*

Down South, when a white man has won the displeasure of the "master," a Negro is selected to "whip" him.

When a "colored man" is fallen from grace the "master" designates a "white man" to administer punishment.

Thus race hatred is kept alive.

*

In the industrial world of today some "unions" are carrying whips to the master. One union will be working to defeat another union which is fighting for bread.

For instance: In 1917 the Coast Timberworkers knew the slogan of the I. W. W. They knew the Wobblies were out to organize the "eight-hour day." What did they do? Did they come out for a "nine-hour day"?

They did—and that was where they carried whips to the master. If they had come out for the "eight-hour day" the master's whip would have been *half cut through.*

As it was, the Wobblies were able to generate sufficient *power* to "stave off" the nine-hour day.

*

But I must get back to my story.

In the school was a young presidential possibility who was in the habit of bringing in whips which were entirely out of proportion to our size. Many a debate we had with him, all to no avail, until one day we organized and laid down rules of discipline.[1]

Thereafter the teacher was compelled to control her temper and handle said whips gently, lest they fall to pieces.

After our schoolboy organization got to going there were less squabbles and fights among scholars; "class hatred" was a dead issue—but of course you cannot expect groan-ups to organize. They must have their "jurisdiction," their "seniority," their "skill" and "graduated" wages—any damn thing which the master can use as a whip to drive others in turn.

*

I'm off my story again—and if I get off once more I'll quit story writing and take out credentials.[2]

The teacher was forced to adopt new methods of torture (at the risk of her own knuckles). She commenced using the "ruler" on our tender palms.

*

Our "master" is still using the same old whips. They'd never get by with it with school children. Organize solidarity!

Industrial Worker, 11 February 1922

---

1 Presumably, they beat him up.

2 This is likely a reference to becoming a formal workplace delegate or organizer in the IWW, or possibly to being an IWW conference delegate.

Sulphur and Molasses

Sixty years ago we were howling, "How wicked it is to have chattel slaves!"

Sixty years hence we will say, "The wage-slave sure did ketch hell in 1921."

Who knows but Mr. T-Bone Slim will write an *Uncle Tom's Hovel* about it?[1]

*

By the way, there is a movement to buy Monticello, the home of Thomas Jefferson, author of the Declaration of Independence, and present it to the nation as a perpetual memorial.

Wouldn't it be a graceful deed if the I. W. W. would purchase one of Fogg Bros.' boarding cars (the home of T-Bone Slim) and place it on the grave of "Jim," the empire builder, as a perpetual memorial to us both?[2]

By the way, again—I request this be done after I am hung.

Industrial Worker, 20 May 1922

---

1 This is a reference to Harriet Beecher Stowe's antislavery novel *Uncle Tom's Cabin* (1852). There is an apocryphal story that Abraham Lincoln described the book as having "started this big war," referring to the American Civil War, which ended slavery in the United States.

2 "Jim" refers to railroad builder and tycoon James J. Hill, who owned a number of the lines that hoboes and others traveled along. By the time he died in 1916, Hill had amassed a fortune equivalent to more than $1.5 billion today.

Overalls

Everybody knows that it is an unpardonable sin and an eternal disgrace to put a patch on a pair of overalls in this, the greatest country on the globe. But it had to be done. I could not stand for the admiring glances of the populace directed at my bobbing knee.

*

For a man of lesser abilities, this task would have proven insurmountable. The idea being to get the patch on and still not commit a sin. That is, to take the "curse off sin" and neutralize the disgrace.

*

Long did I concentrate upon this problem, my feelings rent between loyalty to my country, and mortification. If I "done" this job of patchwork, in the sense that a plebeian would do it, I would disgrace our small but select tribe of brain workers.

*

But the inexorable law of supply and demand spurred me on to action—and I want it understood before we put that patch on, that "conventionalities" had nothing to do with my activities.

*

The weather suddenly grew colder—I made careful note of this. The wind must be prevented from entering my garments . . . Note: I had filed a relinquishment on my "auxiliaries-unmentionables" (some time ago) for very emphatic and lively reasons. Reasons, I said. Yes, there must have been millions of them.

*

On goes the patch! Not as a common tailor would do it. No—I will put it on as a technician.

*

Looking about, I discovered that, the country is prohibition.[1] What has this to do with "patching overalls"?

Wait a minute. With the country gone dry, I have no use for hip-pocket No. 2. I can use it for a patch.

*

1 The U.S. Prohibition era lasted from 1920 to 1933. Though Slim makes negative comments about Prohibition, there is some evidence that it helped him to moderate his drinking.

Now we are progressing, but it takes brains. We will take off that pocket and transport it from the hip to the knee, sew it on (upside down), leave the bottom unsewed.

(Note: Watch this—don't sew bottom seam; if you do, it is a pocket no longer.)

By doing it this way I still have the same number of pockets in my overalls (which my master lets me use) as before.

*

Once again the fair person of T-Bone Slim is hid away from public gaze. Once again the Lake Michigan breezes are prevented climbing my sturdy frame. But I tremble for the day when my pockets will no longer cover my pulsing nakedness—in this fair land of opportunity.

*

P.S.:—Patching is a poor substitute for unionism, but it is a very good reason for organizing.[2] Do it industrially.

Apology: If technicians take offense at this "joke," then the joke stands unchallenged. My candid opinion is that technicians are poorly organized—if at all.

Industrial Worker, 27 May 1922

---

[2] That is, craft unionism is only putting a patch over the rags of capitalism.

The Stuff Heroes Are Made Of

Confession is good for the soul—and my soul, being, as it is, susceptible to good influences, is no different than the general run of souls in my neighborhood. Hence this confession.

*

I realize that in confessing I am running a chance with my reputation and possibly with my complexion, inasmuch as I have not heard of confession being used as a first-aid in preserving the texture of the human hide.

*

If confession would benefit the complexion, wouldn't we be a homely race of people? All the bay rum in Christendom wouldn't make us presentable; opticians would lose their trade and people would buy "dimmers" with their "meed of prosprity" until they went broke.

*

Fortunately, our hide is immune—yes or no—but before I start confessing I wish to state a gentleman friend of mine inveigled me and Shingle Creek Shorty into one of those moving picture places.[1]

Ever have I tried to protect myself against this form of dissipation; these germ-breeding caverns of darkness and filth. Therefore, imagine my astonishment when I beheld on the screen scene after scene of unbridled splendor wherein a bunch of parasites cavorted regardless.[2]

*

Across the silvered sheet struts a man who to my unpracticed eye seemed to have but one ambition in life. At the slightest opportunity he would bend over gracefully to suck at a lady's wrist.[3] At first I thought he was trying to see what time it was by the lady's wrist watch, and I would still be of that opinion if Shorty, who used to be up in society, hadn't told me that the parasites have that habit because time hangs heavy on their hands—having nothing else to do.

*

1 That is, an early movie theater, called a nickelodeon.

2 Early films tended to focus on the lives of the rich—an observation that might arguably be made about today's films as well.

3 That is, the man is kissing the lady's hand in a formal manner.

The hero of the piece got his start in life by tapping a man over the head, going through his clothes and relieving him of his valuables. The man robbed was no good, so I guess it was all right according 'o the bourgeois psychology, although we think it all wrong.

*

He makes a perfect getaway, under an assumed name, and then he runs into a lad who knows something about horses. *They* employ themselves betting on horses, and *he* clears a hundred thousand by the sweat of *their* brow. Again he makes a get-away.

*

Next *he* invests *their* capital in a gambling enterprise, a business proposition, and again he clears a million (and the law) in a "corner on cotton" deal without doing anything to earn the money. It is after getting his hands on this "jack" that he saves the lady from drowning and starts sucking her wrist. He gets *caught up with* by the man he rapped over the head, and that worthy proceeds to return the compliment; puts our hero in the hospital and commits suicide.

*

The ends of justice met!

Our hero recovers, reforms, and takes another suck at her wrist. And the play ends too soon (in an inspiring fade-out)—too soon for the audience to see our hero looking for a job.

Well, anyway, our hero by this time is well along in years. It's too late for him to start working for a living; besides, what's the use of working when you have a million dollars and a wrist? *Too late!*

*

By the way, I was going to do some confessing. It's too late now. The column is finished, and besides, the editor won't stand for any of that stuff———but.

*

If we wanted to be mean we could put in a board bill against these heroes for a thousand years' board. We might be able to collect it, too. But, oh, well, if we couldn't, we could at least get a job as an umpire in baseball.

Ho hum!

You have nothing to break but your chains.

Industrial Worker, 17 June 1922

Normalcy Has Arrived

Normalcy has arrived.[1]

The illustrious T-Bone Slim has projected his scintillating presence onto a job. (Great applause.) Somehow he eluded his caretakers and accepted a flattering offer of a position in an extra gang—as a gandy dancer.[2] This sudden rise of Slim into prominence was an agreeable surprise to his many friends. Nevertheless, his enterprise was not without its "deleterious" side, inasmuch as: Time (in its mad passage) finds Slim's hatband stretched, which is more than can be said of the belly-band around his neighborhood. . . . Thus it is we find him swaying, one foot in the air, doing yeoman service on one of the "trade arteries" of our beloved globe.

*

Contrary to all beliefs, Slim says, he isn't going to bust any criminal syndicalism law on the first day . . . by kicking on the grub.[3] Yet he insinuates that no government inspector is going to be fool-hardy, or hardy, enough to eat any of it. He challenges any governmental agency (from Hoover up)[4] to eat a mouthful of *that material* which is dished up to the dancing proletariat of *the maintenance of the way.* He defies the Labor Board[5] to eat of the plenteous "vittles"

---

1 This is a reference to the key slogan used during the 1920 U.S. presidential race by eventual winner Warren G. Harding, who promised a "return to normalcy" following the crises of World War I and its aftermath.

2 A slang term for a railway construction or maintenance worker. The job was known as gandy dancing because of the peculiar movement workers needed to make while tamping ties, hence Slim's reference to "the dancing proletariat of *the maintenance of the way.*"

3 As part of the repression of the IWW, a number of "criminal syndicalism" laws were passed in various U.S. states in the late 1910s and early 1920s. These laws proscribed membership in the IWW and made illegal the use and propagation of revolutionary ideas and militant tactics.

4 This is likely a reference to Herbert Hoover. A former mining engineer, Hoover was in charge of maintaining food supplies for American citizens in Europe during World War I and was appointed head of the U.S. Food Administration in 1917. After failing to gain the Republican Party's presidential nomination in 1920 he was appointed secretary of commerce in 1921, a position he held until 1928, when he was elected president of the United States. Alternatively, this could possibly be a reference to J. Edgar Hoover, then deputy and later head of the Federal Bureau of Investigation. Since 1917 he had led operations focused on imprisoning and deporting radicals.

5 This refers to the sections of the U.S. Department of Labor, as well as state-based equivalents, that set minimum standards and intervened and mediated in labor disputes. The IWW was critical of such instruments, asserting variously that they were ineffective, that they favored employers, and that they provided minor concessions to workers in order to waylay or prevent more radical action.

provided by the "commissary" and served under the "By-Product Act" in the *models of twentieth century sanitation on "all roads"* cursed with Morgan & Co. management.[6] He issues an invitation to the "board" and requests they allow themselves the privilege of dining with him. The expense will not be great—and if necessary he will look after them. Board is one dollar a day—low, considering the high cost of fertilizer. Bring a dollar with you, O ye Noble Labor's Board, and stay with us the whole day long—eat with us and be merry—that's a good fellow, learn with us.

*

The back of the panic is broken! Let us record that on this day, June 16th, T-Bone Slim had "one day in!"—one day nearer emancipation! Tonight, after a day of toil, he has five cents coming to him, *if the road doesn't go bankrupt!* His expenses have been viz.: Board, five meals, $1.70; fee, $1. How the company came to overlook the *nickel* is a mystery. (Maybe it is intended for tobacco.) If so, then the Co. is too extravagant. Slim's 'head expenses (for snus) are only 3½ cts. per day.[7]

*

Tomorrow is Saturday . . .

Monday morning (if he isn't fired before then) Slim will have 30 cents coming. If it rains Monday he will be owing the company 20 cents, for two days' work. Slim thinks the only reason the company doesn't rob him of his clothes is because the company is afraid of the Labor Board. . . .

*

Slim, you see, is not personally acquainted with the Board members and thinks the Board is a bunch of two-fisted, horny-handed battlers, who wouldn't wait for the "drop of the hat" before engaging in-battle for labor's rights, in valiant defense of labor's prerogatives, which is all labor has left. And that isn't all he thinks (of the board), but space and modesty will not permit the use of such flowery language extolling the virtues of our heroic board of the recent wage cuts.

*

---

6 "Morgan & Co." refers to the banking firm of J. P. Morgan, which at one point controlled approximately 16 percent of U.S. railroads, along with large holdings in other industries. The federal government targeted the firm with antimonopoly cases in the 1900s, but it continued to have a major stake in industry. At this time the firm was owned by J. P. Morgan Jr., the founder's son, who had inherited from his father the equivalent of $2.5 billion today.

7 Snus is a variant of dry snuff that originated in Sweden; it is mixed with salt and placed under the top lip. Slim seems to have used snus regularly.

Well, the second day of hopping is come to an end at last! Such contrary "ties" no one ever saw! No more than Slim would tamp up one, somebody would step on it and tramp it down again—causing Slim great agitation of mind. . . . Upon such occasions he would wax wroth, and in a voice vibrant with emotion he would warn his colaborers to tread lightly, nor mar the scenery his diligence had so laboriously created—a task well done!

*

Let us glance back over our work.

Previous to 1893 practically all roads were controlled by German and English capital. Ham and eggs (and other good foods) were served to the gangs of track-layers. Wages (outside of section men)[8] were $2.25, $2.50 and $2.75 per day. Board was $3.50. A man could clear $12.70 per week.

*

Then the House of Morgan took over the roads. (The panic of '93 was utilized for this purpose.) Then came the 90 cents a day. Since then have come the predigested pigs—slimy, disintegrating things, too far gone to be served uncooked. Since then have come the chicory coffee, lowest grade oleomargarine (untouchable), rancid bacon and pork (maggots withdrawn by special process).

Menu for week: Dogs, cow-lips, beef butts, pig snouts and ears, and redhorse, all of these in an A. No. 1 state of decay. The "poor devils" try to work on bread and chicory—and eggs on Friday (a concession to Catholics, unnecessary, considering the meat is unfit to eat at all times).

*

Nowadays a man working on the tracks, if he actually isn't in a poisoned condition, is at least suffering malnutrition.

Previous to '93, when English and German capital was in control of the roads, we received good board for $3.50 per week. Now we get nothing but low grade swill—and we are charged $7 per week for it.

*

After mature consideration Slim has decided to withdraw his invitation to the Labor Board. He thinks it too risky. They might get hold of food that isn't properly disinfected, get cramps, and die of pellagra before you could haul them to near-beer saloon.[9]

---

8 "Section men" may refer to railroad maintenance and/or construction workers. The term was sometimes also used for the foreperson in charge of a gang working on a section of the railway.

9 Pellagra is a potentially fatal disease caused by poor nutrition, specifically a deficiency of niacin (vitamin B_3).

Then where would we be without a labor board (standing by us) handing out decisions which save the railroads $48,000,000 and reduce our wages the same amount?

*

And then again, by the time the board got together, passed a decision to accept Slim's hospitality, Slim might not be here (or any place else) to show that august body around.

T-Bone Slim

(Note: When the "Milwaukee Road" was put through to the Coast 10,000 ham and egg-eating tracklayers went West with it.[10] When *they* come back, ham and eggs will return also. Get next. . . .)

Industrial Worker, 24 June 1922

10 The Chicago, Milwaukee, St. Paul and Pacific Railroad, known as the Milwaukee Road, connected the Midwest and Northwest regions of the United States during the nineteenth and twentieth centuries.

Das Kapital

In these perilous times, while criminal syndicalist laws are rampant and soups are seasoned with certiorari,[1] it is considered the height of incaution to monkey with profits.

*

Established truths are waylaid and sandbagged, or suppressed. William Jennings Bryan,[2] alive to the painful experiences of Eugene V. Debs,[3] arises and contends in stentorian tones that our industrial captains are not descended from monkeys.

One way of keeping out of jail.

*

Nevertheless, it would seem at this time, while so little is being said about capital, and especially by the men who control said capital, that a word from me would not be out of place. Too often have we trusted the discussion of this important phase of our suffering to those only who have a theoretical knowledge of capital and its many vagaries.

*

People with a mere smattering of knowledge regarding wealth have waxed eloquent, while those who have made capital a study, and an anathema, have been pushed in the corner.

*

I take personal and pardonable pride in pointing out that I have completed a brief survey, a personally conducted investigation of the true nature and habits

---

1 A writ or order by which a higher court reviews a case tried in a lower court.

2 A major figure in the Democratic Party, Bryan had been a congressman and ran and lost as a candidate in three presidential elections. A noted orator, he served as U.S. secretary of state from 1913 to 1915 before resigning when Woodrow Wilson's administration began to break with his favored policy of neutrality regarding World War I. Bryan later became a crusader for prohibition and an opponent of the teaching of Darwin's theory of evolution, famously taking part in the Scopes "monkey trial."

3 The longtime leader of the Socialist Party of America and a cofounder of the IWW, Debs was jailed in 1894 for his role in the Pullman strike as president of the American Railroad Union. His opposition to military conscription led to his being charged again in 1918 under recently introduced sedition laws; he was convicted and sentenced to ten years in prison. In 1920 he campaigned for the office of U.S. president from prison and received approximately 6 percent of the vote. He was freed in 1921.

of capital, and I can say, with the voice of authority, that capital is nothing less than the dollars and cents that the labor did not receive. As to its habits, it is what might accurately be termed "skittish."

*

At this period in our beloved history there appears to be a generous shortage of capital among the working classes—demonetized, so as to say—and it is thought that low wages is the cause of this phenomenon. But I may say in alluding to capital, that capital is only a minor calamity compared to the lack of organization among the workers in conjunction with the "unity-plus" of the shirkers. Even the petty larceny tin-horn "wit worker" despises and adds his mite to the discomfiture of labor.[4]

*

Other things may happen in the sphere of our paper-collared activity which, in a way of heartrending gloom and hydra-headed sorrow, make the large fortunes wrung from labor look like a plugged nicked in a "lead mine." I have in mind the (pitiful) lack of solidarity among the exponents of "Do as you're told," vote as you're told, and die as you're told. It's a poor man who has to be told.

*

Would that I had the gift, even such as has a journalist on our daily papers. Gladly would I oil my stylograph and boldly assail capital in burning words of denunciation, criticism, censure and—and protest. If that would not suffice, I would apologize for distracting the master's mind, just as he was about to send other *workers* to the poor house.

*

Yea, verily would I attack injustice in (every form) in general and exploitation in particular. I would indict the malevolent malefactors and offer maledictions upon their heads.

*

I would pillory them in a flow of language teeming with the misery of centuries of interminable toil, as the most dastardly cruel, inhuman, unsocial, ungodly, unchristian, ungentlemanly and unnecessary affliction, too long suffered by the unprotesting proletariat.

*

---

[4] "Wit workers" are employees who work mostly with their brains rather than their muscles.

But, unfortunately, I have not the gift to properly express my appreciation of the abiding iniquity of the system founded on slavery, permeated with cunning and perpetuated in selfishness.

*

What can I do? I am helpless. My vocabulary is weak. The constabulary is strong. I must ever be mindful of the fate of Debs. (I might lose my citizenship.) Tough, isn't it?

*

When great men like William J. Bryan dare not call the profiteers monkeys, but slightly removed, it is time I withhold my native American spleen and "lay off" this demoniacal system which creeps upon us like a jackal, teasing us and starving half the population of the world, old and young, into submission.

*

What can I do? What can I say? I have much to say but I have no way of saying it. I am stuck.

*

The best way to take what is justly due you is to organize to take, the way the employer is organized to retain, the products of your toll—industrially!

*

Once you are organized he will be "tickled to death" to hand it to you. You will not "have" to take it. He will bring it up to the house. . . .

Tell him to throw it on the shif-fo-nierre. Ask him to take a chair for a change—walking is so hard on a heavy man.

Industrial Worker, 15 July 1922

The Power of These Two Hands

Published for the General Construction Workers' Industrial Union No. 310, of the I.W.W.

The construction workers have made millionaires from coast to coast—Maine to California; Minnesota to El Paso; at all points, projects and places in between wherever undertakings of any size have been completed—"With the strength of this poor old back! With the power of these two hands!" (A "brain" of a contractor never made him a millionaire—cheap lodging houses are full of contractors—unemployed.)

It was these two hands, yours and mine, that finished the job of boosting him into a purple automobile, while we beat our way back into civilization,[1] so-called, in box cars, ice boxes, etc., for, if we "put out" the price of transportation we find there would have been no use of going to the job in the first place. We don't go to these jobs just for the sake of making new millionaires. No. We go there to get something for ourselves and that something is—you'd never guess it in a thousand years—money.

It is a stake we are after.[2] We do not go to these jobs merely to take on some work; we do not go there merely to wear out our old clothes; (old clothes can be worn out); we don't go there merely to eat and sleep—if we did, we would not be on these jobs in the good old summer time, we would sleep under an apple tree with our mouths wide open. No. The only thing that brings us to these jobs in these out-of-the-way places is the fact: "We need the money." It's a question of money, and God knows, too much money never ruined the author of this screed. Too much money never made a tramp of a working man.

Now let us consider that the big mills and manufactories have their own construction companies and that these mills and factories for the first time have started shipping men, construction men, into their gates. Let us see these men as they are on the job: The "alarm clock" wakes us up in the morning to grab a hasty breakfast—pasty breakfast—which, because of its "quality," it would be far better to leave untasted. We grab a nose bag of sandwiches (sand—) and

1 "Beat" is slang for avoiding railroad fares by illegally riding in boxcars, underneath carriages, and on other parts of trains.

2 "Stake" refers to the money saved by migratory workers from their seasonal labor to sustain them during winter and other periods of unemployment and low labor demand.

make a dash for the time-clock to punch in. (Being single we lose no time kissing friend's wife good-bye.)[3]

When we arrived in this camp we found a bunch "quitting" and we wondered if they had quit to make room for us. We found out the boss had requested them to quit.[4] Gladly would they have continued selling their labor—and many of them needed the money as "bad as we did"—for the selling of their strength and skill was the only thing they had left to sell (many of us had "peddled" everything else only to fall back on the old standby—work). So you see, our entrance on the field of action meant a great deal to these men who were compelled to leave it.

We set in. But no sooner are things moving smoothly than the boss can be seen sizing up his crew. He picks out one man who appears a trifle slower, or faster, (doesn't make much difference) and tells him to "go and get it" (this to scare others): He finds one man asking another for a chew of tobacco. "Hey, you two, this is no market house, the timekeeper wants to see you." We see man after man put on his coat and we begin to wonder: "must be another shipment coming in at noon." There is—There was.

Years ago when we had to support our women-folk it may have been necessary to work long hours. Today our women-folk are working same as we, although not on construction jobs, except as waitresses, so **why should we work long hours** to support somebody who is already supporting herself (in a way), and a master (in style)?—tell me that. I fail to see where either man or woman is getting anything more **now** than **then**—yet both are working now.

I will close (like the parasite), wishing you a prosperous year—it is Sunday morning and the boys are getting ready to hold card inspection.[5]

Yours for the One Big Union of All Labor.

Extracts from Slim's pamphlet *The Power of These Two Hands*
(Chicago: IWW, 1922)

---

3 As discussed in the Introduction, Slim abandoned his wife, Rosa, around 1912 and was divorced in 1916.

4 This is an allusion to a phenomenon whereby job agencies, known as "sharks," would sell the same job, such as working as a lumberjack or on the railroad, three times to multiple people: to the worker on the job, to the person traveling to the job, and to the worker returning from the job. This meant that each laborer was typically fired after only a few days of work, with the unscrupulous employer and the shark dividing the agency fee.

5 This is a reference to the IWW's red membership card.

Consistently Speaking

Since the day Vanderbilt first uttered the historical ultimatum, "the public be damned," the public was, is, (and will be) damned.[1]

*

Since then the public has been damned most mercilessly and unmercifully—almost anybody could step out, any day, and damn the public and get away with it—not so today.

*

Since the money pirates began to feel solicitude for the damned public, the public-damners have restrained, and contained themselves—and the public has not been publicly damned since.

*

Since this altered attitude, curbing the latitude of our most fluent and eloquent damners, we feel it no more than right that we should assure the damned-public, (both private and public) that we have never damned the public, in private or public, and that damning the public is one of the last damn things we would think of. . . .

Since we feel that when the public is damned we are damned too.

*

First, let me say that when organized labor wallops the boss with an increase in wages for themselves,[2] the boss sinks down to his knees and yells, "spare the public, for gawdsake men, be reasonable." "Break me if you will," he says, "but spare the public." So you see, the boss is not the public.

*

Labor is not the public. Because, didn't we just now see that when labor was about to receive higher pay the boss feels sorry for the public.

*

1 In 1882, William Henry Vanderbilt, a railway magnate who had inherited $100 million (equivalent to about $2.9 billion today) from his father, Cornelius Vanderbilt, was asked by a reporter whether his limited express trains were profitable or run at a loss for the benefit of the public. His response was, "Accommodation of the public? The public be damned! We run them because we have to." The statement was widely interpreted as evidence of Vanderbilt's arrogant contempt toward the concerns of everyday people.

2 That is, goes on strike.

(If increased pay comes from the public, *what business has the boss with it in his possession*—how did he obtain possession of the public funds?

*

Where did we leave the public? Let's see. Oh, yes—if labor is not the public we must try to find out how the public came to be the nominal owner of that particular piece of money that labor demands for service rendered.

*

(If the public works for a living, it is labor; if it works labor for a living—then, it is a parasite, and deserves no consideration.)

*

Are professional men the public?

A doctor is not the public because it's to his interest to have labor get higher wages. When labor gets high wages the doc. can put in a pill, and a bill—in fact, the missus lets the family doctor fondle the family pocket book in a way that seems sacrilegious to say the least.

*

A lawyer—Is he the public?

No. It is to his interest to let labor have enough wages so that he can hire a lawyer to lose his case in capitalist courts.

No use talking—the public doesn't exist.

No use beating about the bush, this way—There isn't any such animal.

*

No use wasting any space discussing it—the public being non-existent is capable of taking care of itself in this competitive commonwealth, without the hypocritical solicitude of the exploiters of labor.

*

But if it develops that there is a public, then it also develops that the public is unorganized. If this be so, then our sympathy is wasted—let the public organize themselves into a big union of publicans and let them enter into the economic arena (with the proper competitive spirit).

*

I would suggest that public hunt themselves a job and become wage-earners, thus qualifying for membership in the I. W. W.

*

Whether you succeed in getting a job, or not, is not material since "intent" is generally accepted the equivalent of "accomplishment" in such things.

*

I might mention in closing that labor is the only public worth mentioning, the rest all are labors' servants, and for this reason, it is necessary for labor to organize into a one big union in order that they may keep their servants in their proper stalls.

*

Everything that exists has been produced by, and of, labor—labor is entitled to the best of everything.

Organize, and then some.

Industrial Worker, 30 September 1922

Nosebags

Alas! Alas! that I should live to see the day when I must record that underfed freight handlers are in the habit of appropriating eatables (and delicacies even) from freight in process of transportation. Alas!

*

(In Chicago.)

The alleged board, in the alleged camps, fed to "actual" freight handlers is insufficient, and too damn ancient to keep alive that perfect specimen of physical force.

*

I cannot help but feel that a working man should be allowed to eat—even in the harvest fields it has pained me greatly to put a nose cage on a horse to prevent it eating that which it helps to produce—of course I do not mean to say that freight handlers should get the "first crack" at goods in transport. No. I mean to say that equally good goods should be served them on equally good tables in equally good camps (homes).

*

P.S.—Is the capitalist system based on pilfering—When I look in my "nose bag" (lunch) and find therein two emaciated sandwiches and an apple (the apple to keep me cheerful about it) I very naturally open up the sandwiches to find the secret road to wealth—through men's stomachs. And there it is: two slices of tissue of some dead animal. Maybe only a few short years ago this animal was well and able—and now it lies cold in death and in my sandwich. Still we never hear of a sandwich being called a mausoleum.—a grave!

Industrial Worker, 9 December 1922

1923

Best People

Personally, I am in favor of immigration—the more the merrier; the bigger the better. The more that arrive here, the less hours we will have to work to support our "best people"—by heck!

"Best people" is understood to mean the "best fed people"—the word "fed" was dropped for fear it might incite the worst people into ravenous riots of appetite. That would be Les Majeste. . . .

*

Well-fed—ah, that's the word. How very polite-like it sounds.—Anybody is ready to concede that everybody should be well fed—nothing offensive 'bout that. . . .

But, best-fed-people? Nix on that. Drop the fed. . . . Best people!

*

Years ago when we, the "worst fed people," were few and far apart it was quite a task to support our best people. We had to work as high as ten hours per day in order to make biscuits reach around.

*

And then immigration set in; and since then, we have shortened our day to eight hours. Just as soon as a few more ships dock at New York we can go on a six-hour shift and still retain the respect of our best fed people.

*

We, the workers, have just so many to support, besides ourselves. Therefore, every foreigner added to our gang makes it easier to do so. To argue against immigration is to argue for a long day. To argue against accepting their help, is to argue that *you will not put up a fight* to shorten the day; to make room for them in our industries.

*

Years ago it was difficult to keep "all pots boiling." Remember the way the old gang boss used to strut by, a pick handle in his hand.[1] Remember the way he would glare at you! You don't see him any more. Why?

*

---

1 "Gang boss" refers to a railway construction foreperson.

Remember the way our commercial editors used to root into the Italians? The comic pages called them "wops." The news columns called them "guineys," dagos, etc. Why?

*

I will tell you why.—In an unguarded moment our captains of industry sent over to Italy and persuaded a bunch of Sicilians to come here—they came over and civilized the Boss with the pickhandle—they civilized all public work, turned it over to Yankees, and went into business for themselves—Selling the luscious fruit of California.

*

That's why the capitalist papers soured on the sons of sunny Italy and began calling them names. And that is why I'm in favor of immigration.—It seems that our hundred per cent workers are unable to hold their own with the bosses.[2]

*

Again the bosses are crowding the workers.

Again are they hunting around for their old pick handles with which to encourage free born American citizens.—labor—laborers.

*

Let there be more immigrants.

Especially—from Sicily.

Industrial Worker, 20 January 1923

---

[2] "Our hundred per cent workers" is a reference to a xenophobic movement that accelerated during World War I and in the war's aftermath. Encouraged by President Theodore Roosevelt, who in a 1915 speech had rejected "hyphenated Americanism," a revival of nativist sentiment fed into increased attacks on immigrant communities, government limitation of migration, and a comeback for the Ku Klux Klan.

T-Bone Slim Discusses

HORRIBLE! HORRIBLE!

(Air: The Runaway Train Came Down the Track)

I.

'Tis a horrible death: to freeze to
death,
We understand;
'Tis a horrible death to starve to
death,
On Koffee And[1]—
'Tis a horrible death——and don't forget:
More horrible than to drown in
sweat,
Indeed, IT, IS, A, horrible, horrible
death.

II.

'Tis a horrible death to roast to death
Where e'er you go;
'Tis a horrible death to "peel your
neck,"
To "serve" the foe;
A horrible, horrible, horrible death
Like one of those "pages" of Queen
'Lisabeth—
Indeed, it, is, a horrible, horrible
death.

III.

'Tis a horrible death. to flirt with
death,
Without a me'ow;
'Tis a horrible death to lose your
"heft"

1 A slang reference to "coffee and donuts" or other forms of cheap, poor-quality, and minimal food.

Just like a cow;
'Tis a horrible end, my Christian
friend—
Your worldly rations to Not defend
—Indeed, it, is, a, horrible,
horrible end.

IV.

'Tis a horrible death—but WHAT
is left?
A Booby ward?
'Tis a horrible death to bow to
"theft"—
Without a CARD;[2]
'Tis a strictly non-union, unorganized
move
That 'u'd tickle tho 'art of an
Erbert Hoove—
Indeed, she, is, a, horrible, horrible
death.

V.

'Tis a horrible death to land in jail—
Les' sing—a song.
'Tis a horrible death—let no man
fail!
The WHOLE night long.
The citizen by his lonely fire
Shall hear the "smell" of a funeral
pyre—
Indeed, it, is, a, horrible, horrible
death.

(Repeat)

(The citizen by his lonely fire
Shall hear our mel**odious** voice
aspire . . . . .
Indeed, it, is, a, horrible, horrible,
death)

(Repeat)

---

[2] That is, a Wobbly card.

(The citizen by his lonely fire
Shall long to see us all expire
Indeed, it, is, a, horrible, horrible,
death)

(Dedicated to Enid, Oklahoma, bastile.)
(To be sung horridly not hurriedly.)

Industrial Solidarity, 26 January 1923[3]

[3] Because of the scattered and incomplete nature of Slim's archive, there is some uncertainty around this particular publication date.

Between These Two

A man smiling in the midst of his misfortunes is either witless or a . . . philosopher. A broken leg is nothing to smile about. An empty pocketbook is no giggling affair. A cell in a prison is nothing to get comical about. An ingrowing stomach is hardly a suitable subject for laughter. A suit of B. V. D.s[1] in February is nothing to grin over. Carrying the "banner" these cold nights is no occasion for great and prolonged mirth.[2]

*

Adversity may be a "valuable experience" but it isn't marketable—I'll sell all my misfortunes for less than face value, right now.

*

A death in the family may be attended with situations quite humorous—the joke being on the spectators—but, I fail to see, why friends of the departed should utter shrieks of satisfaction.

*

Having your household goods thrown out on the curb is no excuse for jollification—or jubilee.

*

Being run over by a flat wheeled street car may be delightful as an experience, but the celebration should necessarily be short and to the point.

*

The star boarder running away with one's wife may, at first, create a pleasurable feeling—novelty![3] But a certain amount of proper dignified sorrow should be exhibited in front of neighbors.

*

A wife deserting an unprotected man is considered a calamity—therefor, any merry-making, glee or hilarity, is seldom associated with this misfortune.

*

"Adversity Is the Acid Test of Character." You betcha! Yes.

*

---

1 That is, underwear.

2 "Carrying the banner" is slang for being homeless and walking the streets at night, constantly "moved on" by the police and so unable to sleep.

3 This may be a reference to Slim's own parents. See the Introduction for details.

And the fortitude of the working class is the veneer, impervious to heat and cold, dry or damp, hard or soft, acid or no acid—adversity or adipose perversity of those whom it may concern.

*

But there is such a thing as riding a good horse to death.—The American working people have been rode to death; proof of this lies in the fact that the Manufacturers Association is hollering for a certain "net" immigration over and above any exodus of foreigners making their "getaway" from our ideal conditions of servitude.

*

Immigration is, and truly, a remedy but not an ideal one from the viewpoint of the present masters of our industries. The horse that has been rode to death still remains—remains.

*

Full grown foreign workers, raised at foreign expense, are naturally beneficial to our industrial life if properly introduced to the machine and further: It gives our Industrial Kings an opportunity to put to pasture the horse that has been rode to death.

*

Even today the masters are begrudging the pasturing of played out labor[4] and I have no doubt but that their ultimate, ideal conditions call for importing fresh labor to replace stale labor and, to deport stale labor to make room for fresh ones.

*

But, even now, somehow or other, there is a "slipup" in the program.—This is sad.

Last year 40,000 Italians came to this country—53,000 went back. Fifteen thousand Americans, in the same period, had the temerity to commit suicide and dodge all this prosperity, incidentally a pile of work.

*

We are the horse that is to be pastured. All our lives we have worked for "living wages, and no more." Now we can start to earn dying wages.

Industrial Worker, 27 January 1923

---

4 That is, employers are refusing to provide old-age pensions to retired workers.

Unfinished Business

A pastor in New York committed suicide.—We were shocked, so religious are we.—We wonder what's going to become of all the sheep left without a shepherd.—We wonder how this shepherd will square himself with Saint Peter for deserting his flock.—We wonder if he is now sitting in the lap of Abraham with a great, big, self-inflicted, bullet hole in his soul.

*

We are given to understand that if the pastor should have renigged on taking the initiative (and his life) the goats in the congregation had fully decided to protect the sheep against the ravages of present day church tendencies. But, hm, we maintain, ho hom, a man may belong to a church and still be religious, yes, indeed.

*

In Tillamook, Ore., a woman was branded with a red hot *cross*—the form of branding iron leads me to believe religious principles were invoked, to save this woman's everlasting soul. Good Christians (no doubt) pressed the burning steel (ever so gently) to the breast of this woman in the name of Him who never opened his trap in front of his persecutors.

*

Lemon juice is not to be recommended as good for low wages. Try it on pimples; not on principles.

*

"Country degenerating"—So is the sausages—going to the dogs, so as to say.

*

Doc. Garfield, the former coal administrator, has said an unskilled workman should not marry.[1]—Can't see the connection, doctor.

*

What for instance has skill, in pushing a wheelbarrow, got to do with the more or less holy state of wedlock.—What is there in common between the artful juggling of a pick and the manhandling of a woman—or the "her handling" of

[1] Harry Garfield, the son of a former U.S. president, headed up the federal government's Fuel Administration during World War I. He quit the role in 1919 over objections to the settlement of that year's national coal strike, which involved around 400,000 workers and ended in a 14 percent wage increase.

man. Doc. Garfield has lost all his romance in the coal yard. (So have we.)—"He should wait until he becomes skilled" puts the doctor squarely behind birth control. Shake!

*

Not only to take care of the high cost of living, but also the high cost of marriage and the high cost of old age, we must have more wages. A "living wage" presupposes no old age[2]—so the boss sings; You will always be—*"young and fair to me."*

*

A family will make a man do many things he wouldn't think of in his sober senses—single. The advice the boss gives: "Don't join a union, raise a big family."—The advice I give: Soak your head.[3]

Industrial Worker, 31 January 1923

---

2 Pension coverage was patchy at this time, and many Americans, including Slim, did not have access to any kind of pension plan.

3 That is, sober up, meaning, in this context, come to your senses.

Speed of the Tongue

"You're a liar."

How often have we heard this expression of appreciation and admiration from our friends? Total strangers even, at times, have gazed trustingly in to our eyes, and have complimented us on our ability to 'laborate upon truth or what is accepted (by shallow people) to be the truth.—(And then the fun began.)

*

People as a general rule do not like to have their accomplishments paraded in front of less fortunate mental performers (and fellow sufferers).

*

George Washington, it has been stated, although the parent of his country, was one of the worst liars history has known—in fact, he was such a bad liar (in his day of good liars) that great writers (who were in no way gifted that way) have commented on it copiously and piously.

*

Upon occasion, caught with a hatchet in his hand; chips of a cherry tree clinging to his "malones" did he dodge the issue, "Who chopped down that cherry tree?"

*

No, by God, (I should say not) George, as small as he was, saw his limitations—eloquence would not explain away those chips hanging on his woolen pants.

*

"I cannot tell a lie," he said, blushing like a railroad "bull" caught with his hand in the freight, "I did it with my little hatchet."

*

Nevertheless, Washington was showered with honors many and manifest; spiritual and real. A great state on the West coast, an I. W. W. stronghold, was named in his honor; a city on the beautiful Potomac was dedicated a monument to his inability to lie in a pinch.

*

Since then—the beautiful Potomac has been the gathering point for some of the world's greatest liars.—Diplomats of international fame, of resplendent renown, have here fore-gathered to pay homage to Janus; incidentally to "hornswoggle" each other to the everlasting sorrow of their constituents.

*

Lying, today, is classed one of the arts—great universities now recognize its value (as an education) in salesmanship. Every "investigation" is held for the purpose of discovering if some man, or a set of men, has not acquired an extraordinary "power to lie."

*

Lying, to be successful, doesn't necessarily have to be verbal or written.

Paper counters on leather shoes is a pretty good lie.

A dash of water in milk makes a fair prevarication.

Wooden pulp in a cotton shirt; and curled hemp in woolen pants makes a combination of falsehood hard to beat.

Phoney unionism is another way of evading the truth.

LET US ORGANIZE INTO, AND IN, THE I. W. W. (We are the poorest liars of the world!) Let us not depend on the speed of the tongue.

Industrial Worker, 3 February 1923

War

"War is Hell"

Were hell so vile?

I wouldn't dare to crack a smile; but as it is a cozy berth—(compared to war) a place of mirth—I deem it wise to hold my style.—If war is hell then truth is guile.

*

If war is nothing more than hell, then everything is strictly well: no idle chance can do us harm—except, of course, we may get warm. For is it not a proven rule that the northern part of hell is cool?

*

But if "all hell" is like a war, then me for "on the golden shore"—A bayonet, you know my dear, between the ribs, feels kind of queer—It somehow doesn't seem to fit; *and very few get used to it.*

*

It's not the "sticking part" that hurts; (although it ruins a pile of shirts). Nor yet the ugly turn of wrist that gives your frame a sudden twist—The time for mourning, I'm afraid, is when he shakes you off the blade.

Industrial Worker, 13 February 1923

T-Bone Slim Discusses: The Off-Set

Now, a case has been made against the Bum. It has been "proved" that he failed to work steady last summer—and all this publicity probably is intended to encourage him to try again next summer—but it is not shown what became of the work he left undone. Where is it now? How come—did it evaporate into thin air? You say he left it undone and yet, you say, it isn't here now. What kind of arithmetic is that, nothing from nothing leaves one (0 – 0 equals one.)?—Ah-h, you reason, the **other fellow** did the work. That's better—**the wrong man is on the bum.** If this fellow had performed his work and saved his pennies the other fellow would now be on the bum and the *Tribune* would have had a different story to tell the blushing world.

Michael Burke, a labor agent in the days when that business wasn't as raw as it is now, (and I can see he has a kind heart), says the reason for these men being in these circumstances is—and he puts it with one word—"Drink." For his benefit we will point out, drink is The Circumstance.—Its reason is something else—too deep for Mike and the *Tribune.*

Mike's barre' of empty bottles indicates the size, nature, but not the cause of circumstances, (or unemployment for that matter) and serves as an advertisement for his note-worthy hotel—the Workman's Home on Clinton St:

"Drink is the sole cause," he says, "there is no other reason why any man should be down and out this winter."

Alright, to be just as consistent, we will say Eats makes a man poor and Religion makes him honest.

But drink doesn't seem to faze the Gold Coast any.[1] Inebriated Captains of Industry and pickled Colonels of Commerce are still good for a four bit tip in the loop—some of them, even wend their way as far west as Sam's Oyster House where the efficient officers of the law load them into taxicabs and ship them out to Sheridan Road or Wilson Ave., as the case may be. Drunk? I've seen some of them so drunk that if Mike's theory held good they would be in the poorhouse right now.

I believe I am safe in saying that the upper-ups drink more booze than the down and outs, without showing any deterioration in their gate receipts.

Well then, if this be so, it splits an argument. The *Tribune* will now have to admit: It is only poor booze that makes a man poor—that the good booze makes for a steady income; the better the booze the better the income?

Unfortunately, the World's Greatest would not be able to convince anybody

1 Chicago's Gold Coast neighborhood was one of the wealthiest areas in the United States at the time.

along these lines: Consequently, I think it will have to take my theory that Eating makes a man poor. It is quite clear that if we didn't eat we could save about fifty cents three times a day, seven days a week, $10.50 per week.

But it may be men are down and out because they Sleep—because they Flop, as the *Tribune* puts it? Hardly. A ten cent flop could hardly have such a tremendous effect on a flopper's financial standing—he could save only 70 cents per week by swearing off sleep.

Following along this illogical line of reasoning we come to the point where the beans will spill—showing where the argument is open on one end, at least—mebbe on both. We find that we do not grow poor by Breathing? How come—?

How comes it that drink, eats and sleep drives us "down and out"—How come? My Gods! (all of them and then some) does the *Tribune* argue that a drinker, an eater, a sleeper and a dresser shall be penalized, while the desperate "breather" goes unchallenged? If so, what is our journalism coming to?

How about the "Reader"?

Should he swear off reading?

If he does—the *Tribune* will soon be rubbing elbows with the bums and beggars, flops and floppers . . .

Otherwise the *Tribune*'s argument is good.

Industrial Solidarity, 16 February 1923

Golf

Far be it from me to withhold any discovery I may make from the readers of this paper. I simply cannot do it—it is not my nature to be secretive. Being of a scientific turn of mind many things present themselves to me, in my daily intercourse with life, that would never come to the notice of less careful trained eyes.

But my eyes are beginning to get weak,[1] therefore it was necessary for me to take cognizance—did you ever take cognizance, and get away with it—cognizance is harder to take than castoria.[2]

My first impulse was to get a pair of hornbrimmed "sagless gates" for my oggles. But the idea had no more than trickled through the entanglements of my state department when I had to lay it aside as impracticable on account of the recent financial drains upon my department of the ex-chequer.

*

Some other method had to be discovered to rejuvenate the windows of my soul. I couldn't go out and hire a window cleaner to bring out the lustreful (translucent) transparency of my soulful orbits. No.

*

But, as is a custom with scientific gentlemen with watery eyes, I didn't propose to "sashay" into sightless oblivion without making an effort to take a good look at the capitalist system, before I go. I concentrated all the mind I had on my troubles. And you can bet your bi-focal binoculars the preponderance of mind marshaled and focused on said troubles, was prepossessing. The shock alone, of concentration on such a gigantic scale, was sufficient to break the points off them California seismographs you have been reading about. Yes.

*

In troubles of this kind one must systemize his action and thus, ferret out his true condition. My first move was to find out whether my growing blindness was physical or spiritual. I went down to the slave market[3] to test my eyes. I looked over all the signs and couldn't see a thing over 43c per hour,[4] so you see my eyes were physically fragile.

*

1 Slim did wear glasses in later life.
2 A substitute for castor oil.
3 That is, the area of town where employment offices and recruiters were located.
4 That is, he did not see any notices for any jobs paying more than 43 cents an hour.

My buoyant soul pulled a blanket of gloom up to its chin; tears stood in my eyes without power enough behind them to splash down on the cruel pavement of a heartless city.

*

Oh for green fields of Hennepin County! Oh for the laughing waters of Minnehaha Falls! Oh for the placid bosom of some magic Lake Minnetonka, Lake Calhoun, Lake Harriet—Ah! Again would I strop my eyes on the velvety lawn of the Country Club. Again would I whet the mirror of my soul upon the grandeur of nature's handiwork, to regain my vision. I would play—I would play golf (excuse me dear reader, I would cry again). The employment shark has shipped me to a railroad coal chute!

Poor blind, T-Bone Slim, sent to a coal chute!

*

Well, I s'pose we've got to do the best we can. They put me on the night shift. They should have known better—the shape my eyes are in! Sleeping was about all I could do.—A carful of coal is hauled up, the pockets are flung open and the contents slide out in a cloud of dust onto a steel grating; the finer coal goes through but the chunks stop on the grating. It was a part of my duties, in my waking moments, to break up those chunks; breathe this dust, get my eyes, ears and nose full of it. I would reach down in the darkness and feel a lump, pick up my nibblick[5] and address the ball (but there is always the danger that I would slice my drive in the darkness and when that would happen particles of coal would fly up and hit me in the eyes already overstrained). Then I would have to lay down for the rest of the night.

*

Golf, on top of a coal chute, is the greatest remedy for weak eyes. I make this unqualified statement, as a man of science, and offer my discovery free of charge to all blinking book worms. And, even *strong* eyes can be strengthened by filling them full of coal dust in the spring of the year.

Besides: You can get paid 43c per hour until fully cured—that is if you are able to punch a time clock, or get someone to do it for you *if you can't see good.*

*

The one trouble with playing golf on top a coal chute is that your balls get so dusty it is next to impossible to make a mashie shot.[6]

Industrial Worker, 10 March 1923

---

[5] A nine iron golf club.

[6] A mashie is a type of golf club, equivalent to a No. 5 in modern golf, used for short approach shots.

T-Bone Slim Extends Himself to Discuss Education

But you say "if the working class is so darn smart why are they slaves?"

All right again (wait till I take a chew of snus). Here's the way I think it happens:

When the working class is born, it is born a child. It is born into a world full of jails, blackjacks, rifles and bayonets; the most extraordinary instruments of torture and subjugation and, in fact, when each individual member of the working class sticks his nose into this world he finds a ready-made world with a capitalist system under full swing, and going full blast.

The stolen wages and *stolen ideas* have been building this system for ages and ages. *This child is born a slave to this system.* Immediately the child is born the system puts its iron heel upon the little fellow's neck, gently at first, with increasing pressure, as time rolls on. A young colt is never "broken" more painstakingly than is the child of man; hounded on one hand by the parents already broken, on the other hand by bosses, hirelings of the system, etc. The child's spirit begins to droop and what you have left is a wage-slave unorganized at the mercy of organized capital.

*

When I, T-Bone Slim, was born into this world, the capitalist system, with a broad grin on its face, was there to meet me. I and my mother used to go out to do people's washing for them—me hardly three weeks old. How I used to tremble lest she get her breast caught in the wringer and ruin my lunch (such as it was). Baby, boy, and man have I been a slave!

*

"If I'm so darn smart why am I a slave?" If freedom was a question of intelligence solely, then our educators would revolt against the slavery of theirs. Freedom being a result of power exerted, unionism being strength, is it not strange that our educators are practically unorganized? Are we to understand, in our ignorance, that the evident slavery and lack of organization existing among the various tribes of educators indicates ignorance in common with us? (Or is it only the unorganized mucker who is ignorant?) There has been ringing in my ears the past nine days, "Blind leaders of the blind."

*

Someone is playing a joke on my feelings.

*

We are all liable to errors, many of them mortifying in the extreme. I recall an experience I had years ago in a swell hotel back East. It was customary in them days to serve drinks only with meals, as part of the meals. It was also against the law to serve drinks unless there was visible evidence of food on the table. Well, a bunch of us went in to kill time and a few worms.[1] The idea was to "haul on" a few exterminators. We were told to wait a moment, it being rush hour and the place provided with only one sandwich which had to do the "handsome" for all tables. Finally came our turn, our libations and our orphaned sandwich. And do you know, fellow workers, I ate the sandwich. Was I a scissorbill?[2]

You'd think so, had you been there and heard the management rave. "I was an idiot, an imbecile, a disrupter, a sabotager, a general all-round unprincipled reprobate of deepest dye, etc." I had "ate up" the venerable and only sandwich in the house with two hundred customers waiting for their meals.

Also: Let me point out (in support of this) that this custom of serving meals is as old as the hills themselves. Already in the days of Jerusalem Slim[3] it was customary to feed as high as 6,000 people with a couple of fishes.

P.S.—Since writing this I find it slams, but my fellow workers will forgive me.

Industrial Worker, 14 March 1923

---

1 That is, to drink tequila.

2 This is a slang term for a fool or a sucker. Within the IWW, "scissorbill" was often used to refer to a worker who did not believe in industrial unionism.

3 The hobo name for Jesus Christ.

T-Bone Slim Discusses: Sample Camps

On the whole, the conditions in the woods[1] of Minnesota, Wisconsin and Michigan are so bad that the "push" seldom gets a chance to fire a man. He is gone . . .

The conditions are so bad that if I describe them "the editor will refuse to print it"—thinking that I am lying, so as to get him in bad. . . . In the best camps the conditions are bad. We call them "best" because we compare them to camps that have no conditions at all—not even rotten conditions. For, remember, conditions don't begin until a certain amount of comfort is established—sleep is not enough, we can do that standing up when sufficiently tired.

Yes, if I said that the best camp in Wisconsin has only four windows from which 160 men look at the glorious landscape on Sabbath morning—on the day when Jacks should be (?) praising the Lord instead of cussing the company—the editor would say, "Darn that Slim anyway, he's taken to lying, on top of all his other vices."

If I said that 414 pairs of damp sox are drying in this bedroom; if I said 831 single sox are hung around the stove in this bunkhouse the editor would be laying for me in the Proviso Yards when I go back to Chicago. He wouldn't believe it, and he wouldn't print it—and if he did, the G. E. B. would fire him.[2]

If I said that 320 pairs of mitts, in addition to all those sox, are drying in this bunk-chamber the editor would start plotting my downfall right away; he would prevail upon a few strong men to come out here to Pine Lake to find out what's the matter with me.

If I said that in addition to all these sox and mitts there are 98 pairs of rubbers, 150 pairs of insoles, 12 jumpers, 9 suits of underwear, 37 pairs of overalls and 4 pairs of shoes drying in the same place, at the same time he would gasp—wilt in his chair, and be past all human or other help in a minute or two—dead.

If I said that the bunks are muzzle-loaders with room of the deacon-bench for only half the crew and that the other half has to get in bed to be out of way, the editor would say, "It's too bad, Slim was just getting good; it's a pity he lost his mind." Yes. He would think *I* was crazy. He couldn't believe it possible.

---

1 That is, the lumberjack work camps.

2 The General Executive Board, the IWW's main coordination body, was made up of members elected at each convention. Slim never served on this board, but one of his editors and biggest supporters within the union, Fred Thompson, did.

If I said that the lamps are arranged with "devilish ingenuity" so that you can't read; that you have to move a dozen pair of sox before the lamps pale yellow gleam falls on the paper, he would grow sorrowful and say that Slim has been overworked; he should be given a vacation in a house of detention—if I said that you can't sit in under the lamp, and see to read, because the products of T-Pot Dome[3] in the lamp prevent light filtering through and if I said that farther along, on the deacon seat, the light is too weak and that the heads, shoulders and whiskers of those sitting next to you would throw ghostly shadows on your paper, the editor would turn sick to his stomach, pack his clothes in the dead of the night and steal forth into the cruel world to be a wanderer on the face of the globe forever—maybe go as far as Cudahy, Wis.

So you see, I can't go ahead and describe these things for that reason and because I ain't got anything against the man, I can't go ahead and say that I picked up an *Industrial Solidarity* that everyone had been reading and that there on the front page I found a great big crumb,[4] alive and well, whiling away the time looking over the headlines, waiting for someone to turn the page so that it could read T-Bone Slim's great article. I can't go ahead and make such wild statements. If I did the editor would look hard at the business manager and say: "How 'bout this—reports are coming in from the field that our 'Mealy Press' is lousy." He, you know, is in no position to know that these aristocratic lumber jacks, that send their laundry to town to be washed, are too tight to do it every week, with the result that they manage to keep the camp lousy all winter long. I can't say these things no matter how true they are. About all I can say is: **the best camps are bad.** I don't want the business manager to go to the expense of fumigating the press.

If I said that the Wisconsin lumber barons had never heard of "toilet soap" or "bed-sheets—"

If I hinted that common yellow laundry soup was used to wash faces with and if I stated that 160 men wipe on ten towels—as slick as I am—if I "worked it into the record" that Castile soap was not being used—the editor would jump up: "That settles it," he would swear and bring his fist down on the ink-well; cripple his hand for six months and cripple the ink-well for life—he'd have to dictate, after that, his editorials and I, possibly, would be the innocent cause of discouraging him in his literary labors, whatever they be. For remember, a man can't do his best work when he thinks a former reliable man-of-letters is trying to impose upon his credulity.

---

3 A reference to the Teapot Dome bribery scandal. In 1922, Albert B. Fall, secretary of the interior, illegally leased U.S. Navy petroleum reserves to private oil corporations at low prices without competitive bidding. Fall became the first presidential cabinet member to go to prison, though no one was convicted of paying the bribes he was found guilty of accepting.

4 Slang for a louse.

If I said that two men sleep in each of these muzzle-loaders; (and that beans are the important part of the diet, not to be sneezed at)[5] that the blankets are dirty; that there is no way to wash them; that a man is lucky if he can wash his shirt and sox to say nothing about blankets.—If I came right out and said there is no wash room, no bathroom and no dry room, the editor would grab my article, rush to the G. E. B., slam the paper in front of the Board and say, "there's the evidence." He would demand that the Board set aside a young fortune for the purpose of building a headquarter-camp for irresponsible writers.

If I went further, if I undertook to use argument in order to remedy this filthy condition; if I said, I have seen one man asleep in the gutter; that I have never seen two men asleep in the same gutter.—If I horn in with a statement that no two men can agree on the same gutter but that two men get along fine and dandy in a bunk, the editor would—words fail me—me T-Bone Slim.

He knows that if the men will organize—oh if they would only organize—that conditions can be bettered, he knows this, so how can we reasonably expect him to believe, that **the best camps are bad.** We can't.

*

There are a few SAMPLE CAMPS, electric lights and all that stuff, for advertising purposes—sample camps—single beds, etc.—and I know one camp (with electric lights) where kerosene is used for illumination. The bulbs are too dusty for ornamental purposes and the dynamo has been dead two years.

In closing I wish to warn all writers not to describe the worst camps. Stick to the best—mebbe I, too, will one day write an article on them—it's a chance.

Industrial Solidarity, 22 March 1923

[5] That is, the men in the bunks are very flatulent.

Off Colors

There is such a thing as "an ice harvest." To call it a nice harvest would be to depart from our proverbial truthfulness (which, of course, we will not do, even to please the two-faced god, January, Janus). It is everything but a nice harvest.

*

We were placed aboard a train—and after three young men, dressed like time-keepers, had been unloaded on a plea that the company could not use them (as much as it would like to) the train was gotten under way and we were carried to our *destination.*

*

For the benefit of those who do not know the meaning of the word destination, I will go deeper into the subject. But I want it understood that any remarks I may make should not be construed as an endorsement of the capitalist system.

Destination means a ramshack camp, full of lousey beds and dirty blankets, full of dirty cooks and dirtier flunkies; dirty language. Oh, what's the use?

*

The morning is bitterly cold. Outside the camp 'tis somewhat colder than inside—zero inside, seven below outside. The system has provided each harvester with a set of rags for clothing; pieces of burlap do the office of socks, etc.

*

The system has starved these men for years. The very last "feeble kick" has been "drained out" by mal-nutrition and under-nourishment, lack of raiment—and here we are, undergoing the same process in the ice-fields. Great Skads, is it in the hope that we will ketch pneumonia and pass away to the icefields of eternity where toil is not, and consequently no products to fight for. Perish the thought.

*

Difficult, indeed, is the position of our overlords. They would eat their banana and save it for tomorrow; they would have us work but dare not feed us. If they feed us not, we cannot work; if they do feed us we may develop manhood enough to make a decided "kick." Hence, hungry, ill-clad, we step out into the seven below. Brave effort, indeed!

*

Like going into a burning building to save your enemy's poodle. The boss says, go; the winds say, no! The slave says, I will; the thermometer says, you will, like hell! *Not in them wraps.* Was it disobedience that brought these men back to shiver in a miserable camp? Was it a last remaining spark of manhood in them that caused them to risk the company's wrath? I hope so, but think not. I think it was seven below zero that whispered in their ear, "Come to mother; come to the cheerless fireside—the hearth you have always known."

Industrial Worker, 28 March 1923

Odds and Ends

France has invented a warplane that will fly where it is sent—guided by radio—with no one aboard. It is thought that this machine will make life uncertain for the parasites and that they will "call the game" in favor of peace. Don't you believe it. They still can declare for war when they want to thin us out, move into another country themselves, send enemy planes to drop bombs down our collar and leave us to mourn our shredded dead.

*

"With malice toward none and charity toward all."

Industrial Worker, 2 May 1923

All I Know

Well, as usual, it resolves itself upon me to give the slaves an "inkling" as to what industrial unionism is—it seems strange nobody has sprung it on them, before now.

*

It is presumed to be a terrific conglomeration of tissue destroying ideas, doctrines, creeds and programs, all rolled up like a ball of fishhooks, and it is further hinted that its tremendous range and unfathomable depth can only be explored by laborers with 'specially equipped apparatus: such as brains, intuition and perseverance, etc.—yes.

*

How well I remember the first time it was explained to me, way back in '16, great beads of sparkling sweat gathered on my brow as I wrestled with the subject and, thus it is: I point with pride to myself as a man "who came, who saw and who conquered," (venus, wieners and vichy, in Latin). Am I right? Of course, I am.

*

Suspecting no shock I innocently asked him, "What is this industrial unionism over which everybody seems to be going nuts?" Imagine my astonishment when he snapped out the fatal enigmatical reply, "everybody in any industry belongs to one union only."

*

The blow had fallen.

"Everybody in one industry belongs to one union." Holy mackerel and sanctified smelts, how in the world is an uneducated man like myself going to get all that through his noodle! I turned pale; I had to do something to hide my acquired ignorance. (Assuming ignorance is not the basic seat of learning.)

*

"Everybody in one union." Even old heads who have studied unionism for years can't get that through their brain. Is it then a wonder that I was somewhat staggered by the problem? Anybody who thinks industrial unionism is easy to understand (and easy to explain) is off his trolley and on the wrong street.

*

An average worker understands the law of gravity—the theory of relativity is pie for him (with one arm tied behind him)—but the conundrum, the hard cold concrete fact of unionism, "the everybody in one union," is as hard to understand, as is the art of aquatics to a water spaniel—what does a spaniel know about swimming? Nothing, not a thing.

(Stopped in nick of time.)

Industrial Worker, 26 May 1923

The Whole Hog: Of Emotions Raised by Charity

One of the **most touching** things came to my notice today on the streets of our Chicago—ladies fair, and motherly grandmothers, were soliciting, alas, tagging people for the benefit of the "Aged and Adult Charities." Needless to say I was deeply touched in spirit (not substance)—I make this statement so as to dispel any illusion the reader may have as to my tender-heartedness—and, while completely unstrung with compassion I hasten to protest my sympathetic and pathetic nature. My feelings are deeply moved (although my hand remains motionless) on occasions like this, and it is no trouble for me to shed scalding tears (without notice) over these poor Adult and Aged citizens who become too old to support anybody, including themselves.

These poor creatures no doubt have worked hard all their lives and are very deserving—excuse me while I step in the back room to cry—I must not be seen with tears in my eyes—it might be construed as sedition against the system, on one hand; and lack of revolutionary stability on the other—as I was saying, they are a bunch of hard-working men and women who have nothing to show for their work, after all these years, except "the hands all knots and a back all hump," an object of our compassion.

When I get sentimental "I go the whole hog." My frame shakes with emotion (even as I write) as I view the heroic efforts of the people trying to undo what the employers of labor have done—trying, at this late date, to donate to these deserving aged, the livelihood denied them by employers in their youth. And, although I consider begging and soliciting a very wasteful form of production for able-bodied citizens to undertake, I recognize its utility as a temporary relief—at the same time deploring its **ultimate** reaction upon those that give—they, too, some day will be old. They too will be made poor by the same system under which they strive to be so helpful.

I pass the time of day with a beggar sitting on the sidewalk grinding music. . . . I almost hesitate to touch this subject. I have asked him "how many hours does it cost him to earn a living"—and he looks at me in amazement—no doubt classifying me more or less correctly—if not **complimentarily.**

*

The man is allowed this **civilized** privilege, to eke out his living, in order that he may serve as an ever present example for us—to continually remind us how much better off we are than he—to impress us with the "desirableness" of our position and to cause us to become contented with our lot—the miserable drippings of a thorough-rotten system of exploitation.

Now that I have sprung the motif behind this civilized barbarism, I am sorry I did it. They now will be taken from the sidewalks and put into hell-holes they call almshouses—where they will get one meal a year, on Easter.

NOTE:—This cripple prefers the sidewalk.

Ain't we a wonderful people! so civilized! and so well organized!—headed for a poorhouse.

I'm done crying.

Industrial Solidarity, 26 May 1923

Prepare for the Worst

Guilt by Inference

The I. W. W. never has been criminally syndical or syndically criminal. Neither has it been criminal, with or without syndicalism; nor syndical, with or without criminalism. It has never been criminal. Never has it been syndical. It has never been either criminal or syndical, with or without, or within, in any way, shape, time or manner, before or after or at present. It has never wished nor does it now wish, nor will it ever wish, to be any, either, or all these things hereinbefore mentioned.

The I. W. W. always was, is, and will be industrial, so far as we know, so help me. Solidarity on that last Great Day.

P.S.—Call the next witness.

Industrial Worker, 7 July 1923

Must or Not-to-Must, or Freaks of Nature

You "must" organize yourself—a union organized by others will serve others. I speak for industrial unionism because I, too, have tried the old style unionism and found it too light for heavy hauling. Organize yourself. How ridiculous it would be if I, a dirt mover, undertook to organize the professors and teachers in an Educational Workers Industrial Union. I would be sure to fail. They "must" organize themselves, as we dirt cats[1] are organizing ourselves. They must emancipate themselves, as we road slingers will emancipate ourselves. It's a case of nobody can't do nothing for nobody.

*

The saddest words of tongue and pen:
"Our teachers are non-union men."
The most pathetic modern fable:
"Their lectures bear the masters' label."

*

The chief outstanding freak of nature:
The freedomless "EManCiPaTor."

P.S.—When in doubt, join the G. C. W. I. U. No. 310, I. W. W.[2]

Industrial Worker, 18 July 1923

---

1 Slang for road construction workers.

2 The General Construction Workers Industrial Union was one of the various sections of the IWW set up to organize workers in specific areas.

Sweet Charity

It may be of interest to the harvest workers to know that the widow McCormick of Cyrus H., the binder inventor, is dead.[1] She left behind her $9,000,000 worth of wealth.[2] And a million dollars of it is going to charity—sweet charity.

There isn't a doubt but this money will be put to beautiful use—and there is no doubt but there will be thousands of paupered farmers who will gladly accept some of it. Thousands of bankrupt farmers will have an opportunity to behold and fondle once't again their "own" money in the form of charity—sweet charity. But that "little," taken from them in an inconvenient period (which bankrupted them) cannot in this period of convenience put them back on their feet. Alas! Charity is no substitute for justice. Sweet charity.

The farmer has always blamed the harvest hand for his troubles, yet both can prove their poverty. Here is a $9,000,000 jack-pot, a sample pot, one of the twenty or thirty such that exist—and one million dollars of it is going to charity. Like throwing a life preserver into a drowned man's coffin—too late to be of any use. Sweet charity!

*

No Exceptions Taken

I notice lately that Gary's[3] latest proclamation regarding the 12-hour day has aroused the whole United Labor Press to action, even including Sam Gompers,[4] and although I have been looking high and low through all the different sheets for some suggestion of a plan to go after Mr. Gary and his 12-hour day, I fail to find one.

---

1 Cyrus McCormick was a businessman and inventor who founded the McCormick Harvesting Machine Company. He died in 1884, and, as Slim indicates here, his widow, Nancy Fowler, died in 1923.

2 This is equivalent to approximately $162 million today.

3 Having earlier served as a corporate lawyer and adviser, judge, and financier, Elbert Gary helped form the United States Steel Corporation in 1901 and served as its chairman for a quarter of a century. In that role he opposed unionism, and his opposition led to a major strike in 1919–20. Following pressure from the federal government, the steel industry carried out a survey in which it claimed to find that the "12-hour day has not been injurious physically, mentally or morally."

4 Samuel Gompers was one of the founders of the American Federation of Labor and served as its president in almost unbroken reign from 1886 until his death in 1924. He was also the longtime editor of the AFL's newspaper the *American Federationist*. He upheld craft unionism as a key form of organizing, led the right-wing antisocialist faction of the AFL, opposed immigration, and was an ardent supporter of the war effort.

Is it possible that all these "great men" including T-bone Slim, have been so slow and stupid as to let a "common tramp sailor" step in and solve this greatest of all problems? Sh! Here is the secret: Organize the Great Lakes! Break the 12-hour day there and you have played hell with Mr. Gary—(Card X7869).[5]

No one recognizes better than T-bone Slim the insignificant magnitude of the "world's greatest writer." And Slim's claim to greatness rests only on the "much he does with so little." A man is only great, as a writer, if his readers are great. Never was, is or will be a writer greater than reader. Stuff that in your pipe—and Schmoke!

*

Slim, too, has suggested the organizing of lakes as early as one week before opening of navigation. Above writer probably hasn't read *Marine Worker.*[6]

As to Mr. Gary, will say, with many reservations, my knowledge of Gary would not make good literature—as we understand it—hence I have requested Slim to confine himself to "playing hell" with other great Americans—Henry for instance.[7]

But this I know regarding all opportunities to divide ourselves: our press must reflect the views of its readers, not its writers, and then, if it can do a little "shining" for the whole, its duty is overfulfilled.

Industrial Worker, 18 August 1923

---

[5] This union card number indicates that this suggestion came from a union member who wrote to Slim via the paper, which was something that happened from time to time.

[6] A newspaper produced by the IWW's Marine Transport Workers Industrial Union No. 510 from 1921 to 1936.

[7] This is a reference to Henry Ford, whose eponymous company spearheaded the production line in order to increase efficiency and keep production costs low. Ford was adamantly opposed to unions and promoted a form of paternalistic "welfare capitalism." He was also a prominent anti-Semitic conspiracy theorist. In 1920, he published a four-volume pamphlet series called *The International Jew*, which received praise in Adolf Hitler's *Mein Kampf.* In 1938, Ford was awarded the Grand Cross of the German Eagle by the Nazi government.

Walking with the Dead

Public opinion was an expression that found form in the immediate dark ages just past. It was an entirely legitimate expression a decade or so ago. Not a single charge or hint of deception could be brought against its fair name—in that day. That day was the day of unadulterated thought—unadulterated political thought. Politics then were politics—the era of adulterations had not set in.

*

Came the era of adulterations, and politics suffered most of all. The once healthy political thought was ravaged until it was a mere shadow of itself[1]—but people still persisted in calling the shadow by its illustrious parent; even so as we refer to a dead person as Bill or Mike. A great change had happened yet the people had not noticed it. To them a bridge is still a bridge although the flood had torn it down and carried it away. Politics to them was still politics. Public opinion to them was still a thing to be conjured with.

Came an era of Economic Thought following the era of Adulterated Thought—but still we find the people unwilling to accept more appropriate names for the things long dead. Substitute the word chicanery for politics and the people will frown; substitute the words Dormant Thought for public opinion and they will consider you unfriendly, to say the least, and if you escape with your life you are lucky—the good people are in the habit of hanging those who think.

But if you will "only be a sport" and lie down with them in the long eternal sleep they have undertaken, they will snore your praise till Hell won't have it.

Two ages have come and still Politics and Public Opinion remain. Sandals are not shoes; shoes are not sandals—although both are leather footwear. Yet paper footwear is recognized by best public opinion and referred to as shoes.

A common drunk doesn't get so drunk that he refers to the present day concoctions as whiskey—no, he is gifted with a vocabulary—the present day liquid adulterations to him are moon, de-rail and horn, raisin-jack and so on.[2] Where the drunk gets all his perspicacity is more than I can understand.

Politics, for two ages dead, is still politics. Although putrefaction has already set in, it is still Politics. A horse that long dead is a carcass; a cow in such a sad state of putrefaction is carrion—corrupt, rotten, vile and loathsome.

---

1 This seems to be a reference to the creation of the field of public relations, the science of the manufacturing of consent, which before World War I had been called "propaganda."

2 These are various terms for bootleg liquor.

Public Opinion today, like public prejudice, is a (chimerical) ebullition of mind in the throes of a nightmare of chicanery—it is of non-substance and cannot be compared to the Public Opinion of two ages agone.

Ask a man what is his public opinion about a social question and he will inform you, for he can talk, that he has an open mind on that question, that he is just now taking up that question—and if he tells you the truth, he will say his opinion stepped out and did not yet return—nobody home. He hasn't got a public opinion any more than a dressed beef has guts.

Why persist in honoring substitutes with the name of a genuine article? What good purpose can be served by resurrecting the dead? Instead of blowing the breath of life into the stinking mess we should be rearing monuments to the dear, dead, departed Public Opinion that came to an untimely end in the Age of Adulterations—get that: Adulte-Rations.

Let us raise a monument to the dear, dead, departed Political Thought that has persistently and stubbornly rested by the side of Public Opinion, in an unmarked grave. The Age of Adulterations was too long and too strong for these friendly allies and twins to withstand. Peace to their ashes!

Political Thought and Public Opinion are survived by Class Thought and Consciousness.

Industrial Worker, 25 August 1923

Stand without Hitching

Today I went to work in an extra-gang. You may think it presuming in me to tackle a position of such responsibility, and you may garner an idea that, at last, my ambition is taking a definite, tangible form; that at last I am utilizing my vast and unexplored resources in the interest of good roads and safety first.

Now I do not wish to exaggerate my great ability or to throw any bouquets at myself, no matter how conscious I may be of the general appropriateness of doing so. The reader has already learned from my previous protestations that although I am averse to "panning"[1] myself so also am I averse to conducting an "individual petting party" in honor of myself. Therefore I will pass lightly over my various virtues and general all around abilities, outside of actual work. On that score I reserve the right to speak favorably of myself—and when I hit the hay of an evening with conscience clear of all entangling influences, such as doubts and misgivings of a labor well done, I want the *Worker* to open its columns to a few well-chosen words of self-praise. This is something I cannot trust or allow anyone to do for me; you see they might not do justice or they might do me by overdoing both.

It was only after careful consideration that I finally decided to become great. There being so many kinds of greatness (to choose from) it was really difficult to pick out the proper kind of greatness suitable for my complexion. After pawing over all the greatness I finally persuaded myself to become a great writer—tamping ties is only a side line with me.

Naturally I then proceeded to "concentrate"—the idea was to get an idea. To concentrate you close one eye and look with the dark one. Finally a crack appears in the darkness; that's the idea, and people who get 'em are called cracked. You continue looking until the crack widens; then before it can fade you grab a pencil and write it down. If you don't do it "right now" you're liable to forget it and the emancipation would be delayed just that much. I'm telling you it's careful business, this being a great writer. The idea, you see, will look something like this on paper: "No wonder the master class are well organized, there are only few of them!" After writing that down you jot down some words this way: 1. Bucket; 2. time; 3. dinner; 4. too; 5. no; 6. valuable; 7. of; 8. to; 9. account; 10. waste; 11. on; 12. in; 13. it; 14. taking; 15. quit; 16. a; 17. to; 18. job; 19. only; 20. is; 21. a. (The trick is to make them make sense.) With a pair of shears and a little carefullarity you separate them, one from the other, and then keep on "switchen'" them around until they do make sense. This way for

[1] Panhandling, or begging.

instance: Nos. 2, 20, 4, 6, 17, 10, 12, 14, 7, 21, 18, 19, 17, 15, 13, 11, 9, 7, 5, 3, 1.[2] That ought to make sense. If you find that they make sense you may be sure that we have stumbled upon a great principle of technique. But the paragraph only forms what I call a "break" and has nothing to do with our "idea" which is our subject.

It is easy to organize parasites because they are few in numbers with hardly any triplets, so there are no minor factors among these "figures."

Yet, considering sameness of opinion among the plutocrats, it is remarkable the number of difficulties Morgan encountered when he undertook to organize the Harvester Trust[3]—he even had to keep the prospective members "locked up" in separate hotels so as to keep them from fighting until "he" got in his fine work. They simply would not agree, but they *did*; and the "dispossessed" farmer is an eloquent testimonial of "how well they agreed." Labor can agree equally well. They won't agree, but they *will*—and the dispossessed parasites will be every bit as eloquent an expression as is the raggedy Twentieth Century farmer. But labor may agree too late. Nothing like being on time.

Labor may agree only after they are bouncing around in B. V. Ds. But why should we care? We are young and strong; big and husky—we're not helpless, nary one of us; we're not without power—let us organize it. Let every other man take out credentials.

Those delegates who have "become" disgladdened need not remain so. Their work has been the only work that has been *worth while* since history began. Everything else fades, but their work will remain, and they will yet organize the one big union of all labor to emancipate mankind from the wiles of the "special privilege fraternity." The delegates have been doing bigger work than they realize. All else has faded with time but their work stands! Revolutions have come and are gone—slaves are still slaves, but the untiring efforts of these delegates will eventually free them.

"What can we do to hold our membership?" Hand them a shovel. In other words, don't hold them; educate them. It is only through lack of knowledge they drop out. If they drop out it indicates they "dropt" in. Merely a formal call they made.

Don't hold them. Clinching shows a weakness.

Industrial Worker, 29 August 1923

---

2 We recommend that readers work out the answer to this word puzzle for themselves, as Slim intended, so we are not giving the answer here.

3 This is a reference to the formation of the International Harvester Company. The merger of a number of existing firms, including the McCormick Harvesting Machine Company, gave the IH Company control of around 85 percent of mechanical harvesters and reapers on the U.S. market.

An Eighty Year Boy

No, I didn't come over on the *Mayflower.* But I've met a man whose *ancestors did.* . . . He said he could trace his ancestors back three hundred years—I thought that was pretty good considering that police court records were so very unreliable a hundred years back—even so.

He was carrying water for the gang so I readily entered into conversation with him,[1] neglecting some important tamping I was supposed to be doing for the bait money the kindly Kommissary Kompany was in the habit of disbursing. . . .

Being a poor sort of a conversationalist at best, I thought—seeing as how every man is interested in his work—it would be best to talk shop. So I asked him if his illustrious forefathers too had been water boys, and was that noble trade handed down from father to son?

"I'd have you know, I'm an American," he snapped.

"Compose yourself, dad, we know you are an American or you wouldn't be carrying water for 'hunkies,'[2] as you call us; no one but an American would be trusted with such an exalted office—excuse me, dad, if I have another dipperful, you know a new man on the job always drinks more—So your forefathers came over on the *Mayflower*! I'm sure glad to hear it and I'm proud to know you—Here shake, I've always wanted to meet a pure blooded American.

"As you say . . . there were no foreigners aboard the *Mayflower* when it landed; they wasn't fugitives from the law of England that were permitted to embark upon that shaky old tub—the crown being convinced that that was the best way to get rid of them—seeing as how they wouldn't abide by the laws of the land. . . . I see . . . Your ancestors weren't foreigners like mine. Mine, you know, came over on the Thingvala Line or was it the Allan Line and naturally my blood isn't as blue as yours. My grandfather told me that he tried to book passage on the *Mayflower,* but he was told that it wasn't running any more, so naturally he came over on the next best boat.

"He wasn't a very good American for that reason and said the only reason he stayed here was because he couldn't get back—money matters, you know; he never could understand the American currency. He also said, and I was going to ask you dad, if it is true that the original forefathers that came over on the *Mayflower* stayed here because they had no boat to get back with—But, of course, I don't expect you to know about such minor details—It's enough

1 Water carrier was the lowest-status job on a work gang.

2 A derogatory term for people of Eastern European descent.

that you're an American and you can trace your ancestors back three hundred years to the cold inhospitable shores of Great Britain.

"Of course, dad, you ain't quite three hundred years old—I don't mean this as a joke—but would you mind telling me your age—Say dad, this water is surely fine . . . How's that! Eighty-two years of age? Can it be possible? You don't look a day over seventy-six. Now I *know* you are a 100 per cent patriot. No one but an American could have the stamina to carry water at the age of eighty-two. Trot along, dad—the boys are beginning to call for you. They sure appreciate your services—trot along."

P.S. From life; no bouquet!

*

"Too Much" Made Plain

It may not be common knowledge to the reader that I am "well off," well to do, if not exactly a man of wealth. Nevertheless, I think I am the richest Wob in this country. (It is easy to write when one has no financial troubles.)

At this writing, I estimate, I am worth over $40,000.[3] Nice piece of jack. Of course I don't carry it around with me as I go, because there is still so much *wick*edness in this world in spite of the fifth or seventh conundrum.[4] Someone might roll me—in fact, this $40,000 is in the form of *backpay* I got coming for a matter of 30 or 20 years hard labor I have done; being convicted of innocence in the 1st, second and 13th degree.

Investments, too, are so risky nowadays so I think I will just let that money lay where it is until such a time as the last crook is hung. An honest man like myself (myself included) hain't got no show in this world no more—and no more than a jackrabbit has with a mudturtle in a running high-jump—if the purrfessors can be believed—which they can't. Honesty is the best policy when everything else fails.

Thus it is that—it isn't as if a poor man was writing these truths—my words carry weight with the working class. But, even so, my fame hasn't spread as far as it should, and repeatedly when I ask a man if he knows T-bone Slim, he gives me a cruel unseeing stare and says: "No, thanks, I'm just after biting on one—what's the joke?" I ask him if he knows what a polecat is. His face brightens up, "Sure," he says, "he's a tramp lineman." Such is fame.

Now, if I were to say: No man has a right to advocate slowing down on the job[5]—*The Literary Template, The Independent Prevaricator* and the *Miscellaneous*

---

[3] Equivalent to more than $718,000 today.

[4] That is, commandment.

[5] Slowing down, also known as "soldiering," was (and is) a form of workplace resistance whereby workers who earned a fixed rate of pay slowed down their speed of production in order to reduce the surplus value extracted by the boss. The practice

Mandrell would carry extra special supplements in rainbow colors announcing to the palpitating world that "our own T-bone Slim, 140 per cent American, once a poor boy, has now conquered the literary world (single handed) and Stands today at the peak of his profession in the full glare of the envious eyes of such great writers as H. G. Wells and H. Bell Wright."[6]

T-bone Slim, the giant of letters, in answer to the question, "Well, what do you say?" replied, "Save your syllables and the sentences will do the rest."

Yes, if I said no man should advocate slowing down, they would name their cigars and streets after me. But, I am not going to say it. Instead I am going to say: No Man Has A Right to Advocate Speeding Up On A Job. No Man Has A Right To Say Hurry Up. If it is wrong to say, "Slow down, Gabe," it surely must be wrong to say, "hurry up, Jack." Woe is me—no rainbow supplements—I never could tell a lie and tell it well.

A Dutchman once't said, "Too much is too much," which proves Heine was a profound student of "bulk."[7] Too much IS too much. Too much Abundance is as bad as surplus of want. Recently the hardware dealers editing the daily press have worked themselves into a frenzy yowling, "Abundance means prosperity."

Bring out your best type, Stumpy . . .[8]

We'll close debate. Never has there been a shortage of abundance in these United States. Rather, it has been a case of too much abundance—and, "too much" is not "enough." Too much is too much (just what it says) and enough is less than too much. Too much is more than enough and enough is never too much. Sufficiency isn't too much, but it is enough, so you can see yourself, enough is enough and too much is too much. Abundance is too much and not enough; hence it is a very am*big*uous quantity to monkey with. Better stick to sufficiency—be it ever so elegant.

Industrial Worker, 13 October 1923

---

was in direct opposition to Taylorism, which Slim here describes as being told to "Hurry Up."

6 H. G. Wells was a prolific English writer, famous for his pioneering science fiction as well as social and political commentary. H. Bell Wright was a best-selling author of the early twentieth century.

7 Christian Johann Heinrich Heine was a nineteenth-century German poet and literary critic.

8 This is a reference to Clayton E. "Stumpy" Payne, the then-editor of the *Industrial Worker*. A founding member of the IWW, Payne became a victim of the U.S. government's repressive criminal syndicalism laws in 1920 and spent almost a year in prison.

Early History

In the beginning there was MAN—and *there he was*—fat and lousy. Yes indeed, editor, and he was reclining in the shade of a sawdust tree—(you've seen them yourself, haven't you?) The reason Man was in the shade was because the sun had burnt Mr. Oompalala's back—for such was his name, and so, too, he thought himself. "I am Oompalala," he would say in a satisfied way. "I am IT and my most recent wife is the charmful Lalapaloosa—the queen of Sawdust grove."

Mr. Oompalala recognized the symptoms of sunburn and with a great show of injured dignity hied himself to the grateful shade of the tree—there to divest himself of a few greybacks[1] that persisted in turning Oompalala's mighty form into a lodging house. "I am Oompalala, the brainy one," he mused. "I have had the exquisite sense to move in out of the sun—but, I am weary. Oompalala would rest—for it is true the contents of Oompalala's head feels heavier today after tapping an alcohol tree. Oompalala would rest, and if them damned sandflies would let him alone, Oompalala WOULD rest."

*

Hardby in the pasture frolicked a calf around its stoical mother chewing her cud. The weary eye of Oompalala followed the playful antics of the calf and Oompalala felt a feeling of good will steal over him as he dozed off to slumber—to sleep the sleep of those God-favored creatures who have been well fed. How long he slept, he did not know. He only knew that it was later in the day, now that he had rubbed his eyes—much later.

But, was it the same day? He did not know. The cow was still in the pasture—grazing this time—and even as Oompalala gazed upon her the calf was sucking her. . . .

Oompalala being refreshed by his recent nap reasoned correctly that the calf was having its supper and a great sense of sorrow swept Oompalala's soul for was it not up to him to climb yonder sausage tree for his own meal?

"A man of brain," said he bitterly, "and I've got to climb that tree."

"It's an outrage," he roared, "that's what I calls it."

But hush! Oompalala has a thought.

"What's the matter with me impersonating that calf? What's to prevent me, the mighty Oompalala, getting on my knees and sucking that cow?"

*

[1] A slang term for lice.

Oompalala is all excitement. He springs to his feet—congratulates himself by pounding his chest and eases toward the cow. With sundry endearing terms he approaches the cow, "So bossy; that's a good girl—are the flies bothering you?" he murmurs, for Oompalala could be reassuring when the spirit moved him. "This beats running down a board or climbing a tree," reasoned Oompalala, as the even half a dozen thoughts he was familiar with went swirling through his head. "I wonder how it will taste and if the damn fool cow don't kick my head off I'm lucky."

Oompalala had made a great discovery. Further laurels had been added to his crown.

The brains of the universe had functioned again to save Man's footsteps . . . and the calf had lost its supper; for in the returning plump Oompalala, the fair and buxom Lalapaloosa failed to recognize the idol of her heart.

What of it if the mighty Oompalala had been on his hands and knees gypping the calf "of one meal"? What is one meal anyway—why, anyone would give away a meal. "What's the odds anyway," reasoned he, "and Lalapaloosa don't have to know anything about it."

Thus it was that Lalapaloosa can be pardoned for being slightly "taken" with her charms, for was not the supperless Oompalala more affectionate that night than he had been since she saved him from the wild and woolly "dinosaurcuss"?

*

Oompalala never intended to keep secret the facts of the health giving qualities of cow's milk, although he did resolve to never mention that he, the mighty Oompalala, had impersonated a calf. And let it be known that he being an observing creature had noticed that the rich fluid flowed from the cow's bag at his slightest touch—in fact he only to hold his mouth open and it would almost strangle him—So, Oompalala would build himself a pail and catch the milk in it—and thus with one operation he could gather enough milk for two or more meals—to have on hand, in case of a rainy day.

Furthermore Oompalala wasn't going to stop there. Indeed not! Oompalala would show Lalapaloosa how to milk and then he himself could catch up with some of the rest he lost chasing that latest bunch of pork chops. Ideas crowded one another in his head and finally he decided to build a three legged stool and train one of Lalapaloosa's children to do the milking for the family on the grounds that the dewey grass is healthy for the kid's feet. That would release him, Oompalala; and her, Lalapaloosa, from all responsibility in regard to the family budget.

They then could, if so disposed, work to support the speculators and bankers—which they proceeded to do. And civilization had begun.

Industrial Worker, 31 October 1923

Starving amidst Too Much

Poets and Pearls: A Rhapsody

Our poet came near landing another job today. He was walking along the street, wondering whether he could raise the price of a Turkish bath to match his cleanly raiment, when his eyes lit upon a sign.

"Dishwasher Wanted, Experienced."

Dear Reader, let me interrupt you while I tell you I can see the Editor's eye gleam *bale*fully, as he anticipates the harrowing tale of his crack poet cracking dishes.

He will rise up in his sanctum, paw the air and distribute hands full of hair in the wastebasket—the mere thought of our poet entering the "field of art"! Spasms of suppressed Emotion will shake his frame and he will utter words no Mule Skinner need be ashamed of, even though the Editor may repent, and deny them later.[1]

He will try to argue that a premier poet, with fine spelling and comprehensive punctuation, is frittering away his time diving for pearls in a restaurant, when he might be making himself useful wheeling sonnets on a Construction job.

But our poet will cite authorities to prove that former great poets have reached dizzy heights in the fertile plains of Art, on the verdant pastures of Science.

Robert Burns, the brilliantmost star in poesy's constellation, won greater fame as a wielder of the broom than our modest bard can hope to ever win—washing dishes.

"Dishwasher Wanted, Exp."

Here was my opportunity for a Turkish bath. Our poet might enter the sweatbox kitchen, perspire to his hide's content, and get paid for it. Wash six thousand dishes for pastime, scrub the floor, compliment the cook, and while away the rest of the day discussing the relative merits of chewing gum as essence piquant added to soup, with or without celery.

All this for $1.42 6–7 per day, and bath and coffee, and beans, and comebacks and never arriveds, etc.

I entered—and in my best voice, and choice words, I informed the proprietor that his anxieties from this moment on would be banished; that I, even I, the inimitable immaculate T-Bone Slim, had resolved to emancipate him

---

[1] A "skinner" is a worker involved in hauling logs and other goods, originally with a team of horses or mules, later with a bulldozer or other machinery.

from the drudgery of the sink; that I would undertake to bathe his superb china (and in the sweet water of Lake Minnetonka, if necessary), to maintain the spotless purity of the "hot dog" joint, Le Par Excellence—would he kindly reveal to me the nature of the wages I would be honor'd with?

"Certainly, my friend," (I had won a friend already—though I hadn't touched the dishes). "Certainly," he says, "we are paying ten dollars a week and we furnish all the soap and water."

"Why, damn it, man, you don't want an expert dishwasher—what you want is a *common* dishwasher." (I had reverted back to my mother tongue.)

"Are you an experienced man?" he inquired.

"Why, man alive," says I, "I've cracked rock on some of the leading rock-piles all over the country." (This, of course, was a lie. Little indeed "moots" a lie when facing the realities of life, when a man wants a job, and good sweat over a tank of dishes—little indeed.)

"Well, if that's the case," he says, "I'll give you eleven dollars and a quarter."

"What in the name of benevolence is the quarter for?" I inquired. "Make it eighteen dollars a week and free pie a day—I'll take it."

"Goodness gracious!" he exclaimed. "Eighteen dollars a week—that would be 77 dollars a month, 800 dollars a year. Eight hundred dollars, just think—with eight hundred dollars you would be able to support a family. No, no, this place cannot afford to support a family—excepting, of course, my own dear family. Leave me," he pleaded. "We—we couldn't afford to let you eat any custard pie, anyway. Good day," he says, as he hit me in the eye with a fresh doughnut.

With my remaining eye I saw that if I prolonged the "conference" he would still hang on to his money, but lose his mind, so I went (as is the custom with great poets) down to the river—but not to drown myself.

I'll get a chance to wash dishes yet—when the weather gets warmer.

*

And when I say "man," they[2] will know I mean a "worker."

According to my ideas about the fitness of things, a man, woman, or child working for a living is a "man" viz—a horse is a horse whether it's male or female. Why should I make distinctions? Why indeed? Thus. The beautiful and gifted young ladies of the south-side slaughter-house are organizing themselves into a debutante organization of the feminine uplift circle, with the avowed purpose of coaxing Armour and Swift etc., etc., to contribute a few pennies extra into their forlorn pay envelopes. No. I don't see them as misses; I see them as workers doing work that would stagger a man. (But I do not see them getting a man's pay.)

*

[2] That is, Slim's female readers.

Waiters rush to and fro as if life depended upon their ability to dodge around the tables and slide along the counter. A bedlam of orders vibrates the air—shorty-brown, "knee deep" or "three high," whatever the case may be, and your meal is slammed in front of you one-tenth done. Every trick in the trade is there. Every adulteration. Every imitation. Every substitution. Dare you argue that this is not industry—that the waitress or waiter is not an industrial worker? . . .

Everything is fast becoming specialized.[3] And it seems a good deal "crazier" than it really is. For let us understand, specialization is the mother of efficiency. Efficiency, if directed into the proper channels, is a great help to mankind, but when directed to benefit those few who profit from the system, it is useless. Less efficiency would mean only less profits. For let it be understood: The master stands at a "pinnacle of profits"; the worker stands at the "level of living." *Between the "level of living" and the "pinnacle of profit" lies a stretch of unnecessary work, and the degree of efficiency or specialization practiced by the worker determines the amount of profit the master will receive. . . .*

In the foregoing I have intended no sarcasm—I am on the verge of hysterics because of my seriousness . . .

If we once admit the "Public" causes us to hurry then we must admit the Capitalist System is the Public. In the case of the Waiter and Waitress we are inclined to think they are holding a "wrongful opinion" about the cause of their "rush." Why we should think so is more than I can say—we do not consider ourselves smarter in any way than is the average waiter or waitress—we imagine that an average waiter thinks that he or she is obliged to rush things because the public demands quick service. If that is the case, he or she is mistaken. The public has all kinds of time; so much indeed, that on Sunday morning, when the system is "laying him off" he won't get up (out of bed) until noon. It is the system, the Capitalist System so called by courtesy, that is in a rush. The public can wait.

If profits drive the system and system drives the public, is that justification for the Public to drive the waiters and waitresses? A halt must be called somewhere, and the waiters and waitresses may as well call it. They can do this best industrially—many of them have already said as much. Personally I recognize no public. I see only working men and women, terribly driven by a ruthless profit-grabbing system.

Extracts from Slim's pamphlet *Starving amidst Too Much* (Chicago: IWW, 1923)

[3] This is a reference to Taylorism, the scientific management of work.

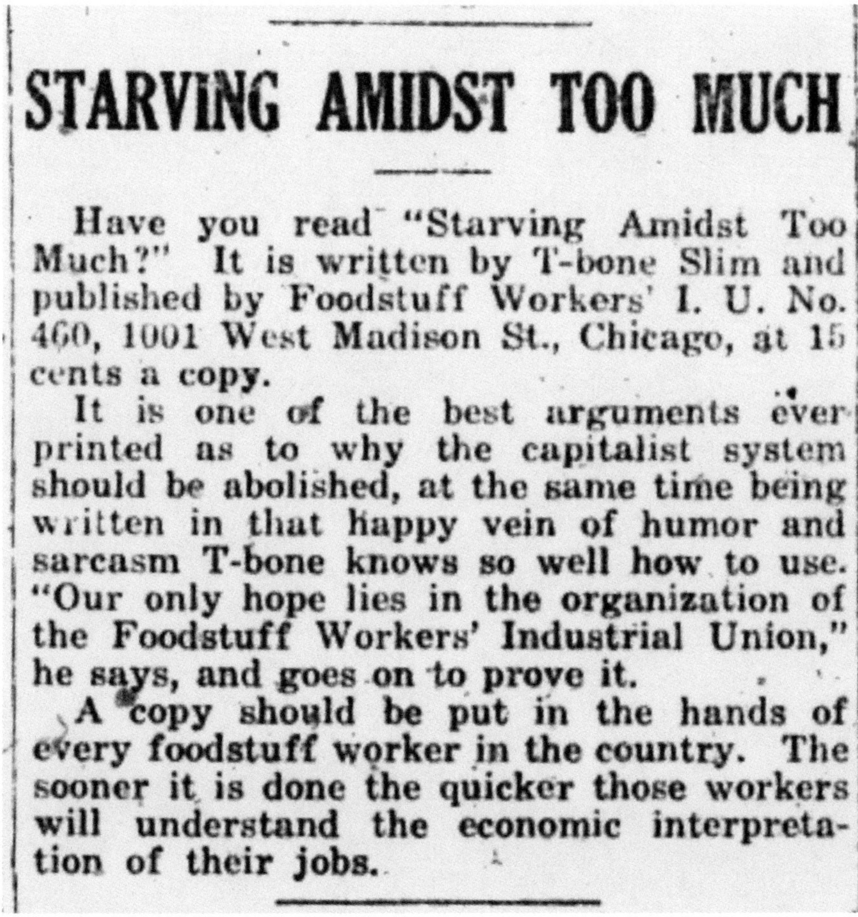

STARVING AMIDST TOO MUCH

Have you read "Starving Amidst Too Much?" It is written by T-bone Slim and published by Foodstuff Workers' I. U. No. 460, 1001 West Madison St., Chicago, at 15 cents a copy.

It is one of the best arguments ever printed as to why the capitalist system should be abolished, at the same time being written in that happy vein of humor and sarcasm T-bone knows so well how to use. "Our only hope lies in the organization of the Foodstuff Workers' Industrial Union," he says, and goes on to prove it.

A copy should be put in the hands of every foodstuff worker in the country. The sooner it is done the quicker those workers will understand the economic interpretation of their jobs.

Advertisement for Slim's pamphlet *Starving amidst Too Much*, in *Industrial Worker*, 4 August 1923.

1924

Mr. Hammond Deggs

(A Novel)

Our hero, Mr. Hammond Deggs, is descending the front steps of his palatial residence with a light heart, head and step. Alas, just as he is about to reach the common level with mankind—swish, his feet go out from under him; his head strikes the cruel curbing at the base of the neck, and at the base of the brass lion—Alas!

He expired—alas—before we could get the arms of the heroine around his neck.

*

We are shy one hero and the novel is just started! Oh, well, we novelists have to run them chances with our characters—we can't be guarding them all the time.

Night and day we are worried lest our heroes get tanked up, half shot, or shot up by unreasonable husbands. Of course, it is very "awkward" to lose the hero right off the reel—and, indeed it puts a big hole in the novel.

But we digress—let it be remembered; we still have the heroine, the beautiful Margarine Raisinpunk, of pure but harnessed parents—harassed parents, beg your pardon. At the moment our story begins, the beautiful Margarine, with her hair awry and golden, is trying to boost a tub of rain water onto the back stoop.

Yet, even, while she stoops to conquer, the icy stoop slips from under her "off" foot. Splash! The tub is empty. Bang! Clang! Down the cellar stairs clatters the tub, maid and twelve gallons of rain water into the basement. Darn the luck! We're shy one heroine. Her last words sounded like a siren—but wasn't. . . . And, isn't—no more.

Both, hero and heroine, are gone!

We didn't even have time to haul them into a hospital and let 'em expire eyeing each other.

Now the quest arises. Where is the villain? What is he doing all this time? We have lost two of the sweetest characters conceivable. And, now we want to meet the villain. Let us now get a hold of the villain!

Ha-a! He approaches. See him skulk along the hedge—and no card in his pocket. What shall we do with him?—r'remember, we've lost Margarine—we've lost Marse Hammond . . . We better lose him, too.

See him sneak, would you! An ever-ready blade in his teeth. Notice the way he throws his feet—Ha-a! He's done it! He's done it! He's stepped on that board—right smack on the rusty nail!

That settles him.

If he doesn't die a horrible death, I'm no judge of death, or a rusty nail—I know what it will do. He's as good as dead right now. That makes three.

We ain't got no hero, heroine or villain, so the rest of the cast might as well eat poisoned crabs or do away with themselves some how—I have a half a mind to hang 'em or make them die of broken heart over the untimely demise of our "love battery," and over their graves—or, have the villain, who by this time has the rabies, bite 'em.

I don't have to do that, mind you. No one is compelling me to do so. I still can continue this novel if I want to. With a few strikes of my pencil, I could resurrect Margarine and Hammond, start them off towards a parsonage, put a wooden leg on the villain—what show would he have chasing a taxicab with one leg made of hemlock? No chance at all.

But we're not going to resurrect them. They've been dead too long, and not long enough, already. The villain, as tough as he was, just now breathed his last and the rest of us will live happy ever after, the better physically, mentally (and maybe) financially.

(end)

*

The millionaire, camouflaged as an old broken down working man. I met him, this morning, and he inquired; do I "for stay" (Polish)—"Where you work?" was his next question. Being busy burying the dead in my deathless novel, I merely shook my head, at which he took courage, sighed, mumbled: "Me no got no work, no monee." I tried to explain to him, in my frank way, that he should have saved some work for himself last summer. I tried to show him how foolish it was to spend all his energy in the summer months and then be without exercise just when he needs it most—to keep warm.

I went into economics and explained as how the foreigners in this country had produced enough food, clothing and shelter to keep the bosses supplied (for a few months) and that if he wanted work steady, he would have to take "that little work" and divide it equally among the twelve months in the year—he must learn to support the bosses, not by the year but by the day—make them come to you every meal time.

This is a free country and you have an absolute right to work if you want to. No one has a right to stop you.

You say you have no work?

Industrial Worker, 16 January 1924

T-Bone Slim Discusses a Peace Plan

Mr Bok has offered another $100,000 for a peace plan that will be acceptable to the senate of the United States.[1]

Therefore: I, T-bone Slim, do hereby and with these presents, in good and sufficient faith, enter and submit a peace plan for the consideration of the said Senate and pray the said Senate to select from among its active members a sapping committee to see to it that the following plan shall have the thorough consideration its profound parts merit.

My Plan

FIRST: **Quit Fighting.**
SECOND: **Never Commence Again.**
THIRD: **Send The Money To T-Bone Slim,**
care of 1001 W. Madison St.,
Chicago, Ill.
U. S. A.[2]

Industrial Worker, 2 February 1924

---

1 Edward W. Bok was an influential editor who ran a newspaper syndication company, served as editor of the *Ladies' Home Journal* from 1889 to 1919, and won a Pulitzer Prize for his 1921 memoirs. In 1923, he proposed a prize of $100,000 for "the best practicable plan by which the United States may co-operate with other nations for the achievement and preservation of world peace." The competition roused much debate in the United States, and more than 22,000 entries were received. The winning plan, submitted by Charles Levermore, proposed greater involvement with multilateral courts and institutions such as the League of Nations.

2 This was the address of the IWW's main headquarters from 1917 to 1925.

Some Star!
(The Solidarity of Desperation)

Solidarity, after all, means something. It means everything that is worthwhile. And that is all it does mean.

Everything worthwhile.

It means biscuits for our babies; lunches for our ladies; oysters for ourselves; fry-cakes for our friends; epilepsy for our enemies; burdens for our bosses; mischief for our masters; millwork for our millionaires—that is: OUR solidarity means that.—His, the employer's, solidarity and our lack of it means: Manna for him and misery for us; money for him, microbes for us—

Here is about the way it lines up:

(For Him) (For Us)

Ambition—Alms
Bonus—Bones
Caviar—Caves
Diamonds—Die-mounds
Emancipation—Ends and Odds
Friends—Fiends
Gold—Gall

Yes that is what old Sol does—

> "Solidarity admits of no debate
> But fancy figures are cut
> With a single skate."—Moore.

And so it brings the bacon home to them that has it and strips the simoleons from those that have it not.

His solidarity and our lack of it means:

(For Him) (For Us)

Goodthings—Gods
Homes—Holes
Industries—Ills
Joy—Jaundice
Kingdoms—Klans
Love—Lice

Milk—Morgues
Melons—Muzzles
Nuts—Nothing
Opinions—Opium
Palaces, Pensions—Padded cells, Poverty
Queens—Quinces
Roses—Ruin
Rest—Rack
Songs—Sorrow
Twin-sixes—Two-bits
Unction—Underpay
Virgins—Vinegar
Worlds—Woe
Xmas—Xantippe
Youth—Yeast
Zest—Zebrine-suit
Zalsparilla—Zoup

The whole damn alphabet of alimony for him and a alphabet of agony for us—that's what solidarity and the lack of it brings. Choose. You'll stick together or be "stuck" together—choose!

Solidarity means something.

It is the difference between emancipation and slavery.

Education without solidarity is ENVY.

Organization without solidarity—ain't!

Emancipation without solidarity will never be—there you are—some "Star"—Soli-DAR-ity.

A solid front is good—a record of achievement. But a solid front with a hollow rear leaves much to be desired—Soli-darity. No matter how stolid or stoic we may become, solidarity is the all important quality and it has made industrial unionism the outstanding world movement it is. No amount of capitalist maneuvering has been "able to wreck it," its solidarity—which is one and the same thing.

Industrial Worker, 6 February 1924

I See, Says I

No doubt you have noticed, same as I, the California raisins in the coffee rolls. And no doubt you have wondered, same as I, why the bakers put them in when they know it is against the wishes of the I. W. W.[1]

It almost seems they are bearding the lion in his "own ward" when they do this—I couldn't make head or tail of it—as intellectual as I am—so I walked six blocks out of my way to ask a bakery worker.

"Slim," he says, "I thought you claim to have brains—and you can't think that out?"

"What's brains got to do with boycotted raisins," inquires I, kind of sore.

"What! You don't tumble yet!" he almost shrieked—and he *laffed* and *laffed* and *laffed*. Four times he laughed and then he pointed with his finger: "See them cockroaches running along that board. Well, pretty nearly always (what I mean, *not sometimes*) some of them get into the dough and we have to throw in a few handfuls of raisins to make people think they are eating a vegetarian lunch. Yes, Slim, if it tastes, it's raisins; if it doesn't, it's a dry cockroach."

"I see," says I.

*

Idle-Power

February is the best month in the year for to argue in favor of a short work day. This month in itself is short and yet it is mentioned with longer months in the calendar, without discriminations of any sort. Folks speak lightly of it—in fact—in almost endearing terms.

The 1-10th (3 days) sometimes missing from its latter part is hardly noticed—any more than the eighth hour would be on a seven-hour day—it never would be missed.

Although this month is short (which forestalls extended arguments), it makes up in emphasis what it lacks in length.

It is during this month that men become unemployed, which means that

---

1 This is a reference to an IWW campaign that called for a boycott of all California goods, as well as motion pictures, in order to pressure the state to repeal its criminal syndicalism laws and free those imprisoned under them. This was accompanied by strike action on two major infrastructure construction projects, increased workplace agitation, and a general strike on 25 April 1923. Up to 10,000 lumber workers walked off the job in the Pacific Northwest from that day, and strikes were carried out on West Coast docks and in other industries, leading to a new round of arrests in California. Neither the strikes nor the boycott had a major impact, and the state's syndicalism laws were not formally repealed until 1991.

their part of social labor has been brought to a successful conclusion, that there is nothing further required of them—in the way of manual toil. Just why we call them unemployed is not clear, since the very word insinuates they had "slipped the yoke" (which, of course, they have not done).

I think it would be ever so much nicer to call them retired-workers, surplus-labor, former-slaves, future-potentials, extra-help, ex-service-men, or shrdlu-zyxchr[2]—anything but UNemployed. What right have they to be unemployed while others must work!—True, they completed their tasks, but that doesn't prove that the tasks were equally difficult with those who are still in the process of prosecution, unfinished.

Industrial Worker, 27 February 1924

[2] In the era of linotype printing, "etaoin shrdlu," of which Slim's phrase seems to be a variation, was a letter combination produced by moving a finger down the first and second left-hand banks on a linotype machine to make a temporary marker that was not meant to appear in the final printing. It occasionally did appear in print, however, by mistake. This happened often enough that the phrase became part of newspaper folklore and something of an in-joke.

Rights vs. Plights

We have seen lilies growing on dung hills, but that is not where they are found as a general rule. Employers that provide such surroundings for their tender sprouts will find the fragrant flowers burn out in no time . . .

*

We can find amidst poverty and want glorious examples of chastity and virtue—that proves nothing—even as we find examples of wanton animalism among the tribes of money getters, and gold diggers.

*

Our argument is not that riches makes for virtue.

Our argument is not that poverty makes for virtue.

Our argument is not that riches demoralize.

Our argument is not that poverty demoralizes.

No, we are not interested in the "moral plight."

No, we are not concerned about the "immoral plight."

We simply are arguing that poverty is unnecessary in this day of inventions.

We don't give a damn whether girls are pure or impure. We want to know if they are getting the full product of their toil—for toil they do, but shouldn't.

We have heard reformers suggesting higher wages for girls, better working quarters, more sanitary and commodious homes and numerous other remedies as solutions of our moral plight.

We do not argue that way. We are direct actionists and believe the girl is entitled to these things as a matter of moral right and not as a solution for moral plight. We reason that if we, and the girl, labor in this society to help produce these things, we shall be permitted to enjoy them—more so than those who produce nothing.

Regardless of whether high wages, short hours and better conditions contribute to our moral welfare or not; even if high wages, short hours and better conditions sent us all to perdition, we would still insist that they are ours by right—we don't want any blue blooded parasite to go to hell "or our high wages, short hours and better conditions—" We acknowledge the corn. Never mind the moral phase, come across.

There is no excuse for rotten economic conditions. The standard of living can be raised to something that approximates perfection with but a slight effort on the part of organized labor . . . once installed, its upkeep will require less energy than the present rotten arrangement.

Industrial Worker, 8 March 1924

Mostly Song

Man feels in the humor for song only a short period of time, per day, per month, per year and per life time. And the more rotten the conditions, up to a certain point, the less he feels like singing—the less he feels like doing anything.

When in humor, he will go along humming a tune until about 4 pm.; then suddenly he goes flat.

Before conditions became rotten, before life began to pale upon him we found him singing like a meadow lark upon a May morning—in September. Yes indeed, men would sing in September like a lark in May—and as a result of this singing, many low-browed intellectuals have gotten themselves into an opinion that singing is the cause of man's present condition. They reason that if man had refrained singing instead of singing refrains, he would now be as free from worry as are they who never hummed a tune in all their lives. . . .

If not that—then, at least, they bewail the fact that singing has brought sorrow to all hands, including themselves. Now, methinks MacBeth, yon song hater has a hungry look. Methinks, oh noble Cassius, that yon song hater hates himself. And, lastly, methinks he has fallen in love with the ideal of our Lord and Master. Oh, ye songless slaves: "Sing nothing and saw wood."

Now, it happens that I have written a few songs—a few songs as rotten as the system itself—no more and no less—ROTTEN. And, I maintain that under proper conditions my songs would have been SWEET as the voicings of an unsuccessful candidate cooing under the protecting wings of the administration. And since this be so and since my songs can not be blamed for the conditions that are, I stand unsullied of any taint of responsibility for the terrible straits in which labor finds itself today and the singing of my songs can not make things any worse than they are.

Industrial Worker, 5 April 1924

Indiana Moon

The saloons used to open at 5 a.m., and I, having become accustomed to rising at that time, find it difficult to lie in bed (like bankers do) until 8 o'clock. A habit acquired by long practice is hard to break, and humiliating it is indeed to wake up at such an ungodly hour—now that there no longer is a need for a long day. To be frank with you, fellow worker editor, my drinks used to cost me in the neighborhood of 25 cents for eye-openers; 15 cents for appetizers, and 45 cents for nightcaps—you can see yourself I wasn't always the virtuous angel that I now am.[1] My drinks used to cost me 85 cents per day.

To generate 85 cents requires considerable time; about two hours' work on the job. But now, since my drinks are with me no longer I hardly know what to do with the two hours per day that are not needed for my upkeep—it's a cinch I cannot sleep them off for I've tried that. . . .

I've been thinking that if I could bring myself to accept "smaller pay" I could still continue to work the long day (for my board and lodging), eat "dry-combinations," etc. and let the boss keep the 85 cents as a sort of "testimonial" of my faith in him—Yea, Bo, so I reason, and what's the matter with it? Isn't it sound reasoning? Two hours' worth of drinks taken away from me—confiscated—without so much as consulting with me to see if I could survive the "raid." Yes. What does it mean? Does it mean that private property is no longer *inviolet*? I'm afraid it does. I'm afraid we are breaking away from the glorious traditions of our rum-guzzling forefathers—mind you; I only fear this, I know better.

I know that we were not consulted about denaturing our shoes with paper heels; adulterating our sox with Alabama wool and rectifying our sausage with screenings advertised as cereals so why should they not Foolstedt[2] us a little with moonbeams and canned heat[3] in our department of the refreshments; in our Bureau of Beverages?

The standard of refreshments has been lowered to conform with low-life living. We are now in the hair-oil-lemon-extract age, on one hand, imitation sausage and one-half of 60 per cent bread on the other (the next thing to be

---

1 Slim's divorce notice accused him of habitual drunkenness. For more information, see the Introduction.

2 This is a reference to the 1919 Volstead Act, through which Prohibition was introduced across the United States at midnight on 17 January 1920.

3 A nickname for Sterno, a brand of denatured alcohol sold as cooking fuel but also drunk by those unable to buy alcoholic beverages. The drinking of canned heat is associated with alcoholism and blindness.

lowered will be our manhood, the existence of which I very much doubt since nobody seems to be making any great holler—watch your step).

But we have them "two hours" that we do not need to labor, since we are not a drinking man—we are distinctly a distinctive eater, like the Frenchman says, "If I cook myself"—well done.

Our standard of living is now one-third of what it was in the good old days when Doc. Wiley's battle flag was dragged in the dirt, Doc., protesting like a colored landlady in the fact of bribe-takers.[4]

Our dollar is now worth about 40 cents; less the two-thirds quality missing from the things we need, use and must have. Divide 40 cents by three and you will find the usefulness of the dollar today, compared to the dollar of twenty years ago, is in the neighborhood of 13⅓ cents.

And when buying moonshine (that infamous substitute for whiskey) the value of the dollar equals the price of a yeast cake—two cents.

Oh America, thy clothes are patches, through the toe of thy shoddy sox thy great American toe is making its debut. Thy food is by-products and thy disgrace a by-word. Thy gospel is hollow-sounding. Thy press is a misleader and a misnamer. Pull yourself together for Christ's sake; join the Wobblies and inscribe on your banner the words: The Best Is Not Good Enough for the People.

Industrial Worker, 12 April 1924

---

4 Dr. Harvey Wiley campaigned from the 1870s onward against the adulteration of food and other products. He headed up the Division of Chemistry of the U.S. Department of Agriculture from 1883 and, following the public outcry caused by Upton Sinclair's description of the Chicago meatpacking industry in his novel *The Jungle* (1905), successfully lobbied for the passage of the 1906 Pure Food and Drug Act.

Don't Threaten

(Note—Opposition press carries Papini's "Life of Christ,"[1] hence our author considers it appropriate to conjure up a picture of a "proletarian martyr"—for the once't—'pproximating truth and promising never again. Introducing: Jerusalem Slim.)

*

It came to pass that day that there was a man in Judea whom the stiffs called Jerusalem Slim.[2] He hailed from the small town of Bethlehem, on the Palestine Central and was a son of a patternmaker in that burg. Now it happened that Slim had a line of economics that was the despair of the chin-whiskered scribes that hung around the Labor Temple—and it is said of him that at the age of eight Slim could quote Karl Marx and Zoroaster faster than the Pharisees could digest it.

But it came to pass that the rank and file of the people living in that terribly exploited country took notice of the lad's gift of gab and gave ear unto his sayings—and became terribly worked up over them.

It was not long before wind of these proceedings were carried to the Chamber of Commerce, the Boa Constrictor Copper Company,[3] the Lebanon Cedar Company, (the latter which had furnished to the Solomon Construction Company every stick of timber used in the construction of the famous temple in Jerusalem) and to the various civic bodies and manufacturers associations including the executives of the Arabian Fruit Growers Equity. They got together and decided to black-ball Jerusalem Slim "on all jobs," behind his back, with the result that it was not long till they had Slim leaning against walls to hide such apertures as were given birth by the ravages of time in the seat of his wardrobe. A job he could not get. Slim, like Wilson, was too proud to steal.[4] He could have visited the clothes lines in the suburbs of Jerusalem but no, Slim says no, I will organize a One Big Union and I will show these malefactors whose dog they's been kicking. So he got himself a soap-box or an empty

---

1 Italian futurist Giovanni Papini's *The Story of Christ,* a novelized biography, was translated into English in 1923.

2 "Stiff" is hobo slang for worker.

3 This is a parodic reference to the Anaconda Company, which owned the copper mines in Butte, where the infamous murder of Frank Little took place.

4 This is a reference to President Woodrow Wilson's 1915 "Too proud to fight" speech, in which he argued for continued neutrality in World War I, despite the fact that 128 American citizens had recently died when the German navy sank the British passenger vessel *Lusitania.* Although he would successfully run a reelection campaign in 1916 on the basis of his having kept the United States out of the war, Wilson eventually led the nation into it following attacks on American ships.

beer keg and proceeded to address the multitude saying: "Come unto me all ye drys and I will make ye wet," or words to that effect, always winding up his speech with the words "follow me"—and they did. "Do unto others as they do unto you" was one of his favorite slogans and, considering he was no mean scrapper, this creed was a source of great trouble to him. One day, having worked up a peeve, he got himself a sap and raided the temple single handed, striking right and left, quite forgetting to turn either cheek for the parasites to land on, he cleaned up on them something proper—talk about action! For this escapade he had to take a fishing trip up the River Jordan for a couple of weeks till the thing had quieted down. Unfortunately, upon his return, he started another free speech fight[5] and denounced the powersz that be with a vitriolic flow of eloquence. He recounted instance after instance of injustice practiced upon him personally, and on the laboring men generally. He recounted how he had been black-balled; how he had been beat out of his wages and how he had been hounded from place to place till he had no place to lay his head. He had been called "a radical" repeatedly and was driven from the shops merely for that reason. And so, in an incautious moment while overcome with his miseries he made a threat. Looking right in the eyes of the stools and dicks he shook his fist and said: The Sins of the Fathers Shall Be Visited Upon the Sons to the Third and Fourth Generation. (That was enough.)

For that he was grabbed and eventually crucified and so ends our story.

Moral: Never make a threat! If you are in that habit, break it. A threat only serves to cause unnecessary worry to those you threaten; it does you no good; it does him no harm—if you do not threaten he will worry about something else anyway. Why waste a threat, besides, "It's against the law." If you must have an outburst, SWEAR.

Jerusalem Slim might be alive today if he hadn't threatened so much. Again I say, Don't Threaten.

Don't tell them what you've DONE nor what you WILL DO. History records the former and the future will prove the latter—as to the present: What are you doing to help the boys in the can.[6] Isn't there something we can do right now?

Industrial Worker, 19 April 1924

---

[5] A reference to the successful "free speech fights" held by the Wobblies in the years before World War I.

[6] That is, the Wobblies still in jail.

Rock of Ages

What would the cold sullen stones in a prison wall say if they could talk? Would they burst into poetry lauding nature's wonderful favors or would they rise in denunciation of a most damnable system of society; wherein nature's noblemen perforce must linger and languish within a dark, loathsome Heritage-of-an-Age otherwise forgotten? Prison.

It is now Centuries and Centuries since prisons were invented and they appear to be the only establishment that defies the Law of Change. Jails and more jails appear to be the rule in our maudlin society to the end that now our fair land is dotted with them. At the end of a good day's walk you will arrive at a jail or a cluster of jails in certain localities, but in industrial centers an hour's walk is sufficient. So the question arises what would the cold, sullen stones say if they could talk—and they can talk. They do talk. They talk a fluent universal tongue that everybody can understand. Their words may not be as polished as the words of a Daugherty or a Fickert or a Cowan, but talk they do. And what does these sullen stones say? Ah fellow workers, I'm a poor hand at reporting speeches—my memory is so poor. I'm afraid I can not put the words down on this paper in the order they were given me by a cynical block of sandstone in a penitentiary wall . . .

Feeling flippant one day I asked the block: "How long you in for?"

"I'm in this wall until everybody gets the full product of their toil," replied the stone.

I was completely taken aback by its answer and begged it to explain more clearly.

"Well Slim, you see it's this way, most of these human beings that I am restraining are of an independent sort and would not knuckle down to work for overalls and snuff—they refused to labor long hours for small pay—work became irksome to them because there were no rewards—everything they 'earn't' went to build their body so that they might work more—a dull, drab, slavish existence stared them in the face—so, like Brodey, they took a chance. Visions of love, comfort, pleasure and rest vanished with the vision of a cottage at the foot of the hill, paid for—a home. They saw it would take several life times to pay for a house that could be whittled out in one year with a jack knife, so they took a chance—they took individual action and realized too late their error—if they had organized they wouldn't be here and *I wouldn't be here.*"

"But," I interrupted, "surely you have some union men in here?"

"Why yes, Slim, but you don't seem to get my drift, I'm trying to tell you, without making a too long story of it, that jails serve to keep the wage-slaves 'contented'—of course we've got union men, but they're mostly organizers—

the idea is to keep them away from the workers, so that the workers can be skinned more thoroughly. Yes, Slim, it's a damned shame too—they only wanted what was right and, now, here they are with those that murdered to obtain the money that would not forthcome through the efforts of manual labor. Here they are with those that killed in passion soured by an inequitable system of compensation; or over woman for reasons traceable to same cause. Here they are with those that raped having been brought down to the level of an animal—'no front,' malnutrition, self-abuse, atmosphere laden with demoralized 'psychology' and suppressed desires are the causes (in the main) acting directly through victim of the deed or through agency of misguided womanhood possessed of false notions created by unequal system—thousands of reasons that remain fostered instead of exterminated—

"Here they are with those that were framed to save the reputation of police officers—some one had to be sent up; the 'guilty' one could not be caught so they sent up a coward—frightened him into confessing—tricks in every trade you know, Slim, and this infamous industry is no different. From time immemorial slaves have been cast into dungeons for rebelling against their drivers. Educators have been jailed for letting slip enlightenment to slaves. Poets have been imprisoned for inspiring hope in the breast of those that toil and moan. Philosophers have been incarcerated for disproving the fitness of existing customs. Christ was crucified. Joe Hill was shot.[1] Frank Little was dragged behind an automobile—can you then wonder that Ford and Suhr are in jail;[2] Mooney and Billings are in the can.[3] Can you wonder that the Centralia boys

---

1 The IWW's most famous songwriter, Joe Hill was born Joel Emmanuel Hägglund in Sweden and immigrated to the United States in 1902. Living as a migratory worker, he joined the union around 1910. He produced cartoons for the union's press and wrote songs that would become labor standards, including "The Preacher and the Slave," "There Is Power in a Union," and "The Rebel Girl." In 1914 he was framed for murder in Salt Lake City, Utah, and executed by firing squad the following year, becoming the IWW's (and the left's) most famous martyr.

2 In 1913 an IWW campaign was undertaken by workers harvesting hops at the Durst Ranch in Wheatland, California. Richard Ford, a former IWW member, was spokesperson for the strikers, while Herman Suhr, a current IWW member, was secretary of a recently formed local chapter of the union. During an attempt by authorities to end a mass meeting and arrest Ford, a police officer fired a shot into the air, triggering a firefight that left two workers dead, as well as the local district attorney and a deputy sheriff. In the aftermath a hundred arrests were made, and many workers were assaulted and tortured. In the trial that followed over the death of the DA, two defendants were acquitted but Ford and Suhr were given life sentences. Following much activism by the IWW, both were pardoned in 1924, although Ford was retried and then acquitted over the killing of the deputy sheriff.

3 In 1916 a bomb went off during a "Preparedness Day" parade held in San Francisco to advocate for U.S. intervention in World War I. Ten people died and forty were injured. Labor radicals Thomas Mooney and Warren Billings were convicted of

are in the pen for protecting their property according to law—(as it happened to be)—their hall, the hall which was objectionable to the lumber companies.[4] Yes, Slim, there are organizers in here and yet these stones will lay, one upon the other, until organizers unite the great working class into a one big union and inaugurate a more equitable system of 'returns' for labor. But, let me give you a tip, Slim: so long as American working men compete with child-labor so long will you all be slaves . . ."

It was quite a talk we had with the old piece of mountainside, but of course I can't be expected to remember it all.

"Watch your step" was its last words and I confess they gave me a start—I recalled the time I was in a workhouse. . . . as I was being released, the kind-faced superintendent took me by the hand affectionately, gazed into my eyes and said, "Slim, get yourself a job and make an honest living."—Next week he shot himself for misappropriating prison funds—so I resolved to be honest even if they hang me for it.

Industrial Worker, 30 April 1924

involvement, with the former sentenced to death and the latter to life imprisonment. Allegations of perjury by witnesses and manufactured evidence gave rise to a long-running international campaign that saw Mooney's sentence commuted to life in prison before both men were freed in 1939.

4 On 11 November 1919, during an Armistice Day parade, members of the American Legion attacked an IWW hall in Centralia, Washington. Attempts by allies and the owner of the property to get police to provide protection failed, and when Legionnaires left their official route and surrounded the hall, a firefight broke out. Four vigilantes died in the fracas. Numerous IWW members were arrested, one of whom, former military conscript Wesley Everrett, was lynched later that night. At trial charges were dropped against one IWW defendant, two were acquitted, one found "insane," and seven sentenced to second-degree murder after the judge rejected the jury's request for the charges to be downgraded. He also ignored their call for leniency, sentencing each of the seven defendants to between twenty-five and forty years in prison.

T-Bone Slim Discusses: Safety First

During these **preharvest** depressions we literary folks have greater opportunities to see more of our beloved America, even with the lesser facilities at hand. Thus it was that our writer weary, gaunt and travel-worn (what wasn't worn was jolted) disengaged himself from a train[1] and alighted gracefully with his ear close to the ground—in a listening attitude.

Hearing nothing he spit the cinders from his mouth and proceeded to take his bearings and a chew of snuff, realizing that cinders are hard on teeth and compare only with bran as **piece 'de resilience** whereas snus preserves the teeth. After brushing himself he discovered he was surrounded on all sides by the beautiful and virtuous city of Cleveland. Hastily wiping all evidence of travel from his face he vowed that hereafter he would boost for the electrification of all railroads, and the electrocution of all parasites, who put in full time working the workers—for he considers criminal-parasitism not a disease but a vicious habit.

Just then two railroad bulls, deeply disguised as jobless workingmen, approached and one of them casually inquired: "How's the crew to ride with" and did I "get off that train?"—Imagine these rising young Burns[2] asking me, my hair grey me at the temples, **if I got off that train**—must have thought that I was some kind of a walking Information Bureau—but I was polite. I told him that it was beyond my powers to know anything about the crew and that I was only a hardworking laborer returning home from work to the bosom of my family. "Where are you working?" he next inquired—(darn these bulls anyway for inquisitiveness). Well,—well sir—yessir, I said sir—**You** ought to **know,** you've seen me pass by here every day (pretty neat, eh!) I'm over here at Isaac Leisy's Brewery, we're changing it into a tabernacle they tell me, I countered. This seemed to satisfy him—I knew it would—and I felt it was my duty to satisfy him even if I had to lie to do it—I'm not drawing any pay for enlightening thick headed bulls and I'm not under oath, yet I imagine under oath I could do better.

Around the corner from Superior Street is an entrance of a bank whose portals are guarded by a couple ladies done in "rock."[3] Both are holding a box—a money box—in the **akimbo** of one arm; holding dagger, hilt end up, which makes it look like a cross, in the other hand. I was not prepared to enter the bank (with all that female militia standing guard) but, and I'll confess, I

---

1 That is, jumped down from the railroad car on which he had been riding illegally.

2 A reference to the William J. Burns International Detective Agency. Founded in 1909, the agency was involved in infiltrating, monitoring, and repressing the IWW.

3 That is, statues of women.

did stand quite awhile admiring (with mouth open) the generous proportions of **the torso**; compared to the size of the head. Then, suddenly coming back to earth, we meandered back to Superior St., and proceeded in our lawful pursuits, athwart the bow of the bank—and then it happened: There on the bank's front porch sat Labor, done in brass, and he had his hammer right along with him. . . . Mighty KNOCKER! Not enough clothes on him to flag a hand car . . . and sitting down! Christ!! Who ever heard of such brazen effrontery? Under the figure behind a sliding panel is a machine gun, a one pounder which slides out whenever a debate commences as to the ownership of the "change" reposing in the vaults of this concern.[4] This layout is burglar proof against all comers except a Tank Corps BUT—if some misguided individual ever attempts to "recruit" his fortunes the slaughter will be terrific! The robbers might not be shot but plenty of citizens will be coughing up machine gun bullets for months afterward. Oh well, it isn't my funeral, if Cleveland enjoys sitting on a keg of powder let her do so. Life insurance rates are going up.

P.S.—Tank of "Nitro"[5] on Public Square would be a reassuring sedative compared to this "one pounder."

Note: Harmless "black powder" must be stored in **isolated places** yet this machine of destruction is brought in amongst the very people—by the very men who preach Safety First and practice it last.[6]

Industrial Solidarity, 21 May 1924

4 That is, in case of a bank robbery.

5 Nitroglycerine, the active ingredient in dynamite.

6 "Black powder," or gunpowder, was by this time a somewhat outdated form of ammunition, having been replaced by "smokeless powder."

T-Bone Slim Discusses

Introduction to Starved Ears

Intro: Canned vibrations, radio, phonograph or telephone are a utility, not a diet—and prolong life about as much as a picture of a banquet . . . artificial. Woe be unto the nation that substitutes anything for the Freedom of Expression.

Starved Ears
(Epic-gramatically?)

Man goes to work, intelligent; comes home, (in the evening) ignorant.

*

In the morning he is "clear"; in the evening he is tired.

*

There is more to a handshake than friendship . . . two handshakes equal a dinner.

*

Handouts, too, have two values—one you know instinctively is food; the other is the trace of a "hand-shake" that clings to it.

*

The germiest handshake is worth more than all the flattery spoken since time began.

*

Printed flattery has no value to the flattered—it benefits the flatterer.

*

Spoken flattery benefits both: The flattered reaps the vibrations, the flatterer feels relieved.

Printed flattery is but reiteration, for the billionth time, of that what is already known.

*

Flattery is the oldest joke sprung. But speech, even when handicapped with flattery, is better than a tubfull of medicine.

Too little speech dwarfs the mind and withers the body—"silent speaker" and his audience both suffer.

*

Too much speech is like too much "turkey," to the hearer. To the speaker, a delirium of vowels is worse than a rupture . . . very weakening.

*

A soundless world is an empty cupboard—A bedlam of noise is more destructive than a cyclone. Cyclones destroy bodies. **"Noise" destroys life.**

*

Conversation, between humans, is the same as two horses gnawing each other's manes—both benefit. Give the boys free speech, and deny not the prisoners.

Why do pigeons hum? Why do dogs bark? Lions roar? Snakes hiss? Hens cackle? Roosters crow? Crows caw? Elephants trumpet?—tell me, oh ye savants! Why do these vibrate the air with their calls? And mice—whose very safety depends on silence—they squeak. Give us, oh my masters, the privileges of a rat. Let your humans participate in and partake of life even as yon rodent at this moment in my room . . .

Silence—death; liberty—chains.—

We are born with a cry and die with a rattle but in the meantime we will speak.

*

Let us shake hands (on it) and speak the word our silent brother is "starving" for. . . .

Denial of freedom of speech is assault (without battery) and is equivalent to life sentence in prison (with prison absent).

Denial of speech in prison is a death sentence in addition to the regular sentence.

I say, let's talk it over—'tis a fundamental right and an absolute necessity.

Freedom of the Press not here discussed, it is another matter and comes under the head of "soaking it in" through the eye.—Our subject was ears.

Industrial Solidarity, 4 June 1924

Bugs and Fords

What is an injunction? Is it a red-light at a dangerous crossing? Is it a "stop, look and listen"? Is it a mother's warning "don't go near the water"? Is it a "no-smoking" sign? Finally, is it a "law-before-the-fact"? Is it a law? Is censorship an injunction and does it serve the same purpose and is censorship bad? Is censorship an injunction-before-the-fact? Are the "two" a part of the capitalist's system? Will law, injunction and censorship be a part of the Toiler's Commonwealth; if so, why kick? Shall we, by our objection, urge that capitalist laws will survive capitalism? Shall we urge that capitalism is O.K. but its laws cause us physical suffering and great mental agony? Shall we organize to change laws or shall we "scrap" (condemn) the source, or shall we do "neither or all of these things"? Is not injunction bad only when used against us, and isn't it perfectly lovely when used in our favor? Isn't it a question of viewpoint, a matter of opinion—a good chance for a split, when we can unite against the system that raises these questions. They have nothing to do with bread and shoes!

*

On our modern American farms it invariably happens the granger[1] distributes insecticide, "vermine" and buggine in the wrong place. Seed-wheat and seed-oats have their formaldehyde-bath, but the hired person's bed-room is a stranger to that labor o' consideration: Slim can not rest, and being of suspicious nature, strikes a match to view the parade of 300 bedbugs—great big healthy ones, and red—bless their little hearts—Crimson!

Slim calls the attention of Shorty[2] to the "Red Invasion." Shorty blinks, and turns a "fresh side" for the bugs to devour. "Keep your shirt on, Slim," he says, "it's just another case of two Daniels in a lion's den."

Darn, Shorty, anyway, he's always speaking in parables. . . . I wonder if he really meant that story of Daniel was a left-handed "dig" about bedbugs? "Yes," says Shorty, "we shouldn't take the bible literally, them ol' codgers were subtle as hell when it came to spinning razzful yarns about crummy flops."

Industrial Worker, 10 September 1924

---

1 Farmer.

2 This seems to refer to a road partner, though whether this is an actual or fictional person is unclear. It was common for male hobos to travel in pairs, in relationships that could be temporary or permanent, sexual or platonic.

True to Form

The "National Defense Day" will go off big.[1] On September 12, I understand, the nation will spring to arms as one man. Of course, you understand, this will be for practice only, training for the citizens—so that they will stand calm *under draught* in the event of another last war; merely training them to repulse onslaught with "sladder"—to repel attack an' how to follow up.

The last *Last War* was a great lesson to us. We found our nation totally unprepared to kill Germans, so fast they showed up. We found ourselves 3,000 miles away from nearest German selected for slaughter, with almost no means of transportation except a few old British tubs, rattle-traps like the *Lusitania,* which had been a *has been* five years before the war started, and should have been condemned as unable to compete with the stately (German) ships of trade.

On the other hand, the flag-waving-profiteers found themselves Unprepared! Many of them were caught short and grabbed 300 per cent profit when they could of had 2,000 per cent just as well. No doubt these self-styled patriots will take advantage of this coming "mobilization" and practice-up their chosen art. Up goes the prices.

*

Y. M. C. A. will corner the cigarettes and Bull-Durham.[2] Salvation Army will pore over the dough-nut recipes. Ex-Politicians will sell Liberty Bonds without consulting the buyers. Yes, indeed, I believe it will go over big. Labor will demand a 10 per cent increase (piker) in wages to take care of a 200 per cent increase in cost of living. Piker!

*

Debs, the G. O. M.,[3] will go to Can.

"Saucy" Kate O'Hare, also.[4]

---

1 National Defense Day was an event organized by the War Department and the federal government to encourage patriotism "in a most practical way and with all the fervor and enthusiasm of which red-blooded Americans are capable." It was held in parallel with the testing of a national radio broadcast system, which included a program featuring speeches and interviews with various military figures, recorded live by Western Electric.

2 That is, tobacco.

3 Grand Old Man.

4 Kate O'Hare was a Socialist Party activist, novelist, and orator who was sentenced to five years in jail in 1917 for involvement in antiwar activities. She began her sentence in 1919 and was freed the following year, going on to campaign for the release of other political prisoners.

The I. W. W. will be locked-up.

Illinois will lynch one bond-toting German, by mistake.

What would happen—if everything goes true to form?

If the lumber barons and timer-morons take mobilization seriously, on "this" day, the price of lumber "products" is due for a "kiting."

*

Hoover may declare for a *dogless* brekfus's.

*

Conscientious obstructicians will raise grey mustaches and limp, flat-footed.

*

Editors will qualify every statement, or disguise them as interrogations. All treasonable words will be blurred with a quick, sharp blow from the editorial mallet.

*

Three minute speeches by merchants of British extraction. Germans will gang-up on all Pro-Kaiserites, and Irish will fight for the King.

*

Emergency boards will "practice-up" on building transparent-transports from box-lumber. Patriotic steel will advance on orders.

*

Revolutionary periodicals will discuss the general uprising of a dobe-builder in Af-Kanistan, and the simultaneous revolt in Congo, of all hands on the numerous plantations of the Belgia Balloon-Tire Corporation. (Both men disappearing between midnight and dawn.)

*

The "twenty-four bought up papers" will come out in squeeling headlines about the very latest atrocity of the enemy—how a heartless fuerst "luff" dragged a motherless orphan, three months old, through a key hole until the child resembled a buckskin belt lacing—RETALIATION! will be the indignant cry of the mortally offended press!—Yes, the press too must be mobilized for instant action. We will live all over again the Lucy Tania HORROR, with all those little children and widows on an innocent visit to the battle fields of war torn Europe. Ach, Poor Belgium, Poor Armenia, Poor Turk.—No, not Turkey—Poor—that is—all those that got it in the neck, whoever they were. Every shot fired by the enemy will hit a church or a hospital or a cradle—darn 'em anyway.

*

Super-patriots will grab bullet proof jobs h'ist their "stinkers" on top the "grand rapids" (So's to prevent red blood warming their feet). Hundred Per Centers will patrol Balm Peach—Peach Balm—Palm Beach. There, I guess I've got it right!

Superannuated "ante-dates" will screech for war (for someone else to fight) and the Red Cross will offer First Aid to the Strangling Fossils by Pounding them on the Hump. It's going to be a big day. War provender will be fed the voracious public until its celluloid belt "melts."

North Dakota bank robbers will be severely censured for trying to get celebration started two weeks early, and for using a man's house for target practice.

Anton ZWACH, south of New Ulm, and his silver toned wife, at same address, will probably give their chore boy something to eat on that day. (Co. Commissioners please note.)

Personally, I will try to mobilize the Lord on our side. I will spend the Day in prayer, if it isn't good drying weather.

The Wobs in Hanley Falls insist that "coming as it does in September, and being as how it is the 12th day of that very same month, it is an ideal day for stamping up the ol' book, in full; 'n' have that much done in case we're attacked or invaded by a horde of parasites."

I fully agree with the learnt fellow workers, if we're to mobilize, we must not forget the essential most features. Hop, skip and a jump.

Industrial Worker, 13 September 1924

T-Bone Slim Discusses: Discrimination

It is becoming clearer every day that we, 180 lb. Americans, cannot compete with child labor; we cannot hold our own with these kids, and it simply means extinction for us—we're done for; just like the dodo and buffalo.[1]

Therefore: I think we've gone altogether too far in protecting infant industry, and it's high time to get together and do something for the adults. And I demand, in stentorian tones (groans) that the government start nursing us heavyweights. . . .

Coming right out, I suggest that we be given a subsidy for poundage. There's no use arguing, we're handicapped with age and weight; we're altogether too heavy for the amount of brains we pack.

*

This will not solve itself. It must be solved. We have been in the process of solution now for a number of years; we have missed meals regularly at regular meal-times, all to no avail—we simply cannot make the weight of these child laborers not with our frame. Sometimes I've thought that if I could get something to soften the bones, the rest would be easy—the thing would be solved. Alas, I'm afraid the solution is in dissolution. It can't be did.

On the other hand, why not compel children to carry weight—leaded shoes, cast-iron cuffs on the ankles—anything to give "equal opportunity" to all, and others.

This phase of the solution deserves profound consideration since it offers **more than hope** of liquidation of labor troubles in this country—weighted down, I'm sure, the children would have no advantage over us grown-ups.—But that seems like a cruel thing to do.

Oh, well, suit yourself—I have still another solution. (I never start out with one or two.) So . . . So you won't subsidize us defenseless grown-ups (groan-ups). All right fer you . . . but remember!! So you won't hang weight on the kids?

Well, if you won't do these, what's the matter with getting out a law against employing 56-lb. laborers? Why not make employers buy their help by the pound—3 cents per lb.—that would give me $5.40 per day . . . no, that won't do, they'd cut down on our chuck, to keep us from raising our wages a pound or two. Sorry. It won't do. Besides, it would be unconstitutional, to say nothing

1 Child labor was not permanently banned in the United States until 1938, and even then agriculture was (and still is) held to be an exception. Today approximately 500,000 children pick a quarter of the food produced in the United States.

about what it would do to our civilization.—Maybe dissolve us instead of the "solving" of the problem.

*

Setting an age limit is also contrary to unalienable rights, etc., as has been pointed out to the supreme judges time and again by employers of **tender help**—childish rights can't be trampled under ruthless dogs, not while the manufacturers' association is hoarseless and able to wheeze a protest.[2]

Looks as if we're up against a stone wall, every way we turn—like the guy who was asked: **"Where were you during the war?"** "Who, me . . . oh, . . . I was under the unconscionable **reperbate,** refusing to become disconcerted—or interested."

So it is with us. Have patience, we'll solve this problem:

I would suggest that all children who are employed in industries (including agriculture) be given a pension including board, clothing, shelter, play and schooling, or its equivalent, and that it be provided: **The pension shall apply only during the period they absent themselves from the point of production.**

Thus, if the tots cannot resist the temptation to work, and assert their God-given inalienable rights, the pension will be discontinued.—Ye$$iree, I'm satisfied that we can bribe these children to quit work.—I have in mind the miracles bribes have wrought among more stable citizens, even in recent months—but we are not going to bribe them. We will ask Congress to sit on 'em, unless other means are found to curb their 100 per cent American pep.

I have other solutions—if foregoing program fails—and, if they all fail but one, we still have a wonderful solution—not in our head—(we carry it on our hips): a red card.

It wouldn't be a bad idea for the fathers and prospective fathers, (the would-be and can't-be fathers) to try the latter solution first—and save time, worry, money and shoe leather.—Without YOU a One Big Union is an impossibility.—Bear in mind: Too much "impossibility" makes for gray hairs, puts a hump on your back. . . . Don't Be an impossibillist. Be SOMEBODY!

I call on every able-bodied citizen to rise and defend our glorious institutions against this "epidemic" of child laborers.—Let the slogan be: "Defend your Jobs" . . . (what do we care for the looks.)—Anyway to get started! Ah'm; m'm; h'm!

Equal opportunity (at least) with the kids. That's what we want. We get to have our exercise; done-up in neat packages of no more than 10 hrs. per package.

---

[2] A 1916 federal law restricting child labor had been reversed by the Supreme Court in 1918. A subsequent attempt by Congress to increase taxation on employers of child labor was also struck down by the Supreme Court in 1923.

Why, it's getting so now that employers knock down dozens of unemployed men in their mad rush to hire a child—mebbe the only unexpected kid in that locality. It isn't fair.

*

We are moved to make these remarks after observing a minor agricultural **worker** performing with three horses and one cranky plow that wouldn't **scour.** And we said, what wonderful conservation of profanity (which would be all wasted were we to attempt the actual tilling of soil too wet to mold well). How much did he plow?

It isn't the "how much?" it's how numerous were the hours?—The horses being of Age, he worked a full day.

How old was the child? Let's see: There's Nellie, age 3; Bertha, age 4; Carrie, age 5; Edmund, age 7; George, age 8; Elbert, age 9; Oscar, that's him, I'm sure,—(in sequence) his age is 10 or 11—yes, that's his age. His weight is 65 lbs. Anything else you want to know?—Think you could handle three horses with nothing stronger than a prayer to lean against.—The good ol' Christian religion! (Every mealtime the old gent would pray over the corn-on-cob, and I would rise and **second the motion** with a most morbid "Amen.")

'Tis said that "Life is a struggle." 'Tis not.

Our struggles don't apply. We live by **permission,** not by struggles. Struggle means "to jump" every time a parasite barks. Struggle **less**—organize **more**—and your living will double itself in no time.

We are doing well, thank you.

Industrial Solidarity, 1 October 1924

Interlocking

The practicability of "the one big union" has been put in question so it is up to me to take up cudgels, (literary-spare-parts) in its behalf and favor. How people can question the feasibility of a "one union," in face of the fact that it already exists, is more than I can decipher, without an assistant—unless I work overtime, which is out of the question. Full time is more than enough for me.

People are a one big union whether they "prefer" to think so or not—inter-related, inter-allied, international, inter-extreme, intermediate and at all points before, after and between—interminably associated together, inseparably—though they may choose to ignore "facts" in favor of "fancies" and cruder grades of B. S. (buck salve)—and Kid themselves with artificial and artful *substitutes* for the Real Thing.

There's no getting out of it, they are "one"—not a "dozen"—not a hundred dozen—not a million dozen—Just one. They are subjoined together by a thing called "soul"—not souls—for "soul" is "life," and life is "one." People do not have "lives"—They are *gifted or afflicted* with "life." Just one—not nine, like a cat—and one life, sometimes called soul, animated them all.

Nature doesn't furnish individual "souls," nor an assortment of "lives"—no indeed, life is like a roller towel—everybody uses it—everybody looks for a clean spot—and many soil the spotless "fabric of life," the soul, most unnecessarily—more's the pity. With every means at hand for the keeping of it clean.

The above view of life occurs to me as it has occurred, and occurs, to thousands of others but that doesn't mean that it is a true view—though it seems plausible enough.

Only recently I am corroborated in this by coming across H. M. Tichenor's *Sun Worship*,[1] a discussion of the leading aberrations and religions, and among them he does mention one Jainist religion, an Eastern affair which incorporates within its philosophy the following none too clear ultimatum: "Everything has a soul within its material and visible manifestation, not only human beings, but all the animal, vegetable and mineral kingdom. The Jainist word for soul is 'Jiva' which means 'life.' Their philosophy presents all cells and atoms as containing life."

---

1 Henry M. Tichenor, *Sun Worship and Later Beliefs*, Little Blue Book No. 204, ed. E. Haldermann-Julius (Girard, Kans.: Haldermann-Julius, 1921). The Little Blue Books were produced to provide workers with access to the world's knowledge. Printed small enough to fit into back pockets, the books could be taken to work or indeed brought along on freight trains.

So, you see, I'm rather tardy with my "dope." The Indians have beat me to it by a few thousand years—but, and this is my consolation, if the Indians and H. M. Tichenor had not said it, I, myself would (and do) say it.

Well, now, if this be so, it follows that people are united by life, by soul, and, if united they must be ONE—One Big Union. Stuck together.

Industrial Worker, 8 October 1924

An Earfull

Only the poor break laws—the rich evade them.

*

Babe Ruth is America's greatest statesman—Jack Dempsey the brightest scholar.[1] Barney Google the most eminent scientist.[2] The greatest writer?—modesty prevents our naming him.

*

No two things in all this world are alike.

Nothing is like it was—there is a continual change. A stone thrown is a different stone when it lands.

No two cherries look or taste alike—nor does the taste linger; it fades, dies.

A pea—one in ten thousand—can be identified.

*

A jeweller offered to charge me two bits for a minute hand for my old reliable Ingersoll[3]—that's as far as he got. I repaired it myself.

Tools used:

One railroad spike, for hammer.
One needle, for punch. (hole).
One safety pin, for material.
One match, for forge (to anneal the pin)
Time spent:
Ten minutes.
Earnings: two bits. Rate! $1.50 per hour.

Imagine the rate the jeweller was charging—approximately 60 times 24 cents. How much is that?

I mention this just to show that the capitalist system has come to a pretty

---

1 Babe Ruth was an iconic U.S. baseball player. In a career lasting from 1914 to 1935, he set a number of records for runs scored and became a major celebrity. Jack Dempsey was a famous professional boxer who fought in the 1910s and 1920s and was the heavyweight champion of the world for seven years.

2 Barney Google was a character in the highly popular comic strip *Barney Google and Snuffy Smith,* which ran from 1919 and was syndicated to more than nine hundred newspapers at its peak. A hapless hustler and would-be social climber, Google was the subject of a major hit song in 1923.

3 A well-known watch brand.

pass when it cannot compete with me and the crudest of tools. Somebody is doing some tall stealing, I verily do believe.

*

Foolish question: Is a Wobblie a Wob after he is dead?

Foolish answer: He is if he keeps his dues paid up.

Here's where our author "pays up ahead"; feeling kind of shakey (?)—a fellow never can tell—what may happen.

*

Apology: I have fallen off on writing because I have too much to do. Lately I have been busily engaged on an invention that will bring me a fortune, I expect.—Some day it will take its proud place, (with my trade mark T-B S, blazoned on its side) alongside of other means of transportation—It travels on one wheel, guided by two shafts (and is intended exclusively for the use of our leading parasites when they go out for a walk) a well padded oval container rests on the shafts; in this the user is expected to deposit his ample bosom, where it nestles snug and comfortable, making both easy and dignified—when not used for this purpose it can be loaded with gravel, concrete or other materials, displacing a wheelbarrow—there's money in it.

Another thing, gentle neighbors: Ford was calling for production. Press was howling for production. Employers all were demanding production, so I, in order to get over a bad period, gave them production—like all production, it was more or less off color.

Industrial Worker, 17 December 1924

1925

Oranges

Doctors will tell you to eat oranges—one would almost get the idea that oranges are a healthful, healthgiving food.

They tell you to eat 'em.

Now, let's face this question: The doctors make their best money from sick people—(when you are well, they don't get one cent). If, therefore, oranges are good for you, the doctors are advising you to eat them against their own interest and welfare—in the face of the fact that many young doctors are already without visible means of support. . . .

It is not reasonable—and oranges are not a good, even mediocre, food. But we need not "doubt" oranges just because the doctors boost them—we can use our own reasoning power and doubt them "on a scientific basis":

Nature never did intend that man live in one country and eat in another country. Nature intended that man eat where he lives, and any and all fruits, etc., that he can reach in four hours of foot travel between meals.

Nature never intended (and could not anticipate) that man would haul his "feed" 3,000 miles before he ate it.

*

Oranges may be a good food in California—in Oregon they are a mild poison—in Montana a stronger poison—in Minnesota, you're flirting with sour stomach, if you eat 'em. And so on. . . .

Remember, the doctors tell you to eat 'em. And remember I'm telling you to lay off. . . .

Furthermore, ('slong's we're making a case against them) oranges are picked green for shipment; colored with acid fumes to resemble a ripe orange—green apples, what!—the acid clings to the fruit—a man's simply plumb crazy that eats 'em.

I leave it to you, reader; isn't it true that you yourself have noticed how sour they are compared to the orange of 20 years ago? Green apples!

Industrial Worker, 21 January 1925

To My Friend

Tho the skin be sorely wrinkled
And the form be badly bent;
Tho by showers often sprinkled
And by crowding moments rent—
Tho the shape be bruised and mangled
Crushed by ages driven hard
It is still with "tokens" spangled—
It is still my Wobblie card.

Tho the cheeks be sadly faded,
All the color from them flown—
(And the "atmosphere" gets jaded,
Like a busted understone!)
Tho bereft of youth and vigor,
Quite devoid of pleasing-looks;
Still—it cuts a *quite a figure!*
It is still my book of books!

Tho the troubles, (by some jinx sent)
Puts a burden on my soul,
And we both grow quite delinquent
In our most engrossing role—
(This is not of "bull" I'm handing)
I will linger by my pard
Even in its "twisted" standing
It is still my union card.

Tho the hand of "thoughtful" passion
Mutilates "what I adore,"
In a most ignoble fashion—
In a mood most awful sore;
Rends my old "side-kick" to pieces,
Throws the chunks out in the yard—
I will still maintain the thesis:
It is STILL A PERFECT CARD!

P.S.—Upon hearing that a violent tempered fellow worker had torn up his card, Slim gets poetical as hell . . .

Some cards are merely tossed away, but an I. W. W. card . . . well, you know how it is, they're worth more attention, worth more attention!

Cool down and get a duplicate.

Industrial Worker, 11 March 1925

The Passing Show

(A souperfishal eggshamination cornducted into a soup-cellar (sub-cellar) by the author at Milwaukee, Wis., while the souphounds, hugging their "identities" (passes) were trailing down to the feast—a decidedly "soupy" supposition.)

Let's go:

Soupposing som soupernatural souperintendent soupereillously soupprest soup!

Soup! souperb soup! Soupblime soup!

Souperlative soup—Soupposing!

And soupposing the SOUPer-MEN, soupprised, souppliantly soupplicate the SOUPPREME SOUP-BONE for souppert, soupstenance and soup-stance.

And souppose the SOUPPREME SOUPERIOR souplements the "soupprest soup" with soupterranean soupulchres, as soupatiture—to said soupceptibe soupbordinates and unsoupspicious soupbalterns and loyal-soupjects.

And soupposing, souprequetly, the soupersticious soupur soupfragettes and unsouplucky soupranos soupply the melefluent notes of We Shall Meat—bye and bye[1] (Note! "O" and "meat" is silent in "soup.") Would that, O mighty editor, be soupfishient grounds to soupspect that our soupfaring (suffering) is souperinjuiced and that we should organize to get the rest—the rest—the REST ... of the good things of life (very festful they are). I pause for reply.

Soupserviantly yours,—T-bone S.

(P. S. May I call this a cuss-word puzzle?)

Industrial Solidarity, 8 April 1925

---

[1] A reference to Joe Hill's song "The Preacher and the Slave."

Cross Word Puzzle

If mud was gold and gold was snow (sniff sniff) and words could emancipate the workers, T-bone Slim would have J. Christ backed in the corner by six columns and a bunch of *pomes*.[1]

*

Dictionaries would find a ready sale among professional saviors and savees.

*

Newspapers would save all their old lead and take contracts in salvation.

*

The Dawes Plan[2] would be a suspended sentence and Cal Coolidge[3] would be a new-fangled leg-iron—if words could emancipate men.

Typewriters would burn up with hot-box, linotypes, also—the mimeograph would be equal to one dozen hacksaws and a bar of soap.

The *Tribune* plant would be a conditional pardon, *Herald-Examiner* a perfect alibi—I. W. W. Press would be a jail delivery if words . . . shucks!

*

Cross-word puzzles would solve slavery, book of synonyms would be a taste of freedom; slang, a mouthful—the alphabet would be license and sub-titles a privilege—headlines, a statute of liberty.

*

Cartoons, (picture words), would be a two weeks' vacation on pay.

*

A four letter word meaning death would be a Saturday half holiday—an eight letter word meaning line-up or co-ordinate would be equivalent to a two weeks' fishing trip—with five gallons of pink bait. Bonded.

(As to last week's solution: Four letter word meaning death is—Rest.)

*

---

1 That is, poems.

2 The 1924 Dawes Plan settled international differences over the level of reparations Germany had to pay to the victors of World War I. The plan was created by a committee led by Charles Dawes, an American financier, politician, and diplomat.

3 Calvin Coolidge, U.S. president from 1923 to 1929.

Our old friend B. S. (a relative) would be allee samee commutation of sentence. Women, Gord bless 'em, with their volley of verbs would be more powerful than a stay of execution or a definite reprieve—the two to run concurrently, indefinitely, Yea! O yea! O yes! if words could emancipate!

*

Phylology would be an absolute power. Phonographs would tear down the walls like Joshua's trombone squad at Jericho; radio would make Gainsborough hair-nets of the steel cell-bars to say nothing about the energy for liberation residing in the puny lungs of a little green parrot. . . . Words, dammit words—we'd have job control on slavery if words could do it.

Words cawn't do it, deontchu know.

Words can only lay the facts, fancies and fakes before the folks—(the folks are the sole judges). The folks will then, immidjitly organize then proceed to emancipate.

Nothing happens without work, effort, deeds and action.

Words are necessary never-the-less. Like a silver (not to kill lions) but as a toothpick. But . . .

When words embody a jumble of facts, fancies and fakes they constitute a controversy. A controversy is possible only in an unorganized bunch of men.

For instance: A controversy is impossible in the I. W. W. because the majority rule settles all questions. Should a controversy arise, it will prove that matters are not left to the membership. This in turn will prove that members supposed to look after such things have been listening to extensive programs of words.

When that happens the membership should proceed to express themselves, at an early date, ere some of their number become as discouraged—one way of wrecking an organization is to put these things off until the membership has dwindled down to an appointed number—a vote after that is not a vote, since the result will be settled in advance. Another way to wreck is to install two, three or a dozen sets of officials and divide their support pro rata among the members—in that case failure to support them settles nothing. It merely settles the organization.

This, of course, cannot happen in the I. W. W., for two reasons. First, because of the majority rule. Second, because the membership will demand a vote at the first appearance of controversial matter—they will decide as a whole and not as two or more factions, or as a fraction.

*

Words are necessary and, in this article I use over many, maybe—if so, it is to show the power of words and compare them with the power of action—and balloting is a form of action (words are not). Be it noted I do not discuss the question "whether it is advantageous to divide organizations"—and it may be at times, when the membership is lax, or too busy, that matters get into bad shape. . . .[4]

*

I am reminded: "Our old members are quitting." They're not quitting—they joined a certain thing way back in—when was it?—They knew what they were doing and SO LONG AS THAT THING remains "The Thing It Was" when they joined, so long will they support it—if they "quit," they merely refuse to adopt a substitute. Nine times out of ten. . . .

*

There is reason to be frank.

If one man "quits" it is a very serious matter and indicates the presence of alterations in the organization. If dozen men "quit" it is a catastrophy and indicates an undesirable condition in the organization.

If great numbers "quit"—what is it?—It would indicate that the organization harbors "skunks."

The above holds true only to such organizations that entertain machine administration of affairs and elections, and cannot hold true as to the A. F. of L. (a heavy lesser) and the I. W. W. That is, in the respect of the above indictments, in full. We have our troubles, true—about 20 of them. But our membership is calloused to such things and is not quitting—though we may be drifting slightly from our course—(this can be verified or disproved by digging up 1914, 1915 and 1916 Constitution By-Laws). Also by determining the sentiments of the membership in regards the three following forms of unionism.

Industrial Unionism (straight).
Departmental Unionism (blended).
District Council Unionism (scrambled).

Industrial Worker, 20 May 1925

[4] This is a reference to the 1924 split within the IWW.

Industrial Unionism

Ind. Uns'm is here explained for the first time by the author himself—uncoached or prompted. It is a deep study and is understood only by a few lunkheads like myself and the dumbest members of society.

It is a situation where *all hands working in any industry are members of a union made up of workers working in that industry*—that's how deep it is. Only the dumbest of us can understand it. (And only the toughest can withstand it.) Brainiest men have fallen down miserably trying to cipher it (or syphon) it out.

Convention after convention has tried to put it over. Brilliant speakers have . . .

Say! Mebbe you think it's simple? *All workers working in one industry "belonging" to the one and same union.* I tell you it never would have been explained if I . . . as I was saying, brilliant men have started to explain it, have grown wild-eyed and wandered off into revolutionary-ardorism (enthusiasmism) and finally wound up their careers selling "Christ on the Cross" in the Alleghany Valley and were rescued for martyrdom only by the super-human efforts of the Eagle Eye squad of the 1917 revolution[1]—and it's easy to be a martyr when you're shackled to oppression, not so easy when your two hands and two feet are free—the hands, to reach across the sea; the feet, to scratch the gravel. . . .

No, Industrial Unionism is quite beyond the ken of those learned gentlemen, long despondent because of enlarged ego caused by long disassociation with normal beings ($2 please for the prescription) come out of it—despise and be not despised ($10 more; attorney fee).

(Unfinished).

Industrial Worker, 27 June 1925

---

[1] That is, the 1917 Bolshevik Revolution in Russia.

The United Affront

"Hans Breiman gifs a barty."

Where is that barty now?

I now admit and announce to the popeyed palpitating world that I'm dumber than I act and foolisher'n I look—I can't understand the Workers party.[1] (Neither do I forstay other political parties or political revolutions.) I cannot see why the Workers party press is "knocking" the Russian revolution that resulted in a change of bosses in that tormented country and at the same time knocking the tormented I. W. W. that is trying to do something for the working class in these tormented states of industrial slavery?

Fellow workers hand me their literature, in hopes that I may overcome my ignorance and be like the secondhand dealers and other petite buzz-saws—alas, all to no avail! My ignorance grows denser and denser, as I read their heartfelt apologies for capitalism: "That it is progress"; (that puts progressives in jail) "That it has merit"; "That it was bound to come in Russia"—as else where—like fleas to a dog. Zinovev[2] discusses it in the "monthly," and "Zino" is the nozzle of the conduit of communist (?) rhetoric when Krassin[3] or "Tchick" Cheering[4] hasn't the floor. He lets out a wail, incidentally, about former brave revolutionists, (that can be heard from Moscow to Hammond, Indiana) and

---

1 Founded in 1921, the Workers Party of America (WPA) served as the legal body for the Communist Party USA (CPUSA) until 1929. Following repression, the CPUSA opted to operate largely in an underground, clandestine manner, with the WPA at various times utilizing united-front work to operate in coalition with, recruit from, and take over other leftist parties and organizations. After the Communist International (Comintern) instituted its "Third Period" approach in 1928, the WPA and other communist-led groups pulled away from joint activity with others and formally merged into the CPUSA. Initially, a substantial section of the IWW's membership supported the Russian revolution, and the Bolsheviks made various overtures based on the IWW joining their international and U.S.-based bodies. Since this would have required merging into communist-led organizations and abandoning key tenets of industrial unionism, the IWW did not do so. However, a substantial number of leading and rank-and-file members did leave for communist groups, and tensions existed among remaining members over how to relate to and report on communist parties and initiatives. Following the 1924 split, the IWW moved in a direction that was primarily critical of communist governments and strategies.

2 Russian revolutionary Grigory Zinoviev led the Comintern from 1921 to 1926. He would be purged and executed following a Stalinist show trial in 1936.

3 Leonid Krassin was a Bolshevik revolutionary who served as people's commissar for foreign trade from 1920 to 1924 and as Soviet ambassador to France and then Soviet plenipotentiary in London.

4 Georgy Vasilyevich Tchitcherin was the Soviet people's commissar for foreign affairs from 1918 to 1930.

explains—explains—as how those former revolutionists are now in reactionary camps but does not mention if, or why, they were kicked out—he merely, and in a most scholarly manner, points out where they landed and the shape they were in before and after. . . . "Struve," he moans, etc. (he reads the whole "backsliding" or catapulted roll call) without honoring the effect environment played upon the mental processes of those estimable gentlemen denied a "team to drive" in the bureaucracy of the reborn political Russia.

I'm not belittling the Russian Rebellion, as I would call it, not being prepared, in view of the dearth of development, to dignify it with the name of revolution, in the higher sense; since, as they themselves say, "capitalism was inevitable"—hence, evolutionary; aided by an armed insurrection unhorsing Nick and mounting Lenin.

It was no inauguration of "new" in any sense worth going into hysterics over.

It was the feudal Russia breaking its bonds, as Vic Hugo would say. It was Russia desperately trying to catch up with and embrace the "inevitable" want, torture and despair of capitalism, that we know so well. It was Russia trying to learn for herself the price of retarded progress, under capitalism.

I only hope—fervently hope—that Russia may not suffer long and as meekly as I . . .

"What thou dost do quickly," since thou art "inevitable." Let not her agony be long.

*

I am enabled to understand Russia, not detracting from her new found misery nor overestimating the glory of her achievement. But the Workers party I cannot understand—it is so revolutionary. It admits itself and if it was more revolutionary it would mention it without further ado. It uses words that curdles the blood in the veins of rulers great and small the like of which has not been heard since stools and agent provocateurs quit paying dues in the I. W. W.

In conclusion: word comes direct from Moscow through *Workers Monthly* to the effect that "further wage-increases will now depend upon increased productivity" only it is said more politely—I cannot bring my pencil to observe all the niceties of revolutionary speech; it wants to put it more bluntly—speed-up. "Hurry up, Ivan."

Why is the Communist mouthpiece exposing the shame of Russia so guilelessly?

What is behind it? It gets 'em nothing.

Why have they tuned in with the master to "knock" the Industrial Workers of the WORLD—why?

Industrial Worker, 18 July 1925

From Murder to Re-Action

"Axman Admits Killing Wife"—headline.

We don't believe a word of it—But if he admitted that his wife killed him we would swallow the yarn whole and call for a second helping. It doesn't sound reasonable.

It isn't the style. The women have been killing their husbands, their neighbor's husbands, stray boarders and even inoffensive batchelors—whenever they could get a shot at 'em without hitting a horse or a dog. . . . I s'pose they thought "long's they won't organize it's best to get rid of 'em."—I won't believe a word of it till I see the body.

Women ain't gonna stand for so much fiddling around! They want direct-action—I want belief.

*

After capitalism is fully developed and civilization has reached its dizziest pinnacle, and when the whole land, all the ponds, and part of Lake Michigan is dotted with tombstones—and all the prairies are graveyards—all the valleys are cemeteries—and all the mountains are mausoleums, I mean—when there is left no place in which to tuck the dead, this will be a good world to live in.

The graves should be dug deeper. Plant the dead two and three deep—sort of "stack 'em up."[1] Square the tops of the tombstones—all of equal height—so that we can build our HOUSE on the remains of the dead.

When monument is against monument.

Note: Since making above discovery and after proposing the remedy for the congestion, a thoughtless fellow worker informs me that it is done that way in Scotland. . . . What's the use of having imagination or conceiving anything when others beat you to it by 900 years—through no fault of yours.

Our house is built, on the remains of the dead—there it is—sticking up in the air—on top of those tombstones. We have no bread, no wheat, no farm? No bologny, no meat, no stock—we're stuck?

Just a second there—we have our radio!

Ha! With its two tube hook-up; its condenser housing stator and rotor; its amplifier superheterodyne; its . . . its . . . stuck again, well I'll be damned . . . its thermo-electric principles. . . . Ha! We shall tune in. Turn the knob to eleven octaves and fourteen degrees LLD Fahrenheit, (do it just as if you was opening a box of snuff) have you got it . . . Darn THAT STATIQUE! (We had the bread broadcasting station, R. Y. E.) Darn that loud-baker, anyway . . .

---

[1] This is ultimately what happened to Slim, when his body was buried in a mass grave on Hart Island in 1942.

I believe they palmed a one-step amplifier on us . . . just as we were about to eat. Static? I should say so! Capitalism! Interference! Sap o dodge![2] Skull-druggery! HELP!!—Try it again:

Place the loud-feeder against your belly-button—hm—now turn the knob. Do you taste it? Is it fresh? Broadcasting from the waters, is it? What station—P. U. N. K.?

Now tune in on the butcher—odd and ends is on the program for tonight . . . Say, ain't this a great life—I'd like to see Scotty, (canny as can be) beat that! Live on air, Humph!—Yesterday I saw a book in a window:

"The Life of Christ."

Wot a life! Wot a lift!

*

"Reactionary! You're a reactionary."

So goes the wail. They think they alone are the only smart ones the "lord awl-mighty" made. "You can't go back." (If you walk out of the house without your trousers, you got to tough it out.) If you go back you're a re-actionary. Terrible! Terriffle!—Oh, well, maybe, you can find a pair of pantaloons on the way; out in the desert—deserts are that way—and, surely, you wouldn't hang around civilization without pants? Surely?

If you run into a blind-alley and if you come out the way you went in—you're a re-actionary. But if you start "milling" round and round, "you're a revolutionist of the first-class." They will say so . . .

And remember: It's quite a temptation to "back out." I recall a gentleman in Chicago who went a bit further than that: Chased "in" by the law he fought his way "out" . . . he must have been reactionary as hell itself.

Industrial Worker, 1 August 1925

---

[2] That is, sabotage.

Beseech and Collect

"Ask—and you shall receive."

In these times, when Bryan[1] tried to establish an alibi (for his feats and defeats) down in Sunny Tennessee, and the several contradictory editions of the bible are getting such an academic overhauling, I think it is proper to rescue the above headline from international damnation. Ask and you shall receive. Yes, yes—but be sure you are organized so s's'strongly that the master of ceremonies can hear you. He's deaf in one ear and near-sighted in the other.

Demand and you shall get.

That's better.

The mere asking doesn't seem to do justice to the subject at hand, for bosses are inclined to terrific listlessness and unaccommodating lassitude. The plea thereformust be emfatic.

Of course, it is against the law to ask—a form of vagrancy. For instance: If you pray one or all the gods for something—a pair of overalls, sox, spectacles or aces—it comes under the head of begging, but is allowed. The law knows you are wasting your wind. In fact they (the lawyers) like to see you do it because they know all you'll get is rheumatism, second-hand shirts and soup.

Yes, indeed, they like to see you "bum" God. There's only one more kind of praying they'd like to see you do—kneel to a telegraph pole and ask for more beans—and some pork—pork from *contented sows.*

By the way—right of way—all the bible's prophecies are coming true—the Milwaukee has laid-off half of its extra gangs as far as Hettinger, S. D. The world's coming to an end.

It is said that prayer is good for the soul—it must be. It must be good for something. It isn't good for the liver, heart, brain or bunions. It isn't good for shoes (3 in 1 is better). It's not good for beef steak (ketchup and salt for mine—when I can get the steak). So it must be good for the soul.

Asking, on the other hand, is a concession to politeness (I won't go into details; an illustration is better).

Ever see one of those little, sweet-faced, yellow, courteous curs; bowing his nose to the ground; licking the tallow from your Florsheims; doing the Hetchy-Ketchy shimmy, its tail safely ensconced beneath its belly—ever see one of these?

Well, that's what I calls doggone politeness.

That's the dog's way of inquiring for a bone or a bologna skin—That's asking.

---

[1] William Jennings Bryan.

That's begging. That's praying. That's pleading—beseeching. Beseech and you will be given the swill, the junk, the rags, the cot (bunk) and the poor house. . . .

I won't go into details—I'll simply write down what you think:

Organize, and you will not have to beg—you can then suggest, propose or demand.

And since you know that beggars are poor—or selfish—I would demand that we, labor, make an effort to broaden out; transact our business in a dignified manner. . . .

Ask and you shall receive is not strictly true—just like fishing: "We threw in our line and waited for a bite."

We're still waiting.

The postoffice doubled the postage on picture post cards, expecting to double its income—it's still expecting.

Why didn't it pray?

Prayer is the final eclipse of the soul.

Industrial Worker, 8 August 1925

T-Bone Slim Says: Figures Lie

XII–XII

I.

'Tis said we cannot (clearly) prove
That two and two is four
And that, no matter how we move,
    It may be less or more.

II.

Since no two things are quite alike,
How can they sum up four?
Indeed, the humble three, or five
    Might be the final score.

III.

Three onions, true, is more than none
Right here is where we cry—
Another man with only one
    Was twice as strong as I!

IV.

One-half of twelve is seven, prex—
Let's with the figures delve:
The VII joined to its reflex
    Transforms itself to XII.

V.

Cut off the lower half of X (ten)
It leaves you even V (Five)
Cut II—it leaves you 2, dear, mon—
    Thus seven we derive!

I II III IV V VI—.—7 8 9 10 11 12.

You will note the half of twelve is not six, the "half-way" is between 6 and 7—the last half of six and the first half of seven—hence, six and one half includes one half of seven and since 3½ is half of 7, 10½ is exactly half of twelve—somebody is a liar.

And figures are unreliable—anything can be proved, and disproved, as fast—It's tough! "Wanted Harvest Hands—Red River Valley—Long Run—$3.50 and $4.00."

What does that mean?

That's figures.

It means that you will work for $3.50 and that the I. W. W. will raise your pay to $4.50. Somebody is a liar.

I think it's mathematics.

*

"Each man kills the thing he loves." (Not knowing when to write or quit.) Each man "eats" the thing he hates—But through no lack of ken or wit. The opening line above was written by one Oscar Fingal O'Flaherty Willis Wilde—what a barbarous name!—England's smartest Irishman.[1]

*

"Man wants but little here below."[2] The little he gets is poor—
Birds thrive on quite a bit less, ye know—
But sometimes it's manure.

*

It is said "mind hangs by a hair." Mine must have dropped. (The hairs, no longer anchored, fell out.) Won't I look like hell going into the harvest bald-headed. Who shall I blame? Is there any provision in the compensation law for the loss of fuzz (fur)?

Industrial Solidarity, 12 August 1925

1 Irish writer Oscar Wilde, born in 1854, was a leading member and spokesperson for the Aesthetic movement. His most famous works include the novel *The Picture of Dorian Gray* (1891) and the play *The Importance of Being Earnest* (1895). Persecuted by the British establishment for his sexuality, he was sentenced to two years' hard labor in 1895 for the then-crime of "sodomy." Protesting the conditions he experienced in prison, he wrote *The Ballad of Reading Gaol* (1898), which Slim quotes here. Wilde died in effective exile in France in 1900.

2 A quote from Oliver Goldsmith's novel *The Vicar of Wakefield* (1766).

T-Bone Slim Discusses: Chop Suey

The best way to spend a loose hour is flirting with a chop suey—but be sure the suey is young and fresh in memory. When you can no longer, and any more, eat American civilization, you can **confront the celestial stew.** Ah, laborers, there is nothing like the lobelia poultice; the mournful looking "special plain"—made from contented onions and martyred suey—there is peace and plenty; cheer, and tears subdued—heroism.

(Editor: Get your hat; we'll go down to the Noodle-Distillery.)

*

Then we'll return and throw our **organized** eye over what's left of the capitalist's system . . . what's that—what's that! You say that onions interprevents the consternation of mind over labor matters? Shame on you! Shame . . . that's just the trouble, heretofore we have not kept faith with the succulent, chopped heelskins and we have fallen into a knowtion that our lot is the rest of a "paradise lost." Impossible!

Impossible, since paradise lost is the same thing as suckers—success—It is lost before it gets started. We can't dream a paradise; we must make it—and with the aid of the lord and onions! we'll build one.

But that isn't what I was gonna say.

But that is not what I'm talking about.

In a subject such as this it is real difficult to pick out what to write—a few words in favor of cherry pie might have the "proper" flavor: I hear denunciations to the left of me, to the right of me, to the rear of me, to the front of me, above me, below me, around me . . . peoples claim that cherry pie is a delusion in size, shape and **materia**; they say the name is wrong; that, instead of cherry pie it should read pied-cherry—so depraved are they.

I took apart one of those cute V-shaped morsels, intending to count the flies in it (to determine by majority rule if the disguised "dish" is not meat pie) and found only four whole flies and three fractions (where the ruthless pie knife had severed their last remains). Checking further, I found three ghastly cherries, one raisin, one genuine pearl button and a spoonful of something that looked like blue ointment (cornstarch, the national custard, probably)—all for ten cents.

Not satisfied with robbing you of wages, sticking you up for money, rolling you and picking your pockets, they now rob your stomach and different parts of your—of your physiology; eyesight, ear-hear, teeth-bite, nose-smell, mind-thought, hair-curl, voice-talk, foot-walk, life-live, etc. They rob you blind, deaf, toothless, smelless, thoughtless, baldheaded, dumb, halt and dead—am I plain?

The system is now so rotten that, unless we organize, we will be compelled to start each a system of his own—every man will have to carry a pie factory and a fly trap; a cherry tree and an oven.

(Ice-cream is frozen corn starch.)

But that's not what I'm writing about—I'm particular, I am.

(If you do your own washing, rub the contents of one cone in the collars, wring dry, stretch and "press" between two hot stones. . . .)

Such are conditions. Things are dressed too much—with a name.

Ah, when I think of it, they take a dozen houseflies and make a cherry pie; they take twelve flies and make an apple pie; six pairs of buzzers make a mince pie—ah—two half-dozens of these playful birds make one **"crusted buggy of the dessert"!**

Ah. . . .

(Editor: Kindly tell your readers how many flies you devoured during July.)

I can't make the point slam!

The point is not that German farmers are feeding **dog and beef,** nor is it the terrible waste of heat (on a windy day) at the jungle fire—the point is that things are misnamed. To illustrate: We are pleased to call men who superintend, oversee, propose (accept or reject) "Executives." How come? They tell me what to do, and I execute the necessary moves, and they are executives. Truly, how come? Who am I? Am I an executor, executionist or an **execu**stiff?

Seems to me that it was I "that grasped his pipedream," in a flash; that it was I (labor) that executes every move—'xcutive!

Improvements in farm machinery has no part in this article—that would be sentimentalism.

The fact that I heard two harvest hands (8 and 11 years old) complaining that "the two of them could not keep up with an eight-foot binder" should not influence me.

Industrial Solidarity, 26 August 1925

T-Bone Slim Discusses

So I will change the subject—I will discuss the inferiority complex, under the head of "insignificancy hoax."

Many workers believe they do not amount to much; many view themselves as nothing—they have been "instructed" in that belief. But belief is not knowledge. . . . Every man is of the greatest importance—they are "alike as two raindrops." Some men reason they are not needed in an organization of labor—supposing all men thought the same way—supposing all raindrops refused to come down. . . .

Men are important—nothing much can be done without them. This attitude that **I belong to** this and that is a delusion.

"I belong to such and such a church" is a lie. The church belongs to you. "I belong to the republican party"—Gee, you've surely got owners. "I belong to the I. W. W."—Isn't it possible the organization belongs partly to you? Lies are not constructive; and a lie, no matter how innocent, is perfidious. Take for example the pure white Sunday school lie that "Santa Claus gives presents to good children." That's sanctified lying. And Sunday school teachers are sanctimonious liars.

We've been lied to since childhood and we have been convinced that **we belong** (and have lied ourself) but the time has now come when we no longer **believe** our insignificance; we **know** our importance—and we know that without the so-called insignificant raindrops there will be no flood.

Further, we know that at the "first drop of rain" the citizen's face blanches and he right shrewdly guesses what's coming.

Industrial Solidarity, 23 September 1925

T-Bone Slim Discusses: War

Tame, Normal, Violent and Abstract

FELLOW SWAMPER:

If I was to say that I never swamp "another log" till the teamster has taken away the one I finished the supreme court would be so astoundished that it would fall off the bench.

The federal undertaker would probably prefer charges against me for blocking the traffic, guiltless as I am.

Now, I would like to know, how am I to swamp "logs ahead" when the teamster is always waiting, ready to haul away the one I'm working on?[1]

I'll bet they'd convict me!

We have intended to say, quite often, a few kind words about the sacredness of work (the Polanders call it **rubbish** or robbish—or robbitch). We have been told, times without number, that "work is very healthful and invigorating." Grate men have assured us they would "go crazy without it." "The human race would perish if it wasn't for work—work is so good." Yes, and then they strain every ounce of their brains trying to invent a machine to do the work—I say, if work is so damn good, let's do away with the machines and pass the work around to all hands.

But, Fellow Swampers, work isn't as healthy as it's made out to be; it isn't fun—may be funny—and isn't lucrative (no money in it). In fact, the statement that work is good for a fellow is a misstatement something like the statement that "water hurts no man."—Many men **believed** that statement and drank deep of the bubbling brook of typhoid fever—.

Work isn't a health conserver; it isn't curative; it isn't a pleasure; it doesn't pay, and . . . it is unnecessary.

Lots of people never work.

*

Disturbing reports are coming in to the effect that "lumberjacks" are being attacked by squirrels in upper Michigan. Upon investigation I find the truth greatly enlargerated.

Peace has been declared.

The facts in the case are as follows: A prestigeful "tailer-down"[2] had voluntarily raised the wages of a squirrel to the extent of one doughnut per day—that he slipped over the end of a broken-off twig or branch—

---

1 Slim is complaining that his lumberjack colleagues are working too quickly.

2 A worker who rolls logs for stacking.

The squirrel, of course, wanted to save the doughnut for "old age" and would "gnaw the branch in two" below the doughnut. One day the "tailer" went "skidding";[3] the doughnut was missing. . . . Say, you ought to have heard the language that squirrel used; how he swore. He called me the most damnable impropate and rascalion; so to appease his wrath I compromised myself and bribed him with a piece of cake—this I did by splitting the twig and inserting the cake in the "split." Oh if I had only known! Oh if I had known the depth of depravity of that unsconcionable rapscallion, he never would have received a bribe from me—I felt like a lumber baron that ships men out for $35 to $45—bribes them to be good: bribes them to "stay" a month—Oh, oh, oh . . . You know, that squirrel in the absence of the doughnut had raided the teamsters' coat pockets where they had stored cookies, tidbits and delicacies for their pure-blooded horses. Actually distained to climb into the pocket, but chewed gaping holes into the "Patrick's and Bennies."

Such was the "attack"—a clear case of ignoring the property rights of human beings—teamsters are more than human—a clear case of vandalism against the peace and dignity of the state of Michigan—a clear . . . clear—

The squirrel will get his doughnut after this in the usual way—impaled upon a spear. War is over.

Industrial Solidarity, 9 December 1925

---

[3] That is, he left the camp to transport logs by skidding them. The road on which logs were skidded into town, which passed through areas that were rife with poverty, was called skid road. This is the origin of the term "skid row," meaning a slum or poor area of a city.

Shortcuts

"Odd, how thirsty a logger gets in town," says T-B. S., as he turns away from the W. C. T. U. water "cooler."[1]

Mebbe that's why they turn to cooked beverages and refreshments.

"The worst burst of thirst thus becomes first nursed, then rehearst and finally cursed. . . ."

*

"Politeness is the life of trade." Now, I'm polite as can be—after I have swamped and swamped for hours; and after I have three logs swamped I don't holler for a skinner to come and get 'em. No; I walk over to him and whisper in his ear, "bring your skilled horses out and try those logs." "Skilled horses!" he roars, "they 'ain't skilled, they're just common laborers—I'm the skilled *hombre* of the outfit," he added.

*

Strange how lumberjacks take exceptions to the most ordinary phenomena: Recently I heard that a friend of mine, a confirmed "self-batcher" and ex-sheepherder was cooking in a lumber camp. I hurried out there as fast as my habitual rheumatism would allow. . . .

When I arrived there he was busy making pies but greeted me heartily. He complained sorrowfully about a severe cold—and I believed him for every little while (while we were talking) and as he rolled the piecrust a clear crystal of "snot" would drop from his leaky nose on the crust in the making and he would roll it in with the rest of the material.

He assured me that I could get a job, as he said, "32 men quit this morning over something or t'other—nothing probably."

That's the way they are, I consoled him, they quit for no reason at all, at all. . . .

He ruined my appetite.

So it goes.

Once upon a time a worker had occasion to criticize "the pie" for being *stiffened* with corn starch—He wouldn't eat it.

The cook, upon hearing about his remark, took him to task about it: "When you have anything to say, I wish you would say it to my face." . . .

---

1 From the 1870s, the Women's Christian Temperance Union and other prohibitionists installed "temperance fountains" offering clean water in many towns and cities across the United States. This was done as a community amenity and to undermine the use of beer as an alternative to the adulterated municipal and rural water otherwise on offer.

"If you refer to my remark about the pie, I wish you would understand that I had reason to kick about the corn starch."

"Well sir," says the cook, "if I don't use corn starch it will *run*—you can't cut it."

"And if you do use it you can't eat it—What do you make it for, to cut or to eat?"

The meeting adjourned.

Lumberjacks don't get much sleep now-a-days—The "newer" men were greatly surprised Sunday to find the camp is painted—and red.

Industrial Worker, 12 December 1925

1926

Hall of Fame

Please record that:

There has been, and is now, but few great men outside of lumberjacks.

If I were to recite a full list of great men, all of them lumberjacks, the editor would purchase a clothes basket for waste paper—and, if he DID print the list, many heretofore respected FAKES would blush their disgrace, redden from shame, turn their face, hide themselves *under a tarpaulin* and *feel naked* indeed. I won't take chances on wearing out my pencil—I will merely mention a few, extemporaneously, contemporaneously: Pegleg Ryan, Abraham Lincoln, Sandy and Grizzly McDonald, Abrahamson, McClelland, Fred Aho, Von Platen "Gallagher," and Swiss Pea-Soup of the Welis-Pori outfit. There! Where in all this shop-blithering world could you find a more imposing list of labor Technicians?

Nowhere—Every one of them "roll-out" boys!

Great men! And all of them drink Japanese tea-screenings, with the possible exception of Honest Abe and Pegleg Ryan—and Ox Pete, whom I didn't mention.

Socrates, a famous lumberjack, used to drink hemlock sap every time he *run out* of oleomargarine.

And so it goes—taste is taste. The gang of gods that used to live high on Mount Olympus drank ambrosia and nectar—for sore throat—it being important that the gods' orders could be heard. . . .

Therefore, being a great man, myself, I would like to suggest (to aforesaid great men, at least) that they cannot expect long to be heard if they persist in stimulating their throat with *Tendust dew of the Rising Sun.*

*

Many of these aforesaid great men have monuments erected in their memory—and, the rest are dead ripe even as the others were ripe dead . . . Jim Pole Smith. Hail!

Bug House Lynch—alas! Peace to his ashes!

Now we're down to the great men—and with your permission I will mention kind of *intimate like* the world's *greatest* living creatures; men who not only can find their way home along the well lighted, paved, named thoroughfares and numbered houses but can remember and find a four-foot skid seven weeks after throwing it into a world of brush: To be brief: The Sawyer, the Swamper, the Skinner, and the Skidway[1] "Ameer"—those are the greater men I am spouting about. If they ever decide to organize, It Will Be Done, and a greater organization It Will Be.

Industrial Worker, 9 January 1926

[1] The term "skidway" was often used to refer to a platform or angled path or road on which logs were stacked and from which they were rolled to a point where they could be loaded for transport. Alternatively, like "skid road," it could be used as a label for the parts of towns where lumberjacks and hoboes congregated.

T-Bone Slim Discusses: Wry-Bread—

We have been requested, editor, to announce to the world the secret of our longevity (whatever that is) and the mysterious persistency of our vigorous and timely health.

All right, I am willing.

But, first, we must make note of the fact that many of our truest friends think that we've, editor, lived too long already—that we have no valid excuse for existing—that our death notice published simultaneously in the three (world's first decent) papers, *Sol, Worker* and *Pioneer*[1] would have a tranquilizing effect upon the World Crooks—boobs that think "one world united is able to stand alone."

I say no, editor, no—they've got to join hands with all the planets, meteors, satellites, **hematites**, mennonites and morphodites—it being proved by Stresemann that "no nation can stand alone," it follows that no world can stand alone.[2]

Huh?

Then they ask us to explain ourself; explain how we are able to stand it—alone.

Gutts, eh?

Here's my formula:

An apple a day keeps the doctor away—there are 7 million doctors—seven million apples a day keeps 'em all away.—Simple, isn't it? Just eat a boatload of apples every day and you will be protected against all doctors.

That's half of your health, right there.

Next. You'll want something to eat with those apples.

All right.

Rye bread.

What? You can't get rye bread? Make it yourself—here's the recipe: Three inches of water, one yeast, two inches of wheat flower—be careful not to use any rye flour—oh yes, stir the yeast and water with stove poker, if you have one; if not, hold an unwashed frying pan in the water tor 3½ minutes—did you put the salt in? You didn't? Don't you **know a thing** about cooking? Would we have to tell you to start a fire in the stove?

---

[1] *Industrial Solidarity, Industrial Worker,* and *Industrial Pioneer,* all Wobbly publications.

[2] Gustav Stresemann was Germany's foreign minister. Surviving various changes of government, he was noted for brokering reconciliation between France and Germany, for which he received the Nobel Peace Prize in 1926. He also helped to steer the Kellogg–Briand Pact, through which a number of states pledged to avoid the use of force in resolving conflicts.

Editor, it's a hard life. What can you do with a bunch of men leave the salt out of the bread?

I agree with you, editor—'tcertainly is!

Le's see, did we put the oleomargarine in?

Well, then she's done.—Just set it to rise in a warm place; throw a woolen blanket over it. . . .

No woolen blanket?

Well, it's got to be covered—rip open an individual invalided undershirt . . . no, not a clean one; no sense in wasting a clean shirt if you have **dirties**. . . . After it is risen; should she not look rye-ish, shake a few empty potato sacks over it, punch it a few times, cut into cute chunks, and bake in a pan—and in an oven.—Remember! Bread should not be boiled, fried, roasted or stewed—it's sinners that are fried; peanuts roasted; lice boiled and men stewed—remember that.

Fellow worker: I feel confident, already—if you have followed my instructions—that your oven will give birth to fine rye bread, I'm sorry only that I can't be with you to congratulate your superlative cooking abilities—the bread I won't miss because I'm getting the same kind right here in this lumber camp.

New life surges through my dilapidated frame and I feel that if the cook don't cut himself and get blood poison I will live long and prosper—I'm starting the new year with twenty-four dollars—if I don't get fired between now and the expiration of the time it-would-take-to-earn that amount—**theexpirationoftimeitwouldtaketoearnthatamount**—an' eager of our too well known prosperity; a midnight eerie of dull thuds galloping in pursuit of health and happiness—seeking health where happiness prowls; hunting happiness whether health skulks—

Finding, work, work, work . . .

The devil finds work for somebody else to do.

*

Speaking about law it has come to my notice that people are complaining that even the rich cannot get justice in our courts. I believe that.

Personally I know of case after case where rich men were tried for one-tenth of one per cent murder and failed to get justice—they were turned loose, a stranger to the noose, their goose uncooked. "Not guilty," this time—but don't do it again. And I know of at least one such seeker for justice that tried it again—under another charge—and failed to fall.

On the other hand, the innocent poor cannot get justice and are "railroaded" for years and years into the can—but occasionally the frame-up is proven, generally years later—**after the victim's life has been ruined.**

*

While discussing courts, I'm reminded—and I ask you, editor, what is that World-Spirit I hear the Swedes talking about?[3]

Is it some kind of cement that is supposed to glue all the rattletrap capitalist institutions together into an association of rattletraps—on the principle that a rotten egg is improved by re-laying it in a nest with other rotten eggs—I wouldn't be surprised, editor, and I fully agree with you.

Industrial Solidarity, 27 January 1926

[3] This is a reference to Swedenborgianism.

Go or Melt

In olden days the good citizens had a nasty habit of cutting *chunks off the forward ends* of kings. Along would come an official amputator with an ax on his shoulder or a cleaver under his arm and proceed to hack away—yes sirree—hack away at the *kink in the king's neck* till the blue blood squirted over the carpet like sawdust from a sawsage—that is: sawdust (ribbons of it; most like Colgate's dental cream) from a fresh cut; the old saw "whining through the pine" broadcasting gleefully: today or'r'r tomor'r'row; today or'r'r'r tomor'r'row. . . . Yessirree, and we thought in those days, What a shame! to thus waste labor power—even for dear old art's sake—upon the king's neck—and muss up the sweet-scented Persian rugs (made in the Cleveland workhouse) . . . so we straightway and etcetera edged forth and organized the society for the prevention of cruelty to animals, their descendants, ante-seedlings and crescendonuts. . . .

Little did we think in those good old days—and we haven't thought much since—that is: little did we think that the guillotine-contraption was the forerunner of the modern bread-slicing machine—ah, fellow workers, little did we realize that the block on which the king pillowed his head *for the last time* was the predecessor of the present-day butcher-anvil. Such ignorance has never been beaten yet, what editor?

'Twouldn't been so sad, editor, if the block—the rock—had been used to sever the king's relation with his head and then have some *son-of-a-gun* hide it on him—but no, editor, they goes to work and wrecks his prospects and clips his dynasty all with one fatal swing—on the principle of *might as well have the game as the name*—headless *king*.

Such was progress—just one thing after another—until today when we blink at our glistening civilization and behold the highly flavored cornflakes—just add cream and sugar (the cream you can get in Canada or Mesopotamia). Sugar is extinct.

But one consolation persists, gentlemen and fellow sisters:

Sourkraut![1]

But woe unto the day that Gus invented it!—he might have known that if

[1] Sauerkraut (which means "sour cabbage" in German, hence Slim's playful spelling) is excellent for gut health, in contrast to many of the artificial foods that he castigates here and elsewhere. A cook himself, Slim was knowledgeable about the health benefits of what today is referred to as a "superfood."

he starts mangling cabbage Battle Creek[2] and Armour[3] would take a new hold on life—ours and theirs—and "wrangle" our "goat"—and feed us corn shavings—so I say, back to nature; back to, no—face to sourkraut; back to the good old days when the meat market anvil first found its conception in our consciousness, as old "Hutch" would say: back, back to the days when the first bread-knife descended for the first time on *punk.*[4] . . .

It is evident that progress has been too much of a high-ball order for most men to keep up. . . .

Today we are living the life of twenty years ago—repeating and repeating the same old stuff without knowing enough to sit down . . . to sit down and think it over . . . shedding tears . . . weak.

Weak! And we can't see that united we are strong.

Cry away—I will go and fetch you a pail. . . .

Did it ever occur to you to join the Industrial Workers of the World and Act with them?

I'm telling you, *gentle stranger of tears and sighs,* that *shedding your sap* is not going to purify the system!

Progress is inexorable.

It's a case of Move or Melt!

Organize your "ways and means" congress!

Industrial Worker, 30 January 1926

---

2 This is seemingly a reference to the Battle Creek Food Company, formed by John Kellogg as a rival to the Kellogg Company, which had been founded by his brother, Will. Both companies produced toasted cereals that Slim would consider to be of low nutritional value.

3 A famous meatpacking firm.

4 Hobo slang, in this instance, for bread, though it also had several other meanings.

T-Bone Slim Discusses the Laughing Dog

(Written after Mark Twain's "Leaping Frog")

The Von Platen Lumber Company, an elite outfit, at Pori, Mich., Camp C had, in addition to the aggressive "Gulliver," obstacle-overcoming, overbearing and overpowering lad the sheik of Hill Creek and positive Lothario of Nett River—as I was saying, in addition to all these things, the Von Platen had a Spitz bitch gifted with a hilarious turn of mind.

No one seemed to know what the dog was laughing at and many theories were advanced as the cause of her mirth, sometimes hysterical but always mysterious—discarded as fast as proposed.

One of the popular theories was that "the dog had caught a **case** of **grins,**" contagious-like from one of the super-intellectual gyppos[1] that had a habit of talking to himself, in a fatherly way, nights, (when he had time) laughing over his own brilliancy and applauding his mental **gyrations** with wreaths of smiles, ebbing and flowing—fading and flourishing—ravishing.

Another opinion that prevailed, but finally perished, was that the dog was highly gratified at the way "Gulliver" ran the works and the amount of logs that were taken out pay between two nights—and for a while the dog was under suspicion of being a "Company man." Said suspicion, too, may have been the cause of the sad demise of the "slut" and mother of five pups—peace to her ashes—rumor had it that the poor dog had caught a chill as a result of her vigilancy in keeping track of the restive gyppos and nighthawks[2] taking observations over the heavenly beauties after hours wondering how much raisinjack[3] the big dipper would hold.

Many were the reasons given—almost every man had a version of his own and it was **hard to know** whom to believe. Superstitious **forty**-niners[4]

---

[1] A slang term for timber workers who were paid based on piece rates, in this case the number of logs produced, rather than a wage. This practice became widespread in the 1920s and was opposed by the IWW, as it increased competition between workers and was used to break down the solidarity the union had built up among timber company employees. Many Wobblies were heavily opposed to the piece rate system, but Slim, and others, argued that since it was becoming established, the workers employed through it should be recruited and organized. It is unclear whether the term had any racial connotations.

[2] A slang term for people who stayed up late at night to drink or sell alcohol during Prohibition.

[3] A colloquial term for bootleg wine or liquor made from fruit and vegetables.

[4] Slang referring to older men generally, although it originated as a name for miners who joined the gold rush of 1849.

were firmly convinced that the dog was possessed of one Beezlebub, if not His Majesty himself,[5] and then was those that insisted that a **doglegation** be sent down to Appleton, Wisconsin to fetch up an official **shagger** of Mephistophelian squatters—a monk, expert in expelling and exorcising Luciferian intruders and microbes of the Satanical-common-wealth.

And the **beauty** of that theory was that it could not be disargued—no question could be raised as to its plausibility since there was absolutely no possibility of a frame-up between the dog and the monk. If Beezlebub was in the dog, it was genuine. (Hearst paper please copy.)[6]

Where was I? Oh yes—anyhow, the dog just laughed and laughed. One morning, I think it was the night before she died, she stepped out the porch to see the boys off as they were getting on the car to be taken out to work and, sure enough, here again the dog just stretched out in convulsions of joy, skinned her teeth way back to both her ears in a most **knowing** smile. . . .

"I wonder what makes the dog do that?" inquires a **new-comer,** deeply interested.

"Why, don't you know?" counters an old-timer, in surprise.

"No. I can't figure it out."

"It's very simple—that dog is laughing at you guys getting on that flat car at half past five in the morning."[7]

Industrial Solidarity, 24 February 1926

5 That is, Satan.

6 This is a reference to William Randolph Hearst's media empire, which was noted for its large chain of right-wing and sensationalist newspapers that targeted the IWW and other radical organizations.

7 Flat cars were part of a train's rolling stock; at times they were left empty and at others they were loaded with shipping containers or goods.

Information

"What is a paradox?"

At one time I thought it was a typographical error for pair o' sox. Only recently I've discovered what it is:

When thousands of men are out of work in all towns; when competition for jobs is keen; when, despite the law of supply and demand, the wages do not drop any lower—that is a paradox.

"What isn't a paradox?"

That's easy! When the wages are so low that men cannot live on less; when working men eat only on five days a week and skip meals on all holidays; when, despite *supply and demand,* wages don't drop lower—that is what a paradox isn't.

It isn't a paradox when wages at the bottom do not fall lower. I don't know where they could fall to, except into the sewer.

Stands to reason, too, that you wouldn't expect an elevator to fall from the ground floor—unless you were going down into a sugar mine.

Wages are now on the ground floor and are known far and wide as living wages.

"What is living wages?"

Wages that can be exchanged for a livelihood is living wages. Anything less than that is not wages at all. Americans are not getting living wages; hence, no wages—what they get is part of subsistence.

"Are you a taxpayer?"

That's a big question.

Although I own no land—not one square inch—I'm a taxpayer. Even though I have no home, I'm a taxpayer. Even though I have no stocks, bonds, yellowbacks, greenbacks, dollars, halfs, quarters, dimes, nickels, yea, even if I haven't a red cent—I'm a taxpayer. My boss pays his taxes from the money that I don't get. With the money that I do get I buy a box of snuff, and my taxes are in the price I pay for that tooth powder.

Thusly:

The landlord pays taxes and *passes the buck* to the dealer; the dealer pays, therefore, higher rent, and *passes the buck* to snuff users. Why it's getting to be so that every time I spit into a coalpail I help to pay the nation's taxes.

Out of every $8 that I spend, $1 goes for taxes, federal, state and local—no matter who actually delivers the dollar to the government.

When I sleep I'm a taxpayer—and I snore like one. Taxes are paid on the house that I sleep in; the landlady gets all her taxes from us sleepers; she has no mint of her own; and so it goes.

What is "supply and demand"?

What man produces, that is supply; demand is the holler he raises when his supply gets away from him.

Both, supply and demand, are created by man, and, therefore, are not a RIGID standard.

He may holler low or holler high, his supply amounts to an overproduction.

The law of supply and demand is the twin rule of "product and prayer"; prosperity and requisition; sufficiency and necessity.

*

"No hobos allowed to loaf in here."—Hocking Valley Depot, Fostoria, O. What does that mean?

It means that the depot is too dirty for self-respecting hobos to visit except with mop, soap and water.

*

The preacher drew a gloomy face
And scorned to toil a tap,
Yet, somehow, reaped the "joys of grace"
And grew rotundly fat.

The financier grew quite insane
With grief "too tough to bear,"
And drank "a tub" of dry champagne
To save his falling hair.

*

Persons having no legitimate business herein are FORBIDDEN to remain or loiter in or about PASSENGER STATIONS, etc.—Blue Onion R. R. *If you haven't any money you needn't come around.*

Industrial Worker, 10 April 1926

T-Bone Slim Discusses: How Do They Do It

I would like to know how these "self-made men" managed to do it without parents—how they managed to make themselves—without first aid from the stork.

I should imagine that making one's self purely by one's own effort would be rather a lonesome job and subject to many a "fizzle."

*

A full-blooded cad is the thoroughbreed that calls a "mulatto" halfbred. (Excuse me.) And refers to redskins (Americans) as quarterbreds—he is the very last word in in-bred frailty and witless pride.

Industrial Solidarity, 5 May 1926

Reporting the Reports

Says Prof. Salvemini: "Fascism is merely Bolshevism of the Right as Bolshevism is Fascism of the Left."[1]

Now wouldn't that scale your cheeks! Here we thought that one was two-faced and the other all face—or no face at all.

Dear—Dear. What shall we do?

Let's see—Right face of the left and left face of the right.

No; that ain't right—I mean, left—the—the right face of what's left and left face of—Goodness Sakes! I believe they're a pair of twins born of separate mothers.

How was that again, professor?

One is the left of the right and the other is the right of the left, is that it?

By the eternal Jimminy! If those were a pair of shoes, a man would have *one historical time* getting into 'em.

Either I'm not right or they ain't right! That's all there's to it.

*

"The poor man thinks that if only he can be rich he will be happy."

The poor man might just as well think he will be fat (instead of poor) when rich. It's the consciousness of not being robbed that makes the crown so light to carry. Poverty and riches are opposite—happiness is in no way related to either one.

Says Bishop of Durham: "Believe me, cottages have a better reputation for happiness than palaces."

So have saloons, for that matter.

Surely the Bishop doesn't advocate the doing away with palaces, on those grounds.

Industrial Worker, 5 June 1926

---

1 Gaetano Salvemini was a Socialist Party politician who founded an underground antifascist newspaper in Italy. Arrested and then freed, in 1925 he fled to France, where he continued his opposition to Benito Mussolini's fascist regime. He visited the United States in 1927 and then returned several times before eventually becoming a resident in 1934. In 1948, following World War II and Mussolini's fall, he moved back to Italy.

Taxing Our Spirit

Railroads are complaining that their pay-toilets are not money-making affairs—even at 5 cents a throw. At the same time they accuse the passenger traffic of "dropping off." Can it be possible the traffic has followed "free toilets"?

Brace up, railroads! The generous public will return to thee as soon as you set free comfort and quit that petty nickel game.

Of course they felt hurt—the public—when they got *caught short* and you, railroads, took advantage of it and squeezed a nickel out of 'em.

In this connection, I'm sorry to say that the public being averse to parting with the jit[1] has functioned in a manner that lays them open to suspicion—where the doors of the pay-as-you-enter do not reach clear to the floor the public is frequently caught on his hands and knees either crawling in or backing out.

Now that looks suspicious, indeed.

An officer of the law extricated one such publican from such a compromising position and asked him, "Wot's the big idea?"

The heinous culprit produced a coin and explained that "just as he was putting it in the slot it slipped and rolled into the closet; that he was only fishing it out."

"Noble man!" exclaimed the cop, slapping the victim of circumstantial evidence on the shoulder so hard that the nickel again rolled into the exclusive booth.

Again, during rush hours, the traffic in this department is so great that the doors don't get a chance to lock before a new candidate has moved in—thus killing two birds with one stone. The railroads consequently lost many nickels that way . . . but I'm sure that the public who gain a nickel *that way,* invariably give it to charity—drop it in the collection box—when they attend the more divine service—especially on Easter morning—otherwise, mebbe, they couldn't attend church owing to financial stringency.

*

When Is a Man Crazy?

Ah, a very proper question, following the above treatise on sanitary taxation. The craziness of man depends (according to a popular bureau of standards) wholly upon the man's own words:

As long as he keeps his mouth shut he isn't crazy—that is, as long as he

[1] Shortened form of "jitney," slang for small coin.

keeps his thoughts to himself he is considered a wise man. If he opens his mouth and speaks his thoughts to somebody else, he is a nut.

But, if he thinks his thoughts resonantly to himself—talks to himself—he is crazy.

A condition wherein his governor-belt has slipped off his "clarifier" causing his annunciator to transmit vocal variations of various mental vagaries "neck and neck" with the production of his deduction motor, idea-oscillators, thought-generator and also his knowledge-dynamo. But a writer, ah, he is never crazy—he may be queer, but that's all.

And so, as I was going to say in regards that lavatory deal, may it please the reader to have me produce right in front of his expectant gaze that the 5 cents tax on our sanitary efforts is merely a step in the direction of taking absolute control over our very lives—and let him note that the exchange reports a terrible slump in Castor Oil (unlimited) as a result of it.

It, the step, is a move to prepare the way for taxing our breathing, in the future. Radio will be perfected to the end that it will register (on a meter) in the Air Corporation's office the number of cubic feet of air you inhaled last month and a bill will be mailed to you—you'll pay it, or do your breathing behind iron bars. Of course, a 20 per cent discount will be allowed for dust and smoke. That's when, not only man, but men and women are crazy—or easy.

P.S.—Our author gathers from the above that capitalism is not yet at the end of its resources—it will approximate its end when it begins to keep tab of our breathing.

*

Anent the British strike,[2] says Wm. Randolph Hearst, a rising journalist for the *New York Journal*:[3]

"A catastrophe which has overtaken England" (you mean, Eng. caught up with said fat-as-trophy?) "in the great strike, a catastrophe which might easily have been averted if only some one of the parties to the original dispute had had the intelligence or the patriotism to avert the conflict."

England should import a little intelligence—we could spare Hearst.

*

2 In 1926, a nine-day general strike involving millions of workers was held across the United Kingdom. This followed heavy reductions in coal employee wages, with further cuts and increased hours supported by the government. Heavy policing and the use of troops, recruitment of strikebreakers, lack of support from Labour Party leadership, and limits on the types of workers called out by the Trade Union Council all contributed to the failure of the strike.

3 Hearst was, of course, the owner of the *New York Journal*, as well as someone long opposed to the cause of labor in America and abroad. He is famously represented in fictionalized form as the newspaper tycoon in Orson Welles's classic film *Citizen Kane* (1941).

Great minds are still booting the "moot question" as to whether newspapers create public sentiment or merely reflect it. (Let me answer that, editor—it is my turn.)

I believe the modern murder-messengers and advertising-argosies, after pruning the public of all sentiment, reflect the shorn—butt! To me the question is not "do they create, or do they reflect—but do they destroy sentiment?"

We know what they reflect—disaster, devastation and desolation. Dissolution, in fact!

And they refuse responsibility—debating as to whether they create or reflect public sentiment. Methinks they're "off the subject"—and "off" other ways, too—not so wise—and, really, it's a shame to pay three cents for all the department store advertisements that's fit to read, and worth printing.

Industrial Worker, 26 June 1926

The Trend

The best way to eliminate congestion in the street cars (elevated trains) is have a preacher deliver a sermon in each car, every trip. Possibly the skipping of sermons on a few trips, if done in secrecy, wouldn't create a relapse of sardine*ism*.

*

The laws of Moses was written on stone so as to enable readers to turn a page on windy days. Very thoughtful!

*

The difference between a STATESMAN and a GANDYDANCER is they gaze at things from a different tangle:

A STATESMAN thinks he KNOWS, but doesn't; a GANDYDANCER knows, but THINKS he doesn't. It's just a case of doesn't, that's all.

*

You know that big cord that holds up the big toe? Well, sir, I have a pain that is camped on that cord and strolls along it just like a gunman on guard. Now, I understand, (am right?) that it is the custom (in such cases) to send for religious consolation. No kidding—the pain is plain and real. Now, editor, can it be possible that it is love?

Industrial Worker, 14 August 1926

A Restaurant Is No Stronger Than Its Weakest Coffee

Yesterday, while eating I had the misfortune to spill half of my potatoes on the floor. You see, I had them balanced on a fork instead of "bayoneted." A sudden jar, from weakness, and lo, the house-dog (leaping nine feet and four inches) had them gobbled up before I could rescue them.

Poor dog!

*

I take pleasure in informing the discouraged members that I, T-bone Slim, am the inventor of that great doctrine "What's The Use"—and the Heartfelt SIGH that goes along with it. *I invented it from my own head* and intended it for my own use—and I defy any man to use it as something original of theirs. I'm going to have it copyrighted just as soon as the payroll *begins to erupt.*

*

Notice to the Public

Methinks there is too durn much of this "Notice to the Public." Every place I go the depot is plastered with placards "Notice to the Public." Look! Listen! Learn!—Just like that.

What do they think we are, a bunch of school kids? For Heaven's sake, why don't they address us properly, sirs and sisters, misters and hers? Why?

There's a traffic department notice.

There's a freight tariff notice.

A motion picture film notice.

Notice! Notice!! Notice!!!

Notice to the public, Baggage service.

Notice to the Public, Safeguard Your Baggage.

Notice to Public, Transportation of Dogs in Baggage Cars.

Public Notice!

Notice!—Notice!—All kinds of 'em. Some of 'em framed.

I noticed 'em!

And I noticed that there was no fire in the stove so I wondered why they hadn't put up a notice to that effect.

Industrial Worker, 11 September 1926

Now-a-Days

These frosty morns may be healthy and all that's claimed for them—and it may be fine exercise to stand outside the cook-car shivering, waiting for five o'clock breakfast. I'm not arguing that it isn't—besides, the dewy grass, later, has a tendency of thawing one's icey feet and makes threshing a highly desirable occupation. . . .

What I'm arguing is that the Society for the Propagation of Kindness to American Animals take into consideration the terrible night of the Great American Mosquito.

Only the other morn I had the pleasure of visiting the great American manure pile, back of the barn; and, would you believe it, I was horrified to espy there a mosquito, half dead from struggling to his feet. He came out of the recesses of the manure where, evidently, he had used a vagrant straw or half-digested oat for a blanket—American farm horses having notoriously poor digestion.

Ah! I said. He struggled to his feet only to fall down again—catarrh, probably. He fell and fell only to rise again. Such wonderful persistency I never saw! Such stamina! Such, such strength of will power! I held a match for him, so that he could thaw himself out—and I was glad to see, would you believe it, that the bug highly appreciated my efforts and actually wanted to kiss me on the back of the neck. . . .[1]

As to the harvest hands, they are well provided for: 12-hour day, 10 pounds of hamburger, 41½ cents per hour and a 1917 model—quilt!

Therefore, let the S. P. K. A. A.[2] throw their benevolent eye upon the poor struggling mosquito, in compassion and aid him in his heroic battle for supremacy.

Industrial Worker, 9 October 1926

---

[1] This seems to be a parody of the apocryphal story of Robert the Bruce and the spider.

[2] This is likely a play on the ASPCA (American Society for the Prevention of Cruelty to Animals), which was founded in 1886.

Boneyard

When a person is drowning he does not need help—he can drown without help. He doesn't need help even to get saved.

The shape he's in—He couldn't do any part of the saving. If he's drowning he doesn't want help—what he wants is a complete performance of rescue. The nerve of these drowning people is the limit, conceited buggers—Help! Help! Just as if they was doing the job and needed but a pull here and a lift there. . . . The next time a drowning man hollers at me, I'm going to point this out to him. When I pull people out of the ocean, I'm no helper—I'm the mechanic—And I want all the credit, or blame.

Pass the medals, please.

Industrial Solidarity, 15 December 1926[1]

---

1 Slim's columns for *Industrial Solidarity* often, though certainly not always, used the title "Boneyard." As well as obviously denoting a graveyard, the term was slang for an area where old ships and other derelict vessels were stored while waiting to be scrapped.

1927

Boneyard

Made-To-Order Deaths.

Inexpensive ways to commit suicide are getting more expensive every day. In fact, it's so expensive that a poor man, (who needs it worst) can't afford it. Guns are too costly just for one operation. Safety razor blades won't do because you've got to have a pair of fifty cent pliers to hold'em—besides you can't buy a lone single and blade, you've got to buy a dozen—that's 79 cents—the rest will rust and spoil!

The best poisons now are so high that a man who is "short" can't reach 'em. Even the lowly rope is **beyond** the means of an average citizen.

Mebbe you've noticed, all the suicides are men who are well off . . . that is, they've got no opposition.

This thing must not be allowed to continue and since the federal authorities are disinclined to supply the people with proper weapons for this purpose, I suggest that the citizens before investing in those high priced auxiliaries consider well the advantages of drowning or jumping in front of freight trains (they're heavier, and will push you further). But if those don't appeal to you, you might overhaul the more "expensive ones" and pick out one that you put to "a dual use"—for instance, buy yourself a post-war drink and thus combine business with pleasure—whichever is which.

D'D'Death is s's'certain, b'b'but you will d'd'die happy in the consciousness that it d'd'didn't cost b'b'but two-b'b'bits—d'd'drink included. (Them's tears)

P.S. Science is on the point of **tapping the mystery of life.** The unknown is **not so far away.** Unfortunately, to get at it, science must pass through about six feet of solid ivory—and there it is. There it was. There it will be.

Industrial Solidarity, 9 February 1927

Concessionaires?

I've been reliably informed that kissing is bad, dangerous, for the lips, health, brain and stomach—because of the germs, toilet-powder, "turkish"-red[1] and nicotine.

Of course I had to investigate this and will say that at first blush it did seem that the kisses were kind of sloppy, slippery and slimey and might have been the hatching place of worms or microbes—but upon second thought I made up my mind "it can't be true"; else less people would be dying of hootch amendment.

Then again, grey-haired or hairless gentlemen, before doddering into office, kiss the bible. (And I always kiss Harry Acton on the "forehead" before submerging my perspicacity in his "On the Gang-plank"—)[2]

Now, if kissing the old calfskin puts new life into those shaky gentlemen, a scorch from a real hectic "mollie-kiss"[3] would make new men of them—and the people would have to rescind their "election."

What! If a one-sided kiss, minus reciprocity and spit, implanted on a finger-printed bible-cover- (misplaced shoe-leather) benefits the **statesmen** and **the nation,** a double-action osculation,[4] as a rebuke to imitational one-sided exercises would put the nation back on its feet.

Sir, kissing a book or a shirt or a garbage can is just like single handed love[5] in a cottage and is not as beneficial as the split responsibility—"two heads are better as one."

Industrial Worker, 14 May 1927

1 A reference to Turkish tobacco and cigarettes, popular at this time in the United States.

2 Acton was a shipping news writer for Hearst's *New York American* newspaper. His slang-filled column was titled "On the Gangplank."

3 A reference to sex work.

4 Latin word for kissing; literally, "little mouth."

5 That is, masturbation.

"Origin of Fatal Explosion Baffles All Investigation"

'Twas ever thus, gentlemanners and gentlemamies, save in my case. I refuse to be baffled, and refuse to use addled headlies 'xcept in "quotes."

The explosion was caused by super-abundance of immaculate cleanliness wedged in between immense areas of high tension sanitation and vibrant harmony, (the whole volatilizing and creating a vortex in the geyser of human virtues) culminating in over pressure backfiring upon the lily pure cleanliness and touching off the whole works.

Baffled? Not me!

I never "pass the buck."

*

Fellow Workers: I've now reached the age when I begin to feel that I ought to be president of the United States and, I warn you, **my feel is law and desire a fulfilled promise.** Nevertheless, in decency, I must enwise the professional electors of my matured availability in order that they may not enscramble the detail by picking some poor devil that don't know any better than to disguise himself with good man's shoes,—leaving me, the logical contender, practically barefooted for four years.

My platform:

I stand, irrevocabularily, for softer seats—and rubber heels.

*

The next step following this present dance of political-oleogarchy (democratic-autocrazy) probably will be satanical-puritanism—but it will be only a step—then the deluge. (Del-uge.)

I'm getting to be quite a prophet.

Industrial Worker, 18 June 1927

Boneyard

Relativities—proclivities, rather:

Man goes up or down, ahead or astern, is never stationary, except as a corpse—who wants to be a cadaver ahead of his turn?—a dead one?—he never sidles, so help me. . . . That being settled to the bottom, man when he has learned to plaster down his hair with perfumed vaseline is a matinee idol, not counting the dirty sox and stinking feet—and when he successfully negotiates the intricate square-knot in his bandana around his neck he is a movie star, provided he can stick to the saddle (if a thoroughbred bone-pile) long enough (between spills) to get his picture taken. . . . that being so, they're gentlemen, social lions (not rats) way up in "G" . . . But we believe their previous condition and status, as a bum or foster guardian to cows (Godfather to cattle) was on a firmer base than their glory of the present.

As I said, man goes up or down.

WiW

Bakers will persist in sprinkling shredded cocoanut on "buns" (rolls) despite the fact that vast majorities of people prefer other kinds of wood—pine, maple, balm of gilead (poplar) or ordinary "excelsior."

But what can we do? In most states it's a crime to kill bakers—no matter what the provocation—no matter how many they kill with petrified cocoanut.

wIw

All has not yet been said about "save your pennies." When your boss or his representathief tells you to do that, tearfully beseeches you to salvage them, your cue is to register great surprise, lift your eyebrows and breathe: "What! is figuring on paying off with pennies?"

Aside from that, we'll groom that slogan a bit: The object of that remark "save" is not to inculcate the spirit of thrift into your vitals, nossir. Nor is it a left-handed accusation against your non-existent "spedthrifticie," nossir.

It is put forth merely as an alibi for the balances of your pocketbook.

Remarks by editor . . . *

*EDITOR'S REMARKS: NONE! This is too good for any editorial attempt at elaboration. When a work of art is finished, it's finished; that's all, and the editor knows enough not to go "bustin" through with a sledge-hammer, or like the vandal soldiers who pulled down and broke up one of De Vinci's most famous sculptures, even while he watched them.[1]

Industrial Solidarity, 13 July 1927

---

1 This does appear to be a genuine editorial comment.

Rough Logic: Seeing's Believing

Politics 'n Pockets

It makes no difference to us, the citizens of industry, whether we are robbed at point of bayonet, point of order or point of desperation; whether it's done by broadcloth, cheese cloth or pure burlap—yea and likewise verily—be it done under *whatflagsoever,* white flag, black flag, rainbow, dishrag, its all the same to us—the mere fact that we ARE robbed is sufficient unto the day if not too much.

But I fear it's too much—more than sufficient and only less than calamity and its attendant HOWL. And what are you going to do about it?

Are you going to howl?

Are you going to lift your beautiful baritone in dirge of distress, or are you going to organize? I was thinking if you're going to howl I'm with you—let's yodle together, that's a mild form of organization: Two souls without a single cent; two lungs that howl as one. Can you beat it?

Aside from that, let me console the unorganized: We know you won't line up, voluntarily—you're too thick headed for so fast a move. You will need lots and lots of encouragement—otherwise you will line up after you are on crutches at the county poor farm or state infirmary. Right now you should be dressed in calico and sent to the old ladies home. I thank you!

Industrial Worker, 16 July 1927

Razzpectability!

Ralph Waldo Emerson and the celebrated Henry David Thoreau once discussed (or cussed) the advisability of paying taxes to a democracy that sanctioned the holding of slaves; they decided they would not "contribute."

In the show-down Ralph Waldo "came across," but Thoreau stood by his principles and was thrown in "the can."

Pretty soon Emerson went "with the money" to get Henry out and as he looked in on poor Hank, behind the bars, he said in mild reproof: "Thoreau, why are you in here?"

"Emerson, why are you not in here?" was Thoreau's scorching "comeback."

Rebels?

*

Our venerable author, while slightly cockeyed, fell overboard and wet his cigarettes. Luckily they were Lucky Strikes and toasted, so he simply retoasted them. . . . This will be a source of great relief and a lesson to all those whose feet need washing. The citizens in Kansas may well take this lesson to heart.

*

"Thanks, God!"

'Tis easy enough to say that—and I suppose God 'ppreciates our politeness—but, nevertheless, it seems one-sided.

We never hear God saying "Well done my noble sergeant," nowdays—do we?

Why is that?

Is it possible that we're just a bunch of stinkers in his nostrils, on his rostrums and no nostrum in sight?

It didn't use to be that way. Years ago the old gent used to get behind our virtuous forefathers and "hock" and "hock" and "honk praises" till the devil got jealous—

Now, I would suggest to our ministers, Fosdick, Empringham, Bishop Brown, Jawn R. Straton, etc., don't be so bashful—stow your modesty. When the good Lord says, "Much obliged, Rev. Straton," as the case may be, get right up on your hind haunches and tell us about it—else we'll lose faith and you'll go the way of Massachusetts courts.[1]

---

1 This is a reference to the conduct of the judge and legal system during the trial of anarchists Nicola Sacco and Bartolomeo Vanzetti in Massachusetts. The pair were found guilty of armed robbery and murder in 1921 and sentenced to death. A cause célèbre at the time, in subsequent decades the trial was acknowledged as unfair and biased, influenced as it was by xenophobia and right-wing fear mongering. Having been denied opportunities for appeal and retrial, the pair were executed in 1927. They would be exonerated by Massachusetts Governor Michael Dukakis fifty years later.

Nobody, of course, expects ministers to take a stand on anything, least of all on the two innocent men about to undergo judicial murder—anymore than the stand they took when Christ was hung—(we expect, rather, that they will hoot resonantly with their trained voices)—dumb creatures.

And when religion, in addition, becomes an opium and is used to lull the slaves into submission, so much worse for religion. Pews are empty. Preachers' feet are under the bosses' table. A complete circle has been made. Evolution has turned once.

O Tempore O Morons!

Industrial Worker, 23 July 1927

Untitled

I have it that Major General Charles P. Summerall took a fall out of the housing conditions of our to-be-respected-men-of-war-soldiers.[1]

"The housing situation of the army," said our tremendous soldier, "is a disgrace. Men are living in quarters at Camp Hearn like workers in a logging camp. The same condition prevails at other places."

H'm!

Here's something to be looked into!

It's a direct charge, that lumberjacks ain't any better off than the poor, poor soldiers—whose battles the doughty Summerall is fighting—and further, it's a charge that lumberjacks ain't any better fighters than the confirmed fighters.

H'm!

Both, of course, are getting about the same pay—nothing; less the better accommodations, pleasures, grub, etc. Both work for the love of the country—purely, merely, only, etc.

Both make the supreme sacrifice once, only—etc.; sooner or later—mostly sooner—weep, citizens, weep!

Now, fellow workers: Just now I ain't acquainted with lumber camp conditions—got discurvied couple o' years ago and moved under the Statue of Liberty on Fat-blush avenue,[2] Brooklyn—hence, I'm obliged to take Summerall's rever-**berating** word on for it. (Editor! Should the linotyper change the word **Fatblush to Flatbush**, show him no mercy—hand him no quarter—unless you have a leaden one. Send all your good quarters to me—we've got to have better quarters like Summerhall says.)

As I was gonna say, it can be understood that a soldier, hooked up to an several-year agreement, finds it his patriotic duty to stand for disgraceful conditions, but nothing like that stands in the way of the lumberjack; he can step out for better conditions at any time.—Anytime, all the time, or between two times.

Never is it his civic, patriotic, or idiotic duty to sleep in any pig pen to oblige a bunch of rollicking lumberkings—that's that.

Lumberkings, being as they are the most reasonable creatures, are always

---

1 Charles Summerall was the U.S. Army's chief of staff from 1926 to 1930. After retirement he became president of The Citadel, a military training college in South Carolina.

2 A play on Flatbush Avenue, one of Brooklyn's oldest streets. Slim had recently moved to New York City, most likely because his health was suffering and he needed to find work that was less physically demanding than railroad construction or lumberjacking. Circumstances would force him back on the road again in a few years' time.

open to lumber-lore and Jack's logic—. They'll listen. Let the lumberjacks organize their arguments and polish their demands and the barons will supply them—yea, even the exquisite flavored "Stay-comb" to lubricate their bristling whiskers.

That's that. Verily, I've said it all. Summerhall.

Have I?

The complaint is that soldiers are living nothing like "Ritzy" because "they live like workers in a lumber camp."

Well.

Now my idea is that lumberjacks should step up and live a little Ritzier and thus, indirectly, the soldiers will be benefitted—seeing as how they're using lumberjack living as a standard to go by—or get by.

Yes; I believe 'tis the "Jacks" sacred patriotic duty to put more feathers in the heroic doughboys' pillow.

What do you say?

Industrial Worker, 3 December 1927

Untitled

Figures of the Ludlow tent colony massacre tend to show the Colorado state militia prefers women and children first—for targets of their half-baked beastliness; six men, two women and eleven children.[1]

Cromwell, in his religious fervor was no different.

"Six hundred hicks, with their shooting-
sticks,
Piled on one starving striker—"

*

The ledger is balanced. Vanzetti forgave them one and all—only guiltless men can forgive.

Prisoner's Song (Air: Boston Burglar):

"Oh if Christ, HE, "the same WHOM we
owe much,"
Was to come once again among men,
Would he pass out the coffee and dough-
nuts
To the guards at the CHARLESTON
PEN?"

Would HE?

He would not! He'd say, "fasting is good for the soul."

A great lesson:

The Sacco and Vanzetti case proves, for all time to come, that marching and denouncing bring no results. Women and men wore themselves out *marching and sighing*; professors drank gallons of water denouncing politicians.

Therefore: I suggest that American labor do all its marching on Sammy Gompers' Labor Day and all its organizing on *the other* 364 days—and devil take the hindmost.[2]

---

1 After coal miners working for the United Mine Workers of America went on strike at the Colorado Fuel & Iron Company in 1913, they and their families were evicted from company housing and moved into tents. National Guard troops were sent in and on 20 April 1914 opened fire on a strike encampment, setting off a battle that lasted an entire day. The attack ended with tents being burned out and at least twenty-five people, including eleven children, killed.

2 Labor Day in the United States had its origins in celebrations of the labor movement during the 1880s, which were held on the first Monday in September. May Day emerged as an alternative point at which to commemorate unionism after the AFL declared the eight-hour workday would begin on 1 May 1886. The repression that

When you kill a philosopher—even if you roast him by electricity—you ain't getting away with a blessed thing. The whole world reacts against it—consciously and unconsciously.

I'm sorry America has reached the stage when it thinks it a part of wisdom to "bump" philos off. The night Sacco and Van went out I could not sleep between the hours of 10 p.m. and 12:30 a.m. Sleep? Ah! So sure was I that Massachusetts had brains.

Industrial Workers, 24 December 1927

---

followed a strike and violence in Chicago as part of that campaign led to radicals embracing the first day of May as a key time for commemoration. This encouraged numerous states to make the September event a public holiday, and the federal government followed suit, declaring Labor Day a national holiday in 1894.

1928–1929

Boneyard

Bulletins:

It's a quiet world, after all. Positively nothing is happening **all the time.** Peace in plenty abounds and contentment o'erspreads the calm of our slackened, sacred, seared, hokum.

Nothing transpires.

Action inanimate, inertia struts victorious. Repose, rampant, languishes in the throes of acute debilitation. Quiet. Silence. Relaxation. . . . Is that death?

No. That's United States.

Wages are cut—labor snores. Prosperity assails the populace. Newsboys wearing silk sox. Satin cascades the supple lines of laboring ladies. Plush covers the observation thrones of Pullman cabooses. . . . Corn beef and cabbage still undefeated. Three million unemployed—the rest loafing. Forty freeze. Thousand starve.

Eight hundred petition Borah for sandwiches—nothing's happening.[1]

I tell you—it's happening.

Soldiers take shots at the people, countrymen giggle. Citizens grin. Such a good joke, eh neighbor? Our boys learn to defend themselves, thataway—we've got lots of people suitable for target practice, eh neighbor? 117,000,000! Wot's vital statistics for anyhow, if not to keep track of "clean hits"?

"Just as if a hungry striker had any rights to be unreasonable," you say—

He should be cool and collected. Bread? Forget it! and think of next summer's watermelon crop.

Very undignified, I'm sure.

Never get rattled, like the army!

A sturdy-minded citizen just now remarked, "This country needs a cleaning up."

Is it, then, that we must build a new society in the hell of the old?[2]

How ingenious!

Industrial Solidarity, 15 February 1928

(Yes, dear; he is back again; he comes and goes with stops and starts—EDITOR)[3]

---

1 Idaho Republican William Borah was the chief prosecutor in a failed conspiracy trial against IWW leader Bill Haywood in 1907. He went on to become a U.S. senator later that year and held the position until his death in 1940.

2 A reference to the Wobbly slogan "Building a new world in the shell of the old."

3 This is a nod to how little Slim had been publishing during this period.

That "Triple Threat"

Mercy? No; just be yourself!!!

To control one's ferocity is not a part in mercy. Mercy is one of those very unreal things that could not be but for the presence of active ferocity. Therefore, exposition of mercy indirectly identifies such "mercifuls" as ferocious citizens disguised as good samaritans, but better hypocrites.

Better far to be yourself; just natural—and strive to outgrow your FRAILTIES—aiming, always, at higher emprise. For, be it remembered, the exercising of thought in realms of hypocrisy is to surrender it to destruction.

Colorado capitalists, to end the coal strike, shoot down hungry strikers at the slightest sign of enthusiasm or show of anything but strictest dignity.[1] Hunger and reason, thus, are supposed to be concomitants—but what can be said of the "shooter" with his belly full of heavy beans? What of the people of Colorado whose hand is on the trigger as much as is the hand that actually commits that crime against civilization?

Have we come to this?

Would mercy apply here?

Is that not murder?

Could we say, failure to commit cold blooded murder is a graceful act of mercy?

Nay.

I maintain a condition of ferocity is there that cries for correction!

*

PENNSYLVANIA—a protegee of the P. R. R.[2] and part of the United States—through its agents the state constabulary, attacks the children of the coal miners and knocks down mothers that rush to the aid of the kids, and drags the whole along the highways to receive first aid from their bountiful stores.[3]

---

1 On 21 November 1927, armed mine guards and state militiamen opened fire on a demonstration of hundreds of strikers and their families at Columbine, killing six and wounding others. The strike, which was for improved wages and safety conditions, saw an occupation of the town by armed company guards. It followed on from industrial action earlier that year by IWW members protesting the execution of Sacco and Vanzetti.

2 Pennsylvania Railroad Company.

3 During a twenty-month bituminous coal strike that began in February 1927, mine owners in Pennsylvania had deployed armed guards and police to harass and attack strikers, as well as to evict 12,000 workers and their families from company-owned housing. At its peak the strike involved around 200,000 strikers nationally. A clampdown on picketing and protest saw injunctions issued that banned the singing of hymns, leading to a U.S. Senate investigation.

Not much mercy there.

Not much sense either—although it may be that the children were about to attack the brave officers and they merely defended themselves.

Be that as it may, I'm inclined to the belief the circumstance IN REALITY was just another one of those outcroppings of pure, perhaps less violent, ferocity; a punishment for making faces and, in the case of the mother, a beating for being accomplice thereto.

I understand one of the heroic CONSTABULES was bit in the leg by a rabbit.

*

New York executes Ruth Snyder and Judd Gray. Elliott did not electrocute them—New York was the man![4] **The people pulled the chain.** Eight million people in New York City helpt to throw the switch, then went to bed, slept soundly and never saw a ghost.

Ghost? Ah! Excuse me; let us write no more concrete examples of ferocity. Let us rather leave unsaid and unthought, HENCE UNTAUGHT, all such items of mental disorder and well meant action of people fighting a losing fight with embattled aberrations. Let us be MERCIFUL in that respect, and make haste to point out the results of all such, well or ill considered, ferociousness.

Does the Christian State of New York know what became of the soul of Ruth Snyder and Judd Gray? No? It acted without knowing what it was doing? It knows where the bodies are. Can it be this great commonwealth was only after the bodies? How strange!

All such ferociousness, active or dormant, makes for the brutalization of the people. If not present personally they get the "tremendous" kick second hand from the cold blooded accounts of the "disinterested" press. It is assumed "the mutts" are better men and women after being thoroughly brutalized by yellow sheets[5]—two and three cents per brutalization—buy your own ruin. Sometimes the citizen is too stiff-necked to be brutalized—the sobstuff gets him. "The widows," "the orphans," "the cripples," "the martyrs," "the sole-supports,"—a-ahh! The symptoms of this attack consists of a lump in your throat the size of a small hen's egg, and your eyes brim with tears. The lump cannot be swallowed or thrown up—you're helpless.

But there is a remedy, if used in time! Unfortunately, you can't talk or notify your neighbor of your terrible affliction—he could help you. As it is, don't turn from him to hide your tears. Face him. That is important! All right. When

4 Ruth Snyder and Judd Gray were sentenced to death in 1927 for the murder of the former's husband. Both were electrocuted, and a photograph of Snyder was taken mid-execution in the electric chair. It was published the following day in the *New York Daily News*. Robert Elliot was New York State's executioner at the time.

5 A reference to sensationalist yellow journalism, a precursor of today's tabloid journalism.

he beholds the tears and your shirt front wet he can guess the "lump" and realize that you're on dead center of a destructive siege of mollycoddleism—emotion—sentimentalism—and if he's any kind of a man at all he'll save you A MODICUM of the "manhood that was" by placing his left hand on your shoulder and unscrewing your nose with his right.

That's the only way to drive the lumps away.

What have we now?

I have three virile points:

No. 1.—Ruined soul, tortured to extreme and finally despatched, somewhere, electrically.
No. 2.—Brutalization by savagery of deeds, and records thereof in bloodthirsty press.
No. 3.—Manhood undermined by periodical sob-stories and mollycoddleized by said perverted and putrescent journals—the sordid, may I say, BRAGMATICAL publications.

All three conditions border on ferocity and make for ferociousness.

Industrial Worker, 18 February 1928

Passing the Plate

Transcontinental Largess

I was indeed, practically seduced, into trying my hand and foot in the game of hitch-hiking, if you know what that is: begging rides from automobile and Ford drivers.

Well, I humped along the high-ways full of hope—nothing else much—and pretty soon along comes a car . . .

Haa! Shall I stop him?

No!

I gave one look at the driver, through the dirty windshield and jumped into a ditch—he looked like a man that would rob the bank of his child; a farmer, probably.

When he was gone I crawled from the ditch and brushed myself.

A narrow escape!

Pretty soon along comes another one—Christ, are they all escaped convicts? Into the ditch, I goes—I'm not gonna be robbed by any car driver if I can help it.

After being in the various ditches all day, after dark I sneaked back into town and caught a train and I'm proud to say, here in Chew City, Iowa, my money (3 cents) is still in my pocket. Damn that hitch-hiking, anyway—you can't tell what's liable to happen to you!

Industrial Solidarity, 15 August 1928

Untitled

A bad ending is better than no ending at all—a beginning is the thing!

A good beginning is the most beautiful thing in the world.

Consider the first steps of a child—what of it if he walks to the gallows, later?

He has at least moved!

A good beginning compensates for all errors and anything accomplished is clear profit.

Action pays no rent.

Lots of people "refrain" to act, not that they doubt their power to "begin," but they fear they cannot "wind-up."

What's the difference? Put a trick finish to it—same as I do when an article gets beyond control.

But I'm not talking about writing—anybody can write—all it takes is paper and pencil, etcetera, dammit!

Writing is one of those backward arts—too much time is lost sharpening leadpencils. Fountain pens will splutter and explode showering "periods" all over great moral truths and table cloth and, if one uses the old fashioned pen, his good right arm, always is on its way after more ink—no wonder us writers are "behind time."

Such contortions will make anybody late.

Use a typewriter?

Do you mean as a cook . . . ?

I don't see no overproduction rolling out of those typewriters.

No. I'm not talking about writing—writing is the long way around; 'tis either entertainment, abstract philosophy or tedious bringing up of the coming generation to the *foothills* of our high position—wage slavery—justified only by the general demoralization existing and necessary for the pointing out of the sore spots in society and bad cuts in the road—but it's *slow work* and harder than stud poker.

We've got to have faster transportation than writing.

We must be credentialed to organize the working class, to reach the top, to arrive there all together—equally scarred, if the Gods so ordain—but together. Our ambition should not be to pave the way for Willie to reach the top, but for US to reach the top—and give Willie a chance to start from *somewhere.*

What if we fail?

A bad ending is better than no ending

Credentials will do the business.

Industrial Solidarity, 19 January 1929

Junk, or Close Quarters

Einstein's "theories" pertaining among other phenomena to time, space, place as well as "fourth dimension" (to supplement length, width and depth) are "pretty much" for an ordinary "mind" that never fell out of a window when it was young.

Now, I've never fallen out of a window but I have been hit over the head with a hammer and other things my dear mother could grasp on the spur of the moment, not understanding my altruistic motives and intricate movements. . . .

So, naturally, I hasten to explain to the uncrippled public the "true facts" about this momentous question—and a question it must remain, I s'pose, till I get through explaining—maybe afterwards, too—if so it merely proves that I deviated from facts (something like Einstein's lines of force or light or something in relativity) to dodge insurmountable obstructions—not dissimilar to the maneuver of a married man sidestepping an installment collector. And it will prove, further, that my dear mother didn't get a good swing at me, on account of the furniture and small quarters.

*

But, to get to that "fourth dimension," I must use an illustration—to save space:

Somebody tosses a safe (not a rubber one) out of a skyscraper window. The cash-box hurtles down to the street. On its way it has weight, speed and distance—but when it lands it has resistance.

Unfortunately it lands on a taxpayer!

The good citizen tries to retreat in four different directions—in this he is only partially successful. . . .

Now, lots of people would think that the three dimensions, weight, speed and resistance, killed him. Nothing of the kind.

How about the impact?

Not so bad, but—?

What really happened, the man was caught in the presence of "absence of space"; squeezed between "tight" and "narrow." (Chances are the safe didn't touch him at all—nothing but compressed air.)

People speak affectionately of the "old" trinity length, breadth and height.

How about short, narrow and low? **There's six dimensions, right there.** And shallow.

Industrial Solidarity, 31 January 1929

"Yes"—Men

The King is Dead!

Duke the Tobacco King Kickt the Bucket.[1]

The Baron of Durham, North Carolina inhaled his last whiff.

Benjamin N. Duke, famous tobacco magnet—magnate, I mean (and don't you dare to read it maggot; he's not dead long enough) died yesterday in New York, age 74. The body will be taken to Durham, N.C.—the assumption being that dead he can rest at peace where he could not bear to witness the misery of his employees while alive. He left $200,000,000, plus.[2]

They called him a philanthropist—(Upton Sinclair, have a look!)

*

North Carolina has salubrious climate, clothes are practically unnecessary and Duke's employees never did wear any—and Duke never could see the sense of providing for any in the pay envelopes. Nothing but sow-belly and corn-bread.

*

"Let the little ones come unto me," appeared to be his pet hobby and many's the little rascal that jumped out his diapers right into the tobacco factory—fell out of the cradle, you might say, in its anxiety to lend Ben a hand. (Durham has no cradles—the kids sleep on ironing-boards. Durham has no flatirons—gotta use the board fer sumthing.)

They called him a philanthropist? The American newspapers, expert judges in such things called him "Philanthropist."

And I, expert judge in such things, call those papers LIARS—just liars—but liars with the mentality of a three year old.

Hypothetical question:

I have five dollars of other people's money, I peel-off thirteen cents, (12½) from this five bucks, to help a college—am I a philanthropist?

Astute Journalistie three-year olds:—Ye need not answer that question—I know ye are incapable of distinguishing the difference between philanthropy and advertisement—ye are too young—too young!—ye undertook to do the serious work of life too early—TOO EARLY!

Your quota of mud pies remain unmolded.

Back to the clay pile, brats!

---

1 Benjamin N. Duke was vice president of the American Tobacco Company, which was based in Durham, North Carolina.

2 Equivalent to approximately $3.6 billion today.

Apology:

My quarrel is not with Ben. N. Duke or his high pressure methods of extracting a few hundred million dollars in profits from the work of his employees and American people, his customers—and thru them from various other channels and sources.

My quarrel is with childish toadyism of the "weak sisters" of journalistic buffoonery; the epicurean "side-kicks" of a plate of hamburger; the abject worshipers at the shrine of two-bits.

When they grow up, I want them to define philanthropy. . . .

Is it the knack of relieving the nation of a billion dollars for the purpose of pensioning a starved-out professor to study the effect of planked-steak on pellagra?

Please do not think me unseemingly brutal to the children of the press—it would never do to massage a dislocated joint with soothing syrup, it must be brought to place with a jerk.

Industrial Solidarity, 2 February 1929

How Poems Are Made

Many people have an idea that I stay up nights and Sunday afternoons writing these heartrending truths for the purpose of uplifting the readers of our otherwise faultless press.

Nothing of the kind.

In the first place I don't write in the night time, in the second place I slumber all day Sunday and, in the third place, our readers don't need any uplifting.

My sole purpose is to enlighten the linotype operator.

Some would think that Slim, mebbe, is trying to slip the editors a chunk of wisdom now and again camouflaged as an innocious countrybution.

I ain't that crazy.

In the first place, even if I convinced them, they still would think of me as a liar, in the second place editors are consecrated to the belief that anything that comes "in is no better than" not so bad and, in the third place, they don't have to read it—they can smell it blindfolded and send it down to the linotyper. That's the man I'm after! He can't dodge it! He's got to read it!! If he doesn't—he'll lose a day's pay (besides the cost of liquids to drown his sorrow).

wIw

I'm reminded of when Crocker was editor of the *Sol.* in that fateful day when August Walquist and myself were attacked by muses, in old 951 W. Madison St.[1] Nothing would do but write a song. August, hemmed in the corner, wrote two choruses that were the direct cause of Samuel Gompers' death—and I hawed in the wings and did the dirty work—three stanzas.

The masterpiece was finished!

"Take it up to Crocker," orders Walquist. "Why, Walquist, has the strain been too great on your brain-pan?" inquires I, in sincere solicitude, "can't we lower it into a waste basket, ourselves?"

"Well, we'll both go up," blurts August.

wIw

Crocker was very nervous that morning after an all night study of economic problems and the participation of too much black coffee to drive the ever creeping slumber away—for those were perilous days and a great responsibility hinged upon our editors. Crocker was keen and alert—as usual. Walquist

---

1 August Walquist was an IWW songwriter and for a period a member of the union's General Executive Board. The address mentioned was the site of an IWW hall, which contained reading rooms.

stood on one side of him; I, on the other—he was seated in the middle (a deucedly awkward position).

"I got a poem for you, Crocker," says I, in my best grave digger voice and funeral-director manner, "care to look at it?"

"Hand her over," groans Crocker, taking his cue from me.

He lookt at it, cleared his throat, twisted his neck and lookt at Walquist (185 lbs), turned his head and lookt at me (5 ft. 11½ inches)[2] "why demmit," says he, "that's better stuff than has been coming up here; take it right down to the printer and tell him that if he don't get that in this issue I'll come down there and kick him all over the place . . ."

So we let him live!

wIw

"There," exclaims Walquist, as we hit the street, "when you've got a really good piece, everybody will admit it."—

"A good piece? How do you know it's good?"—

"Crocker said so."—

"How does Crocker know, he hasn't seen it yet—he merely stared at it for three minutes,"—

"Dammit, I believe you're right, Slim," whispers Walquist, a great flood of understanding lighting his noble face.

But the linotyper did see it and stated that "a rottener piece never went through his machine"—but then, you know how linotypers are—good mechanics and all that—but what do they know about real ART?

Pooh! Nothing—what with lead-poison? Besides, they're bound to be habitually sore because they have to read it—they ain't like me or you that can lift a lid and shove it in the stove—if it doesn't jibe in with our views of true literature.

Industrial Solidarity, 6 February 1929

2 According to the medical examiner's report on his death, this was Slim's actual height. This was above average for the time period, hence Slim here implies (albeit with humor) that he is an imposing figure.

Work versus Ultra Violet

"Work saves U.S. Women from being spoiled."

Isn't that a pretty headline? And true, as a gospel.

They may get humpbacked, of course, and may have to bolster their pretty heads on three pillows when they *lie down for a few hours to rest and spoil.* But what is that when they can set the alarm to arrest the spoiling process, get up and unspoil themselves with a few licks of labor and keep themselves sweet and pure the rest of the day, the same way. But work is kind o' hard on the kidneys—so I got to wondering if ultra-violet rays wouldn't make a good substitute.

I know, one day a butcher gazed into my trustful eyes and sold me two pounds of rotten veal and I thought I was up against it for foul—but, as luck would have it I had a "milk of magnesia" bottle which was blue—naturally I held it up to the sun and let the ultra-violet rays play on the meat.

And do you know that pound and a half of twelve year old steer turned into milk-fed veal of the finest quality, worth sixty five cents a pound of any man's money. . . .

Now, if ultra-violet rays will unspoil veal chops, it stands to reason it will do as much for the women—in case the ladies get fired or laid off—of course they'll have to find a bigger bottle—a carboy—or, dip a K. K. K. uniform into laundry-Blue . . . or a tablecloth.

Undoubtedly unemployed women will spoil—witness the terrible condition of putrefaction in the fashionable society, kept in the royal households:

Here's a princess gone over to Bohemia to study art—under the best medical men the land affords.

A billionaire, overcome by business worries, jumps out of a 49th story window and cures his "dose"[1] with one operation—why germs were splattered against the windows for blocks. How about gland grafting? How about blood transfusions? *Tell me they don't spoil?* Huh! Let's pull the curtain. Let's give no names or dates. Let's print no photos or scenes—sufficient to say, if those unfortunate, unemployed parasites had only thought of a blue magnesia bottle, they would have been completely rejuvenated!

"Work Saves U.S. Women from Being Spoiled."

---

1 Slang for having a sexually transmitted infection, at this time typically syphilis. In another article written in 1929 but not reproduced in this volume, Slim claims to have "locomotor ataxia," which is a loss of coordination of movement caused by syphilis. As is so often the case with Slim's biographical references, it is difficult to determine with certainty if he is being serious. See T-Bone Slim, "Nothing Is Finished but There Is Hope," *Industrialisti,* 3 August 1929.

Not only women, but horses and mules.

Now you take it in a lumber camp, a team of horses that's been laying around the barn since last August doing nothing, gets hi-falluting ideas, kicks out the side of the barn occasionally—just for pastime.

Don't tell me they don't spoil! Showering splinters and twisted horse shoes through the sky-light of the cook-shack! Try to harness them up, and either you or the harness goes to the hospital. . . .

Such is the effect of rich foods and prolonged, virulent unemployment. Part time employment is not so bad. . . .

Now, my point is this:

You may be located at a place where it's next to impossible to find a piece of blue glass (like a lumber camp) and suddenly you start to spoil on one side or the other, all the work is done, what are you gonna do? Kick the side of the barn down? Wouldn't it be better to save a little work and spare yourself the trouble of climbing a high tree or chopping your head off with a grub-hoe?

It's WORK or Ultra-Violet Rays! Nothing else will save you, so they say.

P.S. Of course the regular working class is not so apt to spoil because they, when unemployed, generally abstain from rich foods. As a rule they die a noble, natural death of starvation or commit suicide (which is just as natural but not quite so noble). Whenever the latter happens, the most observant of doctors cannot find the slightest trace of spoilation—such as syphilis, high blood pressure or etcetera.

Industrial Worker, 2 March 1929

Psycholeragising Wealth—and Time

"Wealth isn't all in life."

We know. But it's something!

What else is there?

Wealth of health. Wealth of brains. Wealth of bravery. Wealth of respect and modesty. Wealth of willingness and helpfulness and fellow-feeling. Wealth of sociability, hospitality and tenderness to the stricken and unfortunate.

Wealth of humanity, class-consciousness and solidarity—all wealth.

What else is there?

Why make "cracks" like that without specifying what is, instead of what isn't? Is life to be further complicated, made into a frowning problem, a puzzle and its lines tangled and twisted till they look like a ravenous corkscrew?

"Wealth isn't all in life."

Of course not—bellyache, for instance. Now go on tell us what all is in life.

*

Another Peter came and warmed himself:

"Lost timepieces are never wound again." Haw, haw ha . . . humpf! How about the fellow that finds it? Is he armless?

Can't he wind it with his toes?—or teeth?

Time is never lost and never found—and cannot be exchanged or dealt with. It is stationary. Doesn't come, and doesn't go. Isn't fast and isn't slow. Doesn't fly and doesn't crawl. Doesn't fall—it is every bit as constant as "change" and has less wear and tear.

Mebbe I'm right?

If I am, I'm greatly surprised!

Man does not use time—has no control over time.

Time is the original bull-headed sitting bull—unbudgeabull . . . Rather, time uses and controls man, Man is in the midst of time—time isn't in the midst of man.

When a man says "I didn't have time enough" it's a safe bet that time didn't have man enough—but time is too polite to mention it.

Time needs no alibi—excuse—to wit: "the woman thou gavest me." Man cannot find time because he imagines that time whistles past like an excursion train while he is limping around with a fist full of tools—O MAN!

Many men imagine that yesterday was time.

Nothing of the sort, yesterday was pay day.

Past, present and future are but a crude table of measures man uses in an effort to size up time. "Quarter to Nine," Wednesday, April, 1929, Twentieth century are NOT the NAMES of time.

Time uses no alias.

Huh! "1929," huh—a number!

Awful crust!—they've dressed poor innocent time in stripes—made a convict of him—put a license plate on him—They think they have!

But after all, as I said before, half past three, dog-days, Monday, September, 1895 and stone age are only the suit of clothes we have dressed him in—and a bum fit it is.

But even if poor old "time" is dressed like a scarecrow, under the auspices of mangling mankind, still it is the period under the duration of which we must build our *one big union of genial labor,*—and, I wish to point out, TIME is practically untouched—mebbe one o' the untouchables.

Industrial Worker, 6 April 1929

The Power of Tears

Some time ago in a reckless moment I threatened to weep right in one of our dignified papers—on account of the terrible sufferings of myself and shortage of snus . . . (I see now it can't be done with a leadpencil.)

Many of my kind readers imagine wrongly that I am a merry old soul and that my belly fairly shakes with the violence of my laughter—and rafters tremble . . . Nothing could be wronger.

I'm about as cheerful as a wet blanket or a death sentence in the face of an unspent winter-stake. And my enemies, who know me best, do say that I'm about as lugubrious piece of wreckage it has ever been their misfortune to gaze upon. They're right—whatever that lugubrious means.

I do weep, ladies and gentlemen, in private and public—it don't make any difference to me—that is, when I'm not sulking or scowling and what I mean, when I weep, I weep—none of this suppress grief for me.

I'll have nothing to do with dry grief—when I grieve I want the tears for accompaniment.

Another thing, this "husky" form of crying is about as contemptible piece of wailing as is and, I wish to point out, when sorrow steals over me and sadness fills my soul, I don't start in like a leaky steam pipe or sizzling coffee pot—I bust right out in a full-throated hearty lament. My cries are famous the world over for timbre and resonance. Why, people walk miles just to grab an earful.

I'm writing this very article, uplifting as it is, thru my tears—because I've been severely criticized by hard-boiled fellow workers for tossing my lefthanded harmonies on the air, "broadcasting my woes to an un-sympathetic bunch of unscrupulous scoundrels," as they say; and, naturally I'm persuaded, I must defend myself.

I do most solemnly swear that not only is my crying a noble experiment but a successful one; and a damsite more melodious than half of those busted chords of optimism extolling the virtues of non-existing prosperity and penniless opulence—worshiping at the shrine of that what is not even a bonafide mirage.

I, at least, am sincere!

I, at least, do not attempt to fool myself!

Nothing hypocritical about my voluble emotions—when I weep, I mean it, and I don't mean mebbe.

My tears rise and fall automatically. Now, let me point out, I have a perfect right to weep if I feel like it—nothing in the United States Constitution (as yet) forbidding me the exercising of my vocal chords in tones of deepest distress and agony. . . . But if I laugh, umh—'specially at the wrong time—I'm liable to be locked up as half-wit, be fined for contempt of court (or a hundred other things) and possibly get punched in the face and kicked in the ribs, to boot—for my pains—as a gentle reminder to control my risibilities and excessive mirth.

But if I weep . . . Say! Who's gonna hit a crying man? Who?

Nobody. NO . . . BODY!

Weep it is.

But I don't propose to do all the crying alone.

How would I look circulating among the multitudes, my nose wrinkled, mouth twisted and warped all out of shape and uttering bloodcurdling howls of despair and desperation, all by myself. Not me!

My idea is to step out and organize all the best tear-spillers and militant weepers into a union of grief—"wet front" shall be our slogan[1]—and we shall make the country resound with our wails as it never resounded before—and as it never will resound thereafter.

A wet towel shall be our battle flag and when we wring those flags—towels, I mean—the cities can junk their street sprinklers, for the dust is gonna be laid—in fact, the gutters are gonna run with tears.

Yessir, the country is going wet.[2]

Great big pearls of tears, as big as Bartlett pears, will bounce off our chins and hit the pavement killing forever the fond ambition of many a half-smoked, smoldering Chesterfield and Sluggish Strike.[3]

Weather reports shall read:

"Owing to emotional disturbances, sentimental showers are predicted throughout the Lachrymose States of America today, tomorrow and the next day and the day after . . .

"Great floods are expected in the valley regions—and many may drown in tears. It is feared the brine inherently a part of the flood will kill all the little fishes and bullheads and when the torrents subside the low lands will be strewn with salt herring and pickled pork—a blessing in lieu of the washed-out maize."

I tell you there's gonna be tears what IS tears and wails that won't jell—and any political spellbinder that wants to be heard will have to yell louder than we howl.

You may be sure we'll howl loud enough, for verily these leaky militants, champeen pessimists and weeping geniuses feel as I feel and are unequivocally

---

1 A pun on the communist tactic of seeking a "united front" with other left-wing and anticapitalist groups.

2 This is a play on the country's "going dry" during Prohibition, a time at which those opposed to Prohibition were referred to as "wets."

3 That is, discarded cigarette butts.

committed to the doctrine that brines and whines, if salty and loud enough, will one day emancipate not only the powerful howlers and tear-spillers but the grinning imbecile and pauperized hyena, as well.

Industrial Worker, 13 April 1929

Long Island Sound

"Do you want a state room?" purred the polite purser, sympathetically.

"No sir, I do not—I expect to swim ashore before morning . . ."

Hence it is that I am defying sleep and writing an experimental article just to show folks what a great writer can do when he's dog tired—besides, I do all my best swimming when I'm awake—not that I objected to drowning—drowning is all right in a way—but I most certainly do object to drowning in one of those cubby holes they call state rooms.

When I drown I want lots of room and plenty of water . . .

I see by the paper, "Poet Drowns At Cape Cod"—as good a place as any, and I unhesitatingly recommend that place to Walt Mason and Edgar Guest[1]—why, there you can drown in three different directions not counting straight down—for a poet, he sure showed a live consideration for the feelings of humanity, for which he should be credited and for which the good people will, no doubt, be duly and monumentally grateful. But there is another fly in our blue-ointment—the street lights of Long Island Sound are too far apart—we can't see where we're going—and for the life of me I can't see how those kids up on the pilot-coop can keep the old tub in the wet places—why, I'll swear by the bones of our illustrious ancestors that a couple of times we came near running into a drugstore—I won't say I saw the Gem Safety Razor sign but I most certainly did see the red and green torts in the window and the druggist's bald-pate glistening like an evening star.

Of course, I went up on the cyclone or tornado deck right away and examined the life boats—in fact, it was my idea to "lie down" in one of 'em—purely as a shelter against the wind—I don't want people to think I was stealing a march on the women and children. Unfortunately there was no straw in 'em—nothing but cold, rusty, galvanized iron—and me with rheumatism of the most despicable type.

One of the boats, No. 2, starboard, would have been an ideal crib to flop in, it oscillated in its "V" blocks the tune of the vibrations of the ship—it soon would have lulled my dull senses to sleep, but then!! a dreadful dread gripped my vitals—sposing the "V" blocks have chafed the old iron sides thru? And if I flounder in there I might fall thru one of the holes?

Lord have mercy—and its rusty keel looks as if some one has squirted tobacco juice all over it!—if the life-boat looks like that, in the open—I wonder

---

1 Mason was a Canadian American newspaper columnist, prose poet, and humorist whose work was syndicated to around two hundred newspapers in the early decades of the twentieth century. Guest was a British American poet based in Detroit whose sentimental works were widely syndicated.

how the bottom of the ship looks? And I wonder and wonder what a steamboat inspector looks like.

Has anyone ever seen one?

WHEN—FOR GOD'S SAKE! AND WHERE!

P.S. Let the inspection department send me a check for this month—I saw in ten minutes what has taken INSPECTORS years to MISS.

Industrial Worker, 17 August 1929

The Taste That Tells

Never again!

I swear by everything holy that never again will I enter a cafeteria and pay extra for the privilege of scabbing on the unemployed waiters and waitresses by the way of self-service.

I confess I've done this very thing in my muddle-headedness and I can only hope and pray the waitresses and waiters will forgive and forget my thoughtlessness.

Can you imagine me, a horn-headed freight-handler, trying to juggle those fragile and elusive dishes, trays, half-cups of creosote and chicory—me, whom some nature, in its outraged and begrudgeful moments, so admirably fitted for the lifting of heavy objects and the prying loose of tight materials?

Why, a bull-rhinoceros in a china shop would have nothing on me!

Can you imagine the bantam-weight waiter with his delicate fingers grabbing a hold of my two wheeled truck and self-servicing himself to a row of wealth and affluence? You can? Yes, and you may as well imagine further—those sixteen sacks of cement on that truck would blister his patties, break his back, explode one or both kidneys and bankrupt half the hospitals in the country.

Well, that being that, the fact that I'm able to handle both jobs is not a good reason for hogging his job—and an injustice for the simple reason that he cannot supplant me on my regular job. In other words when I put him on the bum he stays there and gets nothing because I'm not getting enough from freight-handling to help him—and furthermore, the additional expenditure attendant to said self-service weakens my financial standing to such an extent that I can't help him—All in all, the best way for me to do is to quit self-service and give myself and him a better break—and if I must carry food to my mouth with fingers contaminated with that form of insidious scabbery, it is better for me to quit eating and run-in a streak of lean—it might clear my head.

I'm not saying self-service autocratically shunts the waitresses into the shadow of disapproval—you might suspect I have inside knowledge—so I will merely murmur, "self-service" takes their bread and butter away, and in a very clumsy manner.

Industrial Worker, 14 September 1929

Put a Head on It

Being a shrewd politician, I've repeatedly been requested to define the magic terms "Conservative, Liberal and Radical"—well, now, altho I don't want to make a habit of this, I shall humor those nosey gentlemen for the once for the sake of the others that may get snooty on those problems.

But I shall must needs use an illustration—are you ready?

"Liberal" (being the hardest to define in so far as the Liberals themselves don't know what they are) shall come first—

A Liberal is a man of moderation. He believes that if an automobile hits you it should slow down a little, partly skin you and, of course, knock you down and askew on soft asphalt—not concrete because, as they say, "the coarse, rough surface of the concrete might remove too much of your complexion and force you to flash your birth-certificate to draw your pay"—if you've got anything coming. In other words, they want you scratched up just right—no more, no less—just the right number of bones broken and only a few teeth knocked out or in—they're not so bad.

Conservatives believe, "if we're in the business of knocking 'em down we may as well do a good job of it and plaster their hide against the pearly gates with one wallop and put 'em out of their misery with one operation"—it has its merits.

But the radical, he of the low-pressure "Americanism," as they say, he doesn't believe in being hit by the car at all—why, he doesn't want the car even to rub against his leg as it purrs by—he wants a clean miss. What's the matter with him!

Is he trying to take all the fun out of spins?—out of politics, I mean? What's the use of being in politics if you ain't allowed to skin the other fellow or rub his fur the wrong way every so often?

No use at all.

Those several beliefs makes for disputes among the leading disputers of our fair land and to drown 'em out scientists got together and invented the radio, never thinking those cheerful windbags would grab it and use it for their foul and dastardly ends.

Anyhow, all that hellobulloo is extra punishment for our many and intricate sins of omission.

Industrial Solidarity, 9 October 1929

1930

Where Lies Safety?

Lies, Lies, Lies—?

Ten perished in Pathe Film fire;[1] 9 "check-out" in Auburn prisoners' revolt[2]—peace hath its casualties no less than war.

The several that didn't get scorched, toasted, broiled, baked or roasted in the film fire got their picture in the papers. . . .

Now let us see the picture of 1600 odd prisoners that didn't get so much as a scratch in the "riot" at Auburn. . . .

Deucedly unsafe to be an actor.

Imprisonment too has its drawbacks. Guess I'll look for a job handling nitroglycerine or teaching rattlesnakes to do the hula-hula.

Man isn't safe no more, nowhere! I expect to see the "Peace" commission[3] warm up words and cut each other's throat—in the near future.

Unless a man is too skilful, self-destruction appears to be the safest occupation.

Even admitting that many of the actors were "ham" that doesn't signify the "deah public" prefers its actors fried. Every man to his taste however, frinstance parboiled, raw or desiccated.

It's now up to the actors—the law already recognizes them a poor fuel and says "burn no actors except when protected by automatic sprinklers"—some consolation—it's now up to the actors.

Why not join the I. W. W. and smoke out a few of those stinkers that benefit—yea, unto the millions—from your singes and jeopardize of your deah, deah public?

Haiti: Twenty marines fired 250 shots and hit three people among the hundreds present[4]—not bad at all for peace-time markmanship but, nevertheless, the fire hazards of the flaming still hold a high percentage in the column of risks.

---

1 A reference to the fire that occurred on 10 December 1929 at the Pathé film studios on Park Avenue in New York, in which ten people died and nineteen were injured. The fire could have been avoided if the company had not appealed an ordinance, passed six months earlier, that required it to install sprinklers.

2 The overcrowded and aging state prison in Auburn, New York, saw two uprisings in 1929. During the first, which took place in July, weapons were seized from the arsenal, buildings and shops were set on fire, and four prisoners escaped. The second, in December, saw guards and the warden taken hostage and eight prisoners and a staff member killed.

3 This is seemingly a reference to either the 1929 League of Nations Preparatory Disarmament Commission or the 1928 Commission on the Coordination of Efforts for Peace.

4 On 6 December 1929, U.S. Marines opened fire on approximately 1,500 Haitians protesting at Les Cayes against the continuing military occupation of their country, which had begun in 1915. Thousands of rebels had been killed under U.S.-controlled

Even had there been only three people on the island and our brave marines turned in a perfect score, the 250 bullets is quite a lot of lead and augurs well for the general safety and well being of the Haitians—for I reason that if a man successfully dodges 83 bullets he's got no kick coming if the odd one-third of a bullet punctures his expectancy of life and lays him 'longside the immortals—a far more glorious death than being burnt alive by the film companies.

But what of it? What am I beefing about?

What's my argument?

My argument is that those film fires are the "old form of fun," most thoroughly and unnecessarily cruel—death comes too slowly—and if I had my pick as between laying my life on the altar pyre of pictures or electrocution, I would select the chair (even if denied chloroform)—laugh that off.

One of those deaths is in retaliation, for something or other: preconceived, intentional, sudden and complete (even without chloroform or laughing gas).

The other is unintentional, accidental (coupled to neglect) leisurely, a condition of dying by inches.

One a death from shock!

The other a bed of pain!

Well, what of it?

Who cares?

Death in the chair is an act of war.

Death in the pyre is an act, tho indirect, of the same war—the classes at struggle.

What of it?

Nothing much, only, the out and out, direct, war "tax" is a pretty peaceful performance compared to the "accidents" of camouflaged peace.

Both are preventable—if desired; lest death be a pleasure—a major amusement.

The folks can have anything they want—if they have something that harmonizes not with their heart's desire, it was conferred upon them without consultation—if it offends their spleen they can "scrap" it.

Point is: they can get what they want.

*

Spurious hundred dollar bills are in circulation. Let 'em circle—it worries me none! A cold sweat strikes me only when they counterfeit quarters and dimes.

All hundred dollar bills look spurious to me—I have no doubt. One of 'em should be put on exhibition so the millions of workers could see one and

---

martial law, but the new pressure this massacre brought saw American occupation end five years later. U.S. business, military, and diplomatic interests would continue to dominate the nation, however.

mebbe be encouraged to put in a few extra hard licks of hard labor while under its spell, in Satan's name.

No, fellow workers: what's the use of lying about it? You know damned well that you never saw a hundred at one look, to say nothing about a bill of that description—why? I, myself, as highly learned as I am, never studied any further than twenty—and decimals.

P.S. I'll modify a part of that "snapper": you saw a hundred all right—pennies.

Industrial Solidarity, 8 January 1930

The Dizzy Race

It takes all my spare and sparse moments argying it out with the shining lights of organized fiction sometimes called "the press" and then, and again—"Journalism." Said luminaries upon special request by very special people toss their hats in the air revealing an imposing area of bald pate and screaming: "Look-it the progress WE have made! Hear ye! Lookit all OUR solid comforts! OUR wealth! Glorious institutions! Influence! Power!" etc., ad lib. infinitum, the same old gag in the same old way as barren of thought as the day it was born.

I've looked.

I saw millionaires of yesterday jumping from skyscraper windows and penniless paupers drowning their sorrows in the lakes and rivers of our fair land—and I got to wondering, wondering:

Are those suicides a fair indication of the great blessings we are "enjoying" or just about to enjoy?

Let's take this matter up, editor.

Here's a man, Mr. Abraham Appis, 38, a tailor, discouraged over failure of his business, killed himself to-day, but he first thought of his wife and five children.

He tiptoed through their apartment, 463 E. 171st St., the Bronx, and flung open every window.

Assured that the rooms were well ventilated, Appis locked himself in the bathroom, placed a tube in his mouth and turned on the gas-jet.

Lena, 31, his wife, found him this morning.

I suppose the champions of "AS IS," and apologists extraordinary, will let go the lid again and screetch: "Modern conveniences!"

Let's take this matter up, editor.

Mr. Appis tiptoed his way to open the windows . . .

Now supposing Abe's toes had been weak from over-starvation and had dropt his arches or landed on his heels, waking up his wife? The suicide would have been all off, wouldn't it, and the poor man would have had to put in another long day and balance of sleepless night against his will and better judgement.

Wouldst the apologists call a suicide, that hinges on strong arches a convenience? I don't.

A time comes in every man's life under capitalism when he feels a change is necessary—imperative, acceptable or tolerable. The individualist immediately looks to suicide for a way out and leaves things exactly "As IS" for other misguided suicides to follow.

What is this, a program of self-destruction labeled PROGRESS?

That's about the size of it and the forecast is: continued cold and cloudy.

We haven't seen a thing yet. Just wait. It's due to be a national pastime. . . . That's why I say it's an outrage for society to expect its members to pull off the "Big Idea" with poor tools, appliances, such as gas hose, razor blades and bailing wire.

I do not propose to rest till an electric chair graces every home, boarding house and camp—public chairs at public squares and missions, (nickel in the slot affairs, at convenient distances) for the down and outs and "kicked outs"—anyone will hand 'em a nickel for that purpose.

Chairs in colleges should proportionate population of professors.

Death must be placed within reach of all!

Industrial Solidarity, 5 February 1930

A Ghost Story

Today I passed a public school at recess time. Children (most of 'em) were playing tag, white and colored—no color line was drawn and I got to wondering if this nation will be more colorful in years to come.

My prayer was answered: Only a few paces farther I passed an office, "Automobile Insurance," "Let us take care of your troubles," "Money to Loan" . . .

I glanced in and there on the "mourners' bench" sat an old lady, deathly pale. I figured: a long delayed square feed would do her no harm.

Color? I despair of ever seeing color in this nation, or in that little schoolgirl spending her recess playtime, O so carefully, shaking crumbs of something from an oh so small sack. . . .

Somebody is to blame and that somebody has no shame.

Philadelphia's business, always conservative, cautious, is at a dead standstill—but so is New York, for that matter.[1] Upon the waterfront saw three liners, Berkshire and a couple lesser evils and gang after gang of longshoremen waiting, waiting . . . what are they waiting for? For the heavens to open and dump some bread on their heads?

For the first time I was regarded suspiciously—as if I, poor me, could deprive the whole "mob" of their jobs. Why, I wanted only one.

Such are the muchly heralded signs of prosperity. Yesterday saw first spring bird. Made up my mind the bird is demented—what the bird thought of me is not for me to say.

This morning I've got a date with a master,[2] 8:30—visions of great wealth flood my soul.

He fails to show up.

There was great mourning in our camp until an ageing, working mechanic started broadcasting his woes. . . . For 12 years he had worked in the place—week before last he was sent home for two days—last week he was turned back six times—this week, Monday, he is told to go home and, if he has a chance, grab another job.

He did succeed in landing another job, beginning tomorrow—that explains how I came to eat his lunch, one orange and three chicken sandwiches.

All signs of prosperity.

Industrial Solidarity, 7 May 1930

[1] A reference to the Great Depression, which had begun the previous year.

[2] That is, for a job.

Looking Things Over

The greatest laugh in this country is the cry "our communists are imported from Russia."

Poppycock!

Russia isn't shipping out any communists, she needs all she's got; in fact she's in the market for more—caviar is what she exports—and anthracite.

I'm reminded in this connection of a motto I beheld in a "gentlemen's room"–in Texas longhorn country: "step up close; don't kid yourself."

Uncle Samuel may as well quit kidding himself and herald it to the world at large that he's the father of those "commies"; they're his children, his very own, strictly home-made and that they'll outgrow their foaming propensities.

*

"The exxemthraorthie myxxxigger of the Linotype failed to function for a while this week."—*Rexford News.*

Was he drunk, again?

*

Pay no attention to my ravings, it's merely a way I have of saving the lives of the parasites—ungrateful rogues they are. I don't want to see them killed—I'd rather see them nursing a ball and chain across the landscape—and were I not to write these cheerful items from time to time the good people would lose their minds and the carnage would be terrific—something I can't bear. This other way we can hope they will maintain their well-known equanimity and dress the parasites in hobbles,[1] or tether them out in the pastures.

Industrial Worker, 12 July 1930

1 Hobbles are devices used to tether the legs of horses and sometimes cattle to keep them from roaming. Hobbling is less common today than it was in the past, at least in the United States and Europe.

"Sundownitis"

York, Nebraska, "Hoosiers-Up" on Slim

In the famed state of feather beds, Nebraska, where this poor author ruined his kidneys sleeping in the boss' private chamber, in the front room, downstairs, if you please, while the boss chased his rising generation, considerate sons, admirable daughters and good but hefty wife up to the attic (where he followed them) to swelter in the midsummer night's balmy breezes . . . ah, a touch of real humanitarian consideration on his part; no doubt due to his Germanic origin and training. Although his wife formerly was an up-stater from New York, her cooking was marvelous; the only flaw in her art was a slight miscarriage she had in the making of ice cream—a thing that very easily can be overlooked in this age of phoney phreezers. Looking at those meals I made up my mind the Kaiser wasn't such a bad man after all, and that if he starts another war I'm afraid I might be persuaded to pull my punches and die the hero that I am—it wouldn't seem right to slaughter off a nation of good cooks. Well, that's all right, but this same State has within her borders what the boys call "sundown towns,"[1] a very apt term meaning nature's "throwback towns"; among them we might mention Norfolk, York and Fremont (Hastings isn't so bad, but slipping)—Nebraska, of course, is conscious of those weak points in her make-up but owing to her construction is unable to get rid of them and lives in the hope those unfortunate towns will outgrow their mental infirmities and aberrations or hallucinations. . . .

I had the misfortune recently to get off a perfectly good train (free lunch included, silver mounted toppings, but lunch just the same) to find myself in York, Nebr.—darn the luck—the town looked all right, too.[2]

Me, directly from the City of New York on the shores of the turbulent Atlantic, a city of no mean proportions—where I used to stretch my great frame upon the sidewalk, piers or bank-portals and where the city ordinances had to conform with my comforts on sultry nights—where the populace defied upstart patrolmen to make any changes in their mode of spending the night—and where, too, patrolmen consider it the height of folly to disturb a sleeping

[1] Localities that passed ordinances, typically curfews, against communities of color. The effect was to create racial segregation. Slim's use of the term indicates that it could be extended to describe places employing exclusionary practices against other targets, such as white hobos.

[2] At this point, the Great Depression had forced Slim to leave New York City and go on the road again in search of work, despite his age (forty-eight) and imperfect health. He would return to New York again after a few years.

person; a deed so foul that no lower animal will attempt; a peace so profound that neither snake nor tiger will violate.

But in York, Nebr., I had with considerable effort prepared myself a bed that was suitable to my "form of build"; in a box car of course and probably as sanitary as any place in that immaculate village—Hardly had my snores started vibrations in the rafters when in marches three big burlies of the law and apologized for the intrusion but invited me to spend the balance of the night in the town's calaboose. Hm. My rest was ruined; my sleep seduced.

Being very broadminded, 'twas easy for me to see that the officers of the law, paid for being awake nights, saw no wrong in disturbing people tired out by the toils of the day before—a bear would have lumbered on, about his own business; a snake would have waited till morning to sting me. . . .

I guess that is what the boys mean by "sundown towns"; ace in the hole towns, where hospitality is so nil that workers carry their lunches in their coat sleeves for hundreds of miles coming into town—an "ace in the hole"—in preparation against the welcome to come.

I feel sincerely sorry for the good state of Nebraska because of those towns but, can offer no cure for that condition—in fact, I think it incurable and that it will fester and contaminate the whole state.[3]

Industrial Solidarity, 29 July 1930

[3] This article continued on a second page, but unfortunately we have been unable to track down an extant copy.

It Do Seem So—

"No man is wiser for his learning. Wit and wisdom are born with a man."—Selden.[1]

Oh what a bitter pill, Mr. Selden!

A scissorbill packs his head with learning, only to find himself a scissorbill still?

Oh what a wallop! Mercy! Help! Police!!

I cannot agree with Mr. Selden right off the bat on that proposition because of the accepted interpretation given to wit and wisdom in the late years.

But then again, once we admit that environment is a factor in learning we must conclude the present day wise heads learnt to live without labor right on their mother's breast and are following that line of endeavor throughout their life.

I don't know what this country is coming to—what with Heywood Broun[2] running for congress and Henrik L. Mencken[3] getting married—but it's going to be something terrible, TERRIBLE. Will Rogers had better make no bones about it but announce his forthcoming suicide right away.[4]

*

---

[1] John Selden, a seventeenth-century English jurist, scholar, and polymath.

[2] Sportswriter, drama critic, and columnist Heywood Broun unsuccessfully ran as a Socialist candidate for Congress in 1930. He campaigned for the release of various political prisoners and left the *New York World* in 1928 due to censorship of a piece he wrote about Sacco and Vanzetti. He was later expelled from the Socialist Party for appearing alongside communists at a rally over the Scottsboro case. He helped found the Newspaper Guild and was its first president, serving from 1933 until his death in 1939.

[3] Henry Louis (H. L.) Mencken was a highly influential writer who began his career in 1899. He worked as a journalist, critic, and satirist for various newspapers and magazines until his death in 1948. Mencken wrote a number of books, including a series called *American Language* that included an entry about T-Bone Slim. He also founded and edited the influential journal *American Mercury*. His beliefs drew on aspects of Friedrich Nietzsche's philosophy and included atheism and opposition to democracy. Having derided marriage in his columns, he attracted headlines with his betrothal in 1930.

[4] Will Rogers, a member of the Cherokee Nation, started out in circus work before becoming a famous vaudeville actor in the 1900s. He began working in film in 1918 and became a major star, successfully transitioning from silent to sound movies. He penned humorous syndicated newspaper columns from 1922 onward that reached an audience of up to forty million readers. He also wrote books and appeared on numerous radio programs.

Native sons at last are getting "a break." The other day I was sorely in need of a job to get the kinks out of my muscles. I made judicious inquiries in that direction and rolled up my sleeves for all the world to see . . .

"Do you live around here?" inquires the employer, beaming all over, his eye glued to my bulging muscles.

Like a damned fool I blurted out, "No." (I should have invited him up to the house to meet the missus.)

"I'm awful, awful sorry," he assured me, "we are hiring only home grown talent."

My jaw drops.

Damnit, I had to walk out, way out, to the cemetery and read the headlines till I found a name that had been dead just about long enough to fit me.

When I came back I was a different man. A farmer hired me right away and said he was well acquainted with my folks—what he didn't know I told him.

I tell you a little walk like that benefits not only the health but financial standing. Even if it is to the graveyard.

Industrial Worker, 16 August 1930

A Peach of a Story

It seems the peach crop must be destroyed so as to keep the prices from spoiling in cans—couldn't they give them to the paupers in the country poor farms to go with that yearly egg?

Of course not—what am I thinking about—the system would go kerplunk.

Recently I was accused of being "smarty"—that's all right but pay no attention to them people—I'm capable of being worse: when I left for the harvest this year I thought I was the whole cheese and half the macaroni but I soon found out there are other people in this organization—I ain't so much just now. Mistakes like that will happen to the most careful mathematicians.

Last night a perfectly respectable citizen was overwhelmed by a series of errors and disgraced himself intellectually something scandalous. . . .

I was in his garden carrying on some scientific demonstrations—not experiments—removing potatoes from the vines and replanting the vines; my theory being that if the operation is done on a moonless night nature will replace the spuds I carry away.

I had considerable trouble convincing him on that score—indeed it was his opinion I was trying to put him in a poor house. What would I want to put him in the poor house for, an entire stranger to me—he reasons like a fish!

Industrial Solidarity, 9 September 1930

T-Bone Slim Takes to the Air, or Saved in the Nick of Time

A Thrilling Story of the Harvest Fields

Instead of "with a car," our famed author is going to make next year's harvest in an airplane; he's going to buy one of those condemned "Jennies," name it "The Cream of the Tartars" and show some of those pole-to-pole vaulters how to get over the country—I'd have done this sooner but I didn't want to discourage Colonel Lindbergh (a friend of mine—Charlie, I call him—both of us practically driven out of Little Falls, Minn.).[1]

God only knows where I'll get the money to buy that machine and it may not be good policy to question me too closely afterwards inasmuch as I have a terrible temper when fully aroused.

I'm telling the citizens of Rolla, N. D. all about it in advance.

A speck appears on the horizon; farmers are searching the box cars for the harvest hands that starved to death last fall; grain is all cut down and nobody present to shock it and thresh it; 37 farmers commit suicide and the town's leading banker sneaks off to Canada in the excitement, by way of the Indian Reservation, Turtle Mountains.

The gloom grows thicker—but just as the gloom is thickest, that speck grows bigger and bigger and even as the desperate farmers are getting ready to run, or pray, there is a blueish streak in the atmosphere and the great plane hurtles thru it seven miles a minute. . . .

"Saved! Saved!" a great cry arose, "It's The Cream of Tartars come to save us!"

Sixteen women faint, ninety-two kids crawl in under the five elevators for safety and the managers of I. G. A., Red Owl and Red and White stores head a mighty procession to the airdrome south of town.

"The Cream of Tartars circles the county three times, noses down and alights in the multitudes . . ."

---

1 Charles Lindbergh was an aviator whose fame derived from his achievement in making the first nonstop solo transatlantic flight, from New York to Paris, in 1927. His celebrity further increased with the kidnapping and murder of his son five years later, the notoriety of which led Lindbergh and his family to move to Europe, where they lived from 1935 to 1939. Upon their return to the United States, Lindbergh became an ardent opponent of American involvement in World War II and served as the public face of the isolationist America First Committee, although he would fight in the war once America joined the conflict. He was a white supremacist and in some quarters was suspected of Nazi sympathies, the latter accusation being something that he denied.

I was just going to tell about the handshaking and toast drinking when a citizen speaks up:

"Slim, you better get yourself a Ford next year; we ain't going to let you sail no Jinny over our heads—you might fall and hit one of us."

"Fall? Well, what difference does that make to you—if you don't starve to death this winter you'll be so weak by harvest time that you won't give a damn which way you get killed.—Just so it happens thoroughly."

"That's so too, Slim, but I wasn't worrying about myself—I was afraid you might be injured and all that grain would rot."

"I never thought of that," I had to confess, "mebbe I better get a Ford."

Industrial Worker, 13 September 1930

Elastic Transportation

The nearest approach to a covered wagon is a 1930 model freight train—a wheat train. Only yesterday I had occasion to observe a freight train in full blossom, whizzing (not wheezing) along at the terrific speed of 45 miles in 6½ hours. It was loaded from here far into next county with car-boxes and it intrigued me greatly to discover the wherefore of loading those engines down so heavily. After considerable brain work I did propose the shrewd R. R. Co. had resolved to string them out behind the engine in such numbers so as to prevent the high-life engineer from picking up the speed required to pound those rotten box-cars to pieces.

"Wrong again, Slim, as usual," groans a fellow passenger, "the accommodative railroad has strung those box-cars out that way in a desperate effort to give each individualistic harvesthand a private car to ride so they won't have to associate with their fellow mortals and split punk with 'em."

Dumb as I am, I could see the logic of his oration and did forthwith absolve the railroad of all selfish motives—but nonetheless I protest the action of the honorable railroad on the grounds of the delay occasioned in the transporting of the grain from the field to the hungry mouths and hungrier stomachs of free born, full-blooded American taxpayers. I protest on the grounds of the women and children and babes who have been standing open-mouthed waiting for a month and mouthful of durum and mustard seeds. Those mouths should be the first consideration of every right thinking railroad and it should be against the law to provide private box-cars for harvest hands for verily, if they are too individualistic to organize and ride the compartments and cushions, and if they still persist in the demand for privacy, condemn them to ride the rods. . . .

Aside from that, the service is unsatisfactory and even the most amiable of scissors are beginning to lament and complain most bitterly. Undoubtedly the service will get worse next year and the laments accordingly more profound so I may be entirely within reason to suppose the harvesthand next year will circumvent much grief by riding one of those guaranteed, 1920 model, used cars, price $17.50 including crank-twister and fan-belt. No doubt, too, "those ferocious" I. W. W.'s will go in the market for sedans as an improvement on sandals—I'm informed by malicious minded scandal-mongers "the terrible tempered wobs caught up on all their walking this year." I believe it—if they walked at all, it was too much and according to that they are entitled to ride next year—I'm telling you.

I hope I may not be considered sacrilegious for suggesting that next year's drive be put entirely upon rubber and depend no more on the erratic service of evil-minded railroads.[1] Exhibit: Any railroad that locks its toilets and installs spring-faucets over washstands (requiring two men to operate in the event one man's face is sooty) is evil-minded enough to put square wheels on all its rolling stock. I'm not telling that "harvest on rubber" is for the best, I'm merely telling—I'd like to see it tested.

Industrial Worker, 20 September 1930

[1] Migratory workers, including IWW members, had long ridden trains illegally. IWW members and delegates were known to deny train travel to nonmembers, thus enforcing an "800-mile picket line" that largely removed those willing to undermine conditions and solidarity. The efficacy of this tactic decreased as the automobile became the dominant form of transport in the 1920s and the IWW was unable to develop a successful strategy for recruiting "auto tramps."

A Survey

These immortal words are not being read by unorganized men but by organized men. For fifteen years I've been talking industrial unionism to industrial unionists—hallfuls of wobs do the same to one another.

Not much percentage in that!

The grin dries up—what are you going to do about it? And shall "the great one" continue preaching emancipation to the emancipated?

We'll let that matter ride and offer a few praises for the damnable system:

Up till today, noon, I have missed no meals—a marvel of this here workless and supposed to be eatless age.

The clothes I am wearing are too large for me—conclusive proof I did not get 'em from a smaller man.

I take great pride in announcing this publicly, altho conscious of the fact that smaller men are better fighters—let my reputation suffer.

Six short weeks ago I was a well-to-do working man. Today I am—what I am.

Six short weeks ago I raised a beautiful bunch of callouses on my hands—I've got 'em yet.

Four weeks I have been busted! Of an evening when I soften my pillow by crossing my hands under my head, the callouses hurt my delicate scalp.

Kind reader do you get my point? Why is it that the wages I received have not stayed by me as long as the callouses? Isn't there an injustice somewhere hereabouts?

Busted as I am, I'm most heartily ashamed of those callouses and have tried to peel them off.

Oh well, time heals all wounds and welts.

Industrial Worker, 4 October 1930

Measured Tread

Conditions must be very bad when a fount of perpetual joy like myself starts dripping bitter tears and filling the ambient atmosphere with wails of hopping-anguish.

A batchelor, who no doubt experiences a certain revulsion against things as they are, un-burdens his soul thusly: "Before I would raise a kid to go through what I am going through I would shoot him dead."

"What! Would you shoot a baby," interposes the clown of the bunch, "and deny him all the pleasures of childhood?"

"Well, no—that is, I'd let him have his fun—but after that—," What?

He paused and did not indicate just when the lad would cease to be and I got the notion the thought he was dealing with was father of another thought: "Chloroform them at the age of 45 years."

A Dutchman, discouraged, works himself into a destructive mood and roars:

"Gott dammit, if I had a forty-five?"

"If you had a forty-five, Dutch, what would you do?"

"I'd blow my gott damn head off," screams Dutch almost bereft of his senses.

"No need to do that, Dutch, I've got snuff." (I saw he was out of snuff.)

He took a chew and his eyes brightened visibly—everything once again was hunky-dory. It's a good world after all.

*

Across the way, in Minneapolis, Father Dooley is holding forth for Jesus Christ and passing out real, genuine bread to the hungry listeners—bread is still the staff of life and it seems religion with all its modern development has been unable to make of faith its substitute—no meat is trusted with the chunk of bread lest it put faith in "the shade" altogether.

*

In the sumptuous 10-cent eating houses the none too clean and none too learned oracles discuss revolution and the proper way to make "those ignorant workers" toe the scratch. "Starve 'em out, that's the way Russia done," and other "valuable" information.

"But," says I, "suppose THEY take a notion to starve US out, me and you—what then? They might mistake us two for ignoramuses and chop off our lunch, you know"—

A deadly fear gripped his vitals and he hastily tossed the rest of the hash into his mouth. . . .

What was I doing in such a place?

Has it come to this? Our great author was—nossir, nossir, not by a darnsite—our great author wasn't eating there; he was working there. Got to work some place.

*

I have no doubt there is a revolution on tap; that a leaven, ferment, foment is working to that end and that it will be premature, precipitant, unorganized and retroactive . . . as are all unorganized movements.

At this time I am not able to decipher the identity of the parties that are about to wish a revolution upon an innocent people and I am not greatly concerned, for verily if the people fall for it I'll preach their funeral sermon and use the kindest words I can find.

*

True, the capitalist system is plunging headlong into dissolution, inevitable end and will finally fall into the discard; but that does not mean the engineers cannot manipulate that machine and bring on a panic ahead of time and stampede a trusting people into an artificial dilemma—

No? Is that so? You mean to say the egg shell cannot be cracked before the chick is fully developed—well sir, I'd have you know last summer I cracked and ate-up eggs that were developed very little. They tell me, too, it's impossible to eat an egg that has experienced a certain amount of development—I believe it, and it explains why my Ma used to grab a persistent setting-hen and cool its "setter" in a tub of water.

Of course, I do not know the nature of this impending revolution. I can only speculate as to its origin and, if it's anything like I think it is, it would be better for it to die young like the child in the forepart of this article.

It may be another one of those imported things, shipped in from some country that had an overproduction of revolutions—such things are possible; instance the Australian ballot-system and women-suffrage. Revolutions are now a commodity, can be bought and sold ready-made or made to order—social intercourse permits of that much leeway—either kind or several kinds, depending wholly how you like 'em, straight or mixed.

At the present time, if not at all times, several countries in Europe, alone, stand to benefit by a revolution in America—it would put them on their feet nicely and be a paying proposition from their viewpoint—assumption being, a mechanical "revo." is now just finished and another one impossible.

A revolution conceived in Wall Street would find hard sledding for those reasons and be further inconvenienced by having an angular twist applied to the "street" Jiu Jitsu by the strapping racketeers that favor our land with their presence.

It is said the bourgeoisie will start a revolution and discontinue the age old custom of "good morning, sir; howdydo, sir thank you, sir" and that it will be an informal affair. The tired business man will—oh shucks. "Coo-Coo Klan[1] will revolt"—How interesting! Ex-service will go on a jamboree, yea? Unemployed will assault the bread wagons? Odd Fellows, Baptists, bricklayers and bums will all hold a private revolution of their own?

Let me tell you, nothing like that is going to happen—*nobody is going to do nothing for nobody.*

Join the I. W. W. and do away with the things that make you revolt. . . .

That act in itself is revolution—and revelation.

Industrial Worker, 18 October 1930

---

[1] That is, the Ku Klux Klan.

A Touching Story

Sad as my situation is, I could make my pen run with tears—but why cry over spilt millions? Let's laff it off and save our tears for a situation that really needs a good wetting-down.

Tears will of course stir up sympathy (the more sonorous the sobs the greater the sympathy) but let me point out sympathy is one of the hardest things to digest known to contemporary and contemptuous science—it just lays and lays on the stomach like a hen over an ivory doorknob—so what good is it?

As a garment it is out of date and went out of style with Adam and Eve; it is worse than porous-knit underwear, and stops the north winds but very damn little.—A little cheese-cloth wrapped around the ribs is a far better windbreak (not that I'm boosting limburger-nets for everyday wear, or running down the burlaps and ginghams).

Besides, were a man to prance down Hennepin Ave[1] dresst in nothing but sympathy the constables and gendarmeries would lay violent hands upon him and invite the lunacy-commissars to sit upon him. Why I've seen otherwise sensible fly-cops[2] cast covetous eyes at MY bulky form lurching down the boulevard, fully dressed (up to and including four shirts and a superannuated overcoat). I said four shirts and I mean it AND I mean to keep them on me AND I'd advise any man that has a shirt to stay inside it—my motto is "keep your shirt on, Slim."

Nay, we will not dress up in sympathy yet awhile—at least not until sympathy is made from more substantial goods than parrot-palaver.

"I'm sorry, O, so sorry" is NOT the whole truth. He is not sorry at all—he is *going to be* sorry, sooner or later.

But we will not make a song of it.

Some day I shall write a novel about the human habitat, *House of Sympathy*—how the lord and master froze stiff as a herring, in the wintertime and was roasted to a blister in the summer months (I reveal this much, of the novel), fully convinced that I am the only man in this world capable of writing that novel and if the others grab the idea they'll look like monkeys after I get mine done—I'd write it this afternoon but the damn pencil keeps breaking off all the time.

Yessir, sympathy is the phoneyest kind of weather-boarding and as a plaster it is a fly screen minus the netting.

A man would be falling down into the cellar all the time without benefit of stairs to break the fall; for verily, stairs of sympathy drop a man faster than a dog drops a hot cigar butt. A rose under a different title smells just as sweet.

1 A major downtown street in Minneapolis, Minnesota.

2 Slang for plainclothes or undercover police officers.

With or without sympathy pork chops is pork chops to a hungry man.

A rose with a thorn is still a rose.

With or without a "bawl-out" pork chops is pork chops.

Sympathy or denunciation do not alter the nature of pork chops—it takes onions or garlic. I'm not saying sympathy is useless. Sympathy benefits the sympathizer (as much as such fallen creature can be benefitted without complete reconstruction—reincarnation, a general re-conditioning, you know what I mean).

Sympathy is very hard to define, to gauge—no table of measure or rule has yet been stumbled on by science to accurately compute or describe that "finer feeling"—thus it frequently happens a hungry hobo has sardines for breakfast instead of grapefruit, shredded wheat and ham and eggs.

Recently a complaint was lodged with me against a parasite who practically refused to "stand and deliver,"[3] as the saying goes, when approached on the delicate matter of ham and eggs, by a starving scotchman:

"Why should I help you?" moans the parasite, seeking knowledge.

Now, as a public sympathizer, it is entirely within my province to take cognizance of the alarmingly increasing number of complaints and lay down a law of procedure in all such cases wherein the matter is gone out of hand—nobody can gainsay the matter is out of joint when "the prospect" says, "why should I help you?"—the answer is:

"Dear sir, I know 57 reasons why you should not help me, I know them all, I've given this matter much study; but I also know 999 reasons why you should help me—but let us not make this a matter of debate, 'no' or 'yes' is sufficient; debate the matter with somebody who has a full stomach—excuse me, I'm in a hurry."

Keep your shirt on!

Industrial Worker, 25 October 1930

[3] That is, give money to someone begging, expressed as if the begging person is committing highway robbery.

On Popular Sanitation

Am not feeling so good; I'm sick, that's the word—but I guess a man has a right to be sick if he wants to. A man has certain inalien-rights such as strife, tribulation, pursuit of sappiness and among these we find sickness—a man can be just as sick as he damn pleases without offending the sacred statues; for which heaven be praised. That is one "right" not yet taken away from us.

It is early as yet to start celebrating my illness—I may change my mind and become as one of perfect health; altho, I admit, I've been tempted to throw myself away or feed myself to the dogs, if they would have me.

But I'm not squawking about it for, verily, what's the sense of being sick if you're going to squawk about it—why not be healthy and squawk long and lustily on that phenomenon—and well.

*

Being the last remaining champion of the people, alive and able to brag about it, never hung, burnt at stake, crucified or tortured—a playful way the people have of showing their profound appreciation of championships—it behoovers me to announce to the amazed public that indisputable evidence of the presence of civilization has been found in the United States of America—not much, of course, but genuine; which proves conclusively, the rumor, "civilization is all used up" is pure canard or hooey. One can step out of his haze any day and verify my statement by seeing civilization come marching up the thorofare, arm in arm, with barbarism.

To illustrate:

We have no community loafing place[1]—one must either loaf on the streets or seek a loafing place in the fastness of the wilderness. No man can gainsay these times of unemployment call for communal loafeterias—excuse the ribaldry—where the former workers can loaf in an organized way.

But no. Each loafer must needs step out and find for himself a loafing place with the result that instead of one up-to-date loafing place Chicago has 200,000 loafing places minus all conveniences, scattered over the city. Can you imagine—that much barbarism left after all these years!

To illustrate:

There are dirtier people than I am but that does not mean a bath would hurt me. Indeed, as I remember it, yesterday I was astounded to discover I had accumulated a complete set of lice; as a result of sleeping in high-toned

[1] That is, public accommodation, or simply a space, for people experiencing homelessness.

hotels—too high-tone to change the linen—and boycotting the regulation scratch-houses.[2]

Unversed as I am in cootie-culture,[3] I went into consultation with a couple of rising merchant princes and they assured me my trepidation was totally uncalled for in this civilized age, that "we have bath houses, if not in Chicago, at least in South Chicago—you go right down to 83rd St . . ."

Eighty-third St.? Well, that's only two miles from here, is the bathhouse on this street?

"No, you'll have to go to the right a few miles or you can go to 99th St. (98th) if you're traveling that way . . ."

The bath was all that has been said for it, a clear symptom of trenchant civilization—I revealed in its sprays and drowned every cootie, impartially without pity, mercy or remorse. Yes, but how about those seven miles? Barbarism!

The placing of those seven miles between me and the bath may have been miscalculation, (if Chicago placed them there) and denotes poor judgment of distances—then again it may have been well intended to give each "bathee" a chance to walk and raise a beautiful sweat before entering the fountains of sanitation. Yes, but how about those "crums"?

I do not consider it fair to drown them twice; place them in jeopardy of their lives by this preliminary drowning in sweat. . . .

Imagine the feelings of a crum when he wakes up from his after-dinner nap and finds himself engulfed in a torrent of sweat racing south into your shoes?—my shoes?—

Mebbe this art is getting a little too lousy but my dear reader, let me say in extenuation: The population of lice in this country exceeds and out-breeds all other forms of life, as the late lamented census should show.

I make this statement deliberately and argue that if we're going to clutter our pages with most inhuman remarks about other parasites and cockroaches, my gentle reference to the great American louse be put right next to pure reading matter.

Now let me point out we cannot much longer survive if every man must drag along a washtub for toilet purposes; neither does it make for the better sanitation to do your ablutions in a box-car from a gallon tomato can; likewise it is passé to ankle down to Lake Michigan, dampen your towel, warm it over a distant radiator and rub-down in the depot toilet—all that is unscientific, far removed from civilized procedure.

Not only that. The tubs and tomato-cans would aggravate the traffic prob-

---

2 Slang for cheap lodging houses, so called because they were full of biting insects, especially lice and bedbugs.

3 "Cootie" is slang for a louse.

lem and there are those who think there are already enough tincans and lizzies, as it is—on the streets.[4] I subscribe to that viewpoint.

I can not find an ointment
To heal my wounded pride—
My life is disappointment,
My sorrow high and wide.

Industrial Worker, 22 November 1930

[4] Ford's Model T cars were sometimes referred to as "tin cans" or "tin lizzies," but these terms were also used more generally for any basic, inexpensive automobiles.

1931–1932

Three Bottles

Before passing judgment on the Chinese you should visit Chinatown—take down the strange signs and you won't know whose town it is. Passing out,[1] you will notice deterioration in buildings, neatness and sanitation, as you, no doubt, were surprised by the cleanliness and orderliness when you came in. They wear good clothes, buy Ingersolls and eat hamburgers for all the world like great Americans.

*

Ralph Barton, best cartoonist, bar none, is dead.[2] He shot himself and didn't miss. He was best, not because of execution, but because of ideas—he could almost cause "runs" in kinks and make straight hair curl.

Reports have it he was in financial distress. He, himself, gives no reason for his act, but in his report he mentions several, suggests many and says, take your pick—that's Barton.

It is given to me to know why he did it.

He needed one friend more—he admits he already had one.

Finance had nothing to do with it. He could have stepped out at any time and robbed himself a plumber or a druggist, a man of unlimited means, for, if I remember rightly, he had a gun when he shot himself and it was loaded.

But he could not step out and shoot himself a friend. So he shot himself and by that act, he shot himself a million friends he never knew he had—too late.

Friends, like public opinion, always arrive after the ship has gone down—after a cross marks the spot where the body lay; and they weep bitter tears—(I wish to Christ they'd dry up!)

In this age of mass production, mass transportations (sardine pack), mass asininity, mass this and mass that, it is impossible for a friend to exist—a friend is an individual—and *many are Bartons that are fingering their pistols.*

But we need not despair—we can use mass friendship. Join the union of your class and take your friendship by volume.

---

1 That is, upon leaving Chinatown.

2 Ralph Barton was a popular caricaturist and cartoonist whose work appeared in books and numerous periodicals during the 1910s and 1920s, including the *New Yorker, Puck, Vanity Fair,* and *Harper's Bazaar.* He killed himself in 1931, leaving a suicide note that blamed manic depression, stating that his condition had "made it impossible for me to enjoy the simple pleasures of life that seem to get other people through. I have run from wife to wife, from house to house, and from country to country, in a ridiculous effort to escape from myself. In doing so, I am very much afraid that I have spread a good deal of unhappiness among the people who have loved me."

The I. W. W. is the only friend man has now.

Hear ye! Hear ye! The tardy friends now tiptoeing around the bier may as well come down on their heels—the coffin is empty.

They may now take up their pens and draw their own cartoons—see if they'll sell.

Ralph Barton is dead.

Industrial Worker, 6 June 1931

Say It with Flowers

Half the people in these states know practically nothing about botany and can't tell asparrowgrass from a vegetable oyster, so fearfully has their education been neglected. Half of 'em hasn't the slightest idea what garlic looks like and could be sold a bunch of persimmons or caraway seeds instead. And there is only one way for them to find out—go into a feed store and order a dozen bulbs. Is it then any wonder they can not describe the looks of one of the most beautiful flowers, the spondulics—half say it's green, half say it's yellow and there you are.

Here's a flower that makes orchids (they don't know what orchids are; neither do I), makes orchids look like some thing the consumptive spit out and the populace are in blissful ignorance as to its existence. They must be color blind.

I've often wondered why the menfolk on their rounds do not gather a bunch of those lovely spondulics and take them home to the wife to kinda square themselves in her eyes for past, present and future infractions of various moral codes and codicils of deportment; for I have it from undisputed authority that there's nothing like a vaseful of spondulics to keep peace in the family.

Not a woman would have the nerve to peel the bark from her dear hubby's nose with a frying pan if a bunch of fragrant spondulics decorated the dining room table. Peace would be so profound the neighbors would rush in hoping to find the pair of 'em lying dead, battered beyond recognition. And there they are, sitting peacefully beaming at each other like a case of love at first sight. . . .

"Oh, Mrs. Noseby," exclaims the now docile virago, jumping up from her husband's lap, "look at the pretty flowers Hennery brought me."

"My goodness gracious!" gasps Noseby through her sparse teeth, "how beautiful; they must be tens and twenties."

"Yes Mrs. Noseby, there isn't a five or a two or a one in the whole bunch. Hennery said he could have picked up an armload of fives and ones but he thought I'd like the tens and twenties best—especially the twenties—and I do, too," she cooed bashfully.

"But don't you think, Mrs. Knockimstiff, a fifty or a hundred stuck in here and there would enhance the beauty of the bouquet?" says Mrs. Noseby, spitefully. "Indeed it would, Mrs. Noseby, and I'm sending him out to gather a few—ones and twos and fives, as I'm just after telling him, may be all right for a boutonniere, to pin on a coat lapel, but they would never, never do to put on the centerpiece, near food." "I quite agree with you, Mrs. Knockimstiff, you have a rare artistic sense and taste for true beauty." "Thank you, Mrs. Noseby, I'm sorry you can't stay—do so love to talk with you—but stay, take a few of these flowers with you to show your husband what they look like—mebbe he would like to go out and pick a few after he recovers from the beating-up you gave him."

Ain't nature grand!

Perpetual strife, clawing, kicking, mayhem, assault and battery, torture, assassination and what not all turned into a beautiful love scene just by a few stray blossoms of the esoteric spondulics—spontaneous spondulics. But, as I said before, the people are poorly informed as to the powers of those flowers to quell the rising insurgency of the redoubtable female—nip it in the bud, so as to say—and many is the man carried into hospital for major repairs who lies on the operating table fully unconscious of the flower that would have spared him untold suffering, the disgrace of ignoble defeat at the hands of his dear wife and saved the doctor the trouble of stitching him up and stretching his hide to reach over bare spots. Such is the sad state of botanical erudition in this otherwise happy land of ours—people eat a pan full of poisonous toadstools all the while thinking they are treating themselves to a mess of mushrooms; trembling husbands and fathers reach home, after an all-night session at stud-poker debating circle, fondly hugging a delusion and a bouquet of daisies or posies or pansies when they should have an armful of spondulics—ain't I right editor?

Course I'm right—and then David Starr Jordan has the unmitigated guts to say "no use loading a $10,000 education on a 50c boy."[1] (He means by that that you shouldn't spoil a good half-dollar kid with too much useless education—he's subtle.)

Well, now, it isn't going to cost no $10,000 to learn to pick spondulics. The I. W. W. agrees to teach every man that now stands in terror of his wife and the landlord how to distinguish between spondulics and spoilt-bananas.

It absolutely guarantees its instructions to the end that each student will be able to recognize the different kinds of spondulics at a glance and be able to select the harmless from harmful. . . .

Mysterious are the ways of nature and she has so arranged it that some are good and some are rotten—but she also has placed clear markings on all spondulics so it's your own fault if you pick the wrong kind.

The ones and twos and fives are considered every bit as poisonous as

---

1 David Starr Jordan was a botanist and zoologist who served as president of Indiana University from 1885 and then became the founding president of Stanford University, holding the position from 1891 to 1913. A white supremacist and leading advocate of eugenics, he argued for racial segregation and compulsory sterilization of African Americans, Native Americans, Latinos, disabled people, and others. In recent years both Indiana University and Stanford have renamed a number of buildings that were originally named in his honor.

toadstools—indeed, in some places they are called toadskins—too dangerous to handle bare-handed.

It is high time the American people (the workers) begin using these highly ornamental flowers for the purpose nature intended them: to assuage the griefs and calm the feelings of an excited missus. It's the only way—and the only way we can depart this life with a whole skin unmarked by bludgeonings of the better half.

Take out a course of instructions in the I. W. W., the scientific way to gather spondulics—it will cost you one quarter dozen dollars.

What's three bucks, when it preserves your beauty unmarked for all time—you'd spend that much for court plaster alone to say nothing about doctor bills—and it saves you the trouble of trying to convince St. Peter you had a run-in with a wild-cat.

Let us have peace.

Industrial Solidarity, 30 June 1931

Slim Is Dissatisfied with His Looks

I am in the habit of getting parasites' papers free of charge in the subway trains where they are discarded by good and willing workers on their way to their various employments—not that I am too tight to buy them for I am not and even as it is (getting them without cost) I feel that I am losing money. Early in the game I discovered discarded papers were more plentiful during the morning rush hour and I could select any paper I thought would appease my craving for knowledge. But, I also discovered that later on in the morning the same crowded trains neglected to supply me with free reading matter and I didn't have the crust to take papers away from the passengers; consoling myself—there is no justice.

This condition irked my complacency and caused me to wonder why the early birds were so liberal with their property and finally I came to the conclusion they were afraid to carry those papers into their place of employment, fearing temptation might get the best of their caution and the boss would catch them glancing at them in their idle moments.

Shame on me! To all intents and purposes I am making it appear freedom is crippled and lies bleeding on the Broadway Express and that those collared slaves respect, worship and fear their boss more than they do God—shame on me.

To once admit that those workers dassent have a newspaper in their possession in front of the boss is to say an I. W. W. hasn't got the guts to read T-bone Slim's ravings to J. P. Morgan or Johnny Raha-feller[1]—Which they have of course. I'm afraid I have misjudged those men in thus accusing them of cowardice and that there is a deeper and more respectable reason for their desertion of "the last issue" for my benefit—that my very looks stampeded the mob into relinquishing their papers in hopes of dispelling some of my outstanding ignorance; that their action was purely altruistic—noble creatures!

---

1 A reference to John D. Rockefeller, then the richest person in the United States. Having started his family's fortune through war profiteering during the American Civil War, in which he avoided service by hiring substitutes to fight in his place, Rockefeller moved into the fossil fuel industry, establishing Standard Oil in 1870. The company came to dominate more than 90 percent of the U.S. market and was for a time the largest supplier to the world. It was targeted by antitrust campaigners in the late nineteenth century, and so the Rockefellers diversified. A key player in coal production, the family owned the mine in Ludlow, Colorado, at which the 1914 massacre of strikers and their families took place. The Rockefellers invested part of their fortune in churches, universities, and charities, establishing themselves as well-known philanthropists. By 1931, John D. Rockefeller Sr. was largely in retirement, and he would die six years later.

and that those tightwads, on those later trains who retained possession of their disgraceful sheets, were selfish to the core and did not belong, as we thought, to the leisure class—the bosses.

My ignorance is so outstandingly comprehensive that people take pity on me even on the streets, hand me tomes and pamphlets and circulars; to practice on . . . and I've had it happen a man rushed clear across the street and shoved a salvation army "War Cry"[2] under my arm, encouraging me: "Here buddy, you need it worse than I do—."

'Twas useless for me to protest that I've got lots of cigarette papers; he thought I was only dressing my ignorance with words—so unsophisticated and innocent is the appearance with which my well-meaning parents cursed me. There is no justice—I've got to pack these dumb looks the "all of my life"—which I hope is a short one—and, if the people ever find out I know anything, they'll accuse me of betraying them. Where's the justice in such a condition? If the I. W. W. had any sense at all they'd send me to a beauty specialist, to be rebuilt.

P.S.—Upon second thought, I. W. W. need not send me to a beauty specialist—my ignorance is more than skin-deep.

Industrial Solidarity, 7 July 1931

---

[2] The Salvation Army's newspaper.

Slim Gets Nervous

Some men are so fearful of starvation they dare not quit their jobs under any circumstance, no matter what the provocation. They stick and stay and stay and stick till the boss gets tired of looking at 'em and fires 'em—just now you could not get 'em off the job with a crowbar.

This makes it appear the men who now are looking for work have designs on the other fellow's job. "Gee, I wish I had that guy's job" is no idle practice—altho it is prattle of idleness.

Over in France (or somewhere) an idle man felt the time hanging so heavy on his hands he butchered a workingman so as to get his job. He didn't get the job; altho he had opened it—the police interfered—and the job went to another unemployed who had been hanging around, mouth watering and who hadn't so much as lifted a finger to start the wheels of prosperity rolling—I mean, beg your pardon, to start the rolls of prosperity wheeling.

This should not be.

The workers should get together and "splitup" all this work among themselves and not start butchering one another. And while dividing it they should bear in mind the parasite is entitled to his just share of labor same as human beings.

Let us not lose sight of the fact that I am not encouraging men to quit their jobs—that would solve nothing; it would be merely changing butchers—but I have a personal interest in writing this: I am addicted to wearing of overalls and altho I am unemployed (but cheerful) may be mistaken for a workingman and be butchered without giving me a chance to prove my innocence. Now, I do not object to being murdered if the job is done in a nice way and painlessly but I'll be damned if I want to get killed by mistake, without a reason—I want the unemployed to stay their dagger at least until I get a pay envelope in my pocket and can prove I am guilty of having a job. Even then there is no good reason why I should be sent up to disport with the angels for did I not just now say the problem can be solved by dividing the work equally. This, in turn, solves itself by shortening the work day. The shorter work day can be brought about by organization—murder solves nothing.

The working class may as well throw away their whetstones and use their knives for can-openers.

*

Note by the Editor: No doubt the new method of solving unemployment above suggested by Tee-bone Slim will be quickly reduced to an organized racket. The morning classified columns will have such ads as this:

"Several good jobs located by our scouts. Present holders can be bumped off easily. Ambitious young men looking for a start can procure these jobs by putting up a margin to pay for ammunition, police split and flowers for the funerals. Balance of fee on easy terms. See Cauliflower Ike, Racket Building."[1]

Industrial Worker, 25 July 1931

1 Our guess is that this note was indeed written by the editor, rather than by Slim.

A Mosquito's Lunch

Detroit's unemployed once more gathered in front of the city hall as a result of the closing up by the welfare board of the city's several lodging houses for homeless men. The board's action was based on the question of finance, its insufficiency, and the "unnecessary" nature of such establishments in these warm days and warm nights when the wind blows from the sunny Indiana and sweltering Ohio.

Evidently this board never has undertaken to cajole sleep dressed in a pair of torn pants or transparent skirts, as the case may be, in company with a swarm of healthy Michigan mosquitos.

Last night I was swinging at them right and left till the wee sma' hours and this morning when I awoke from my well-earned slumbers I was all but horrified to find about a quart of dead and mangled corpses, mosquitos, under either ear; where they had rolled from my noble brow, never to buzz again. Such was the terrific execution of my mighty paws when my dander was fully aroused.

Now it occurs to me the good city of Detroit longs within its kindly heart to have all those mosquitos exterminated at once as a measure of enhancing civic comfort and can think of no more efficacious way to do it than by turning the unemployed, homeless men loose upon them in porous-knit pantaloons and BVD-less underwear.

What at first appeared a question of funds and municipal thrift turns out to be an undertaking pregnant with great common good and, I'm sure, when the unemployed fully understand the true facts they will most cheerfully subordinate their individual comfort to public welfare and proceed to slap the pestiferous mosquitos without mercy or rest.

But there is a small matter we must not overlook.

What are the homeless men, those public benefactors, to be paid for ridding this thriving community of all those winged-demons of the soft and stilly night?

And let us not overlook, a full-blooded Michigan mosquito is no mean adversary to contend with after business hours and before breakfast. There are those who say a Michigan mosquito is only little short of a foot in length and that a more ferocious and blood-thirsty creature never existed—they go over into Canada and tank-up and then they come over here raising hell in our law-abiding purlieus, sapping up the very life blood of our dynamic citizens and endangering the very republic.

A gold medal or a bowl of soup would never compensate those heroic homeless for their noble, unselfish battle for human rights and meritorious service in behalf of suffering humanity.

They must have money.

I knew that question would pop up again same as it did in the council chambers—it is a ghost that will not stay put or stand unhitched. Quite readily I can conceive as to how the council was more than willing (anxious) to bed the boys down but it could not bear the idea of parting with real money. For them to say, "a lodging in summertime is unnecessary in the absence of soul-killing frosts," is to say a lodging house in winter months is unnecessary in the absence of vein-tapping mosquitos—a sweet way of passing the buck.

My reader will think me ridiculous for taking up so much valuable space. But my reader is all wrong, it is my subject, not me, that is ridiculous. I will admit, tho, I should know better than to undertake the discussion of such ethereal matters so solemnly.

I do not belong to Detroit and Detroit does not belong to me—no part of it is included among my possessions. I came here yesterday from Toledo and swear by all that's pure and holy that I did not bring those mosquitos with me—and for those two quarts of mosquitos killed, I expect no emoluments other than a cup of good coffee (six cups of bad coffee) and a little buttered toast.

The unemployed homeless are down at the city hall craving excelsior mattresses. The communists are down there with 'em, telling 'em all about the thick soft cushions in Russia. The city fathers are on the verge of civil war. Passing people honor the occasion with a fleeting glance, little recking a great drama is unfolding and the fate of the republic hangs in the balance.

To ignore this is to invite chaos, or worse.

Today the unemployed are marching for mattresses; tomorrow they'll march for matches; next day for mutton; and so on for milk, melons and millionaires.

Tonight they will fight mosquitos; tomorrow night the law of logic ordains they shall seek bigger game—and only chaos can result.

The gathering at the city hall in itself is not chaos but a very elementary form of orderliness—they know of no better way to win a bed for themselves. An attack against such a gathering is an attack against orderliness in its cradle. It need not surprise anybody that people adopt this old form of petition; it's not so long ago the people prayed the moon—as successfully.

Personally I think they should try the moon once more and then join the I. W. W.

Well aware of the fact that Detroit is gripped by a deathly fear that she is getting more than her share of unemployed, I can only say: every city in the country is affiliated with the same fear, an unholy respect for their treasures. Nevertheless this attitude indicates a healthy regard and pride in their geographical subdivision. The condition is new. No precedent cue or hint intruded to inform the councils as to the nature and extent of this panic. Detroit's council can not know that every shade tree in the state of Ohio shelters two to three workers whose jobs are abolished forever.

The council can not know, the only way those men can be re-employed is by shortening the workday of those men not working or by abolishing child labor, baby-snatching and female help—nine months of the year a woman should be free of the burden of supporting a bunch of brainless, silk-hat parasites; the other three months she should be supported by those same parasites.

God in his wisdom did not make these hard times. He had nothing to do with it. The same people that wrote the bible wrote this panic. A bunch of maniacs who mistakenly thought themselves intelligent—right now they are standing finger in their mouths wondering what it's all about—and history is moving in a circle.

Legal minds cannot grasp the significance of these times because there is no precedent—the precedents all lie west of the problem: Romanoff, Kaiser-Bill, Sultans and several kings, including Alphonso,[1] got their walking papers only to leave the problem untouched.

Detroit in the infancy of its reasoning, destitute of thought, undertakes to solve the problem by feeding the unemployed to mosquitos; by raising a flock of big, fat, happy and contented mosquitos.

But I cannot understand why a city should be so deeply concerned about the welfare of such a thirsty bunch of bloodsuckers.

When the nation's business is in such shape that a part of its citizens have no bed and must serve as mosquito bait the disgrace is more than any free people can bear; those people are no longer united by any ties, whatsoever and are justified in getting together and jumping in the lake—in a body.

Industrial Worker, 8 August 1931

[1] Known as the "playboy king" for his hedonistic lifestyle and involvement in funding pornographic films, King Alfonso XIII of Spain fled the country following municipal elections in April 1931, leading to the proclamation of the Second Spanish Republic.

"Will There Be Another War?"

Why not? Arrangements have already been made for several wars. The kind of war it will be depends on which arrangement fructifies first—the other wars will follow in the order they are able to generate the necessary acidity between brethren.

But that should not worry us in the least—the worst that can happen to us is to be killed and that, in turn, is not as serious a blow as it might have been when Fido was a pup.

But who's going to pay for that war? Ha! That brings the matter into private concern; it touches a sensitive chord in our make-up—but the question is not pertinent: the war has already been paid for by the workers and will be paid for the second time by the workers after the war is over. Nifty arrangement ain't it?—a condition wherein labor finances its own extermination.

Now don't get huffy—could anything be more humorous?

I think labor should hire a bookkeeper. It wouldn't be so raw if a man had had his fight and then magnanimously paid the expenses, but when you have to pay for it in advance before the show and then pay for it again after the show and keep on paying for it over and over, that is carrying the thing too far into arithmetic. No wonder a guy screamed, "What Price Glory!" Note: under modern methods of cancellations, interests, destruction of war materials etc., a war worth, say, 10 billion dollars can be made to cost labor 50,000 billion dollars—no wonder they are poor.

I suppose you would like for me to produce a sample of that war (those wars) that I was so cocksure about. Senator James A. Reed[1] has the floor: Condemns Hoover moratorium plan[2] as "sheer foolishness."

"The interest on the $260,000,000—due us from Germany will have to be paid by the American taxpayers."

Minneapolis Tribune takes the floor: Declares "splendid isolation" a myth.

"American investors and American business have the largest stake of any country in the world in Germany."

"Our long term investments in Germany are exceeded only by those made

---

1 James Reed was a Democratic Party politician who served in Kansas City, Missouri, as a city council member, mayor, and prosecutor in the 1890s and 1900s before being elected to the U.S. Senate in 1910, a position he held until 1929. He was an isolationist who led efforts to prevent the United States from joining the League of Nations in 1919 and thereafter.

2 In an effort to stabilize world markets, U.S. President Hoover proposed in 1931 that Germany and U.S. allies be given a year's break from repaying their crippling debts associated with World War I. Despite widespread opposition, the plan was eventually pushed through, but it did not have an appreciable effect on the Great Depression.

in Canada, they represent only one-third of the investments our citizens have made in Europe."

(The "largest stake" and the "long term investments" represent the baby's milk "our" children never did gargle.)

There's your layout for war, Uncle Sam is farming foreign soil—few, few mortgages wind-up bloodless. And when they do the result is bad-blood. Bad-blood, in turn, can be transformed into war under any pretext whatsoever, pertinent or otherwise.[3]

Industrial Worker, 29 August 1931

[3] Slim is prescient here, since war reparations were certainly a contributing factor in German hyperinflation, which would in turn encourage the rise of the Nazis and lead to World War II.

Roosevelt Was Right

How many times do I have to tell the working class to organize? That is hard to say—not many, I hope. I am still young and the working class isn't old. In fact the working class is in its teens (the master's last stand) and, unless I am mistaken, this very morning I saw a mother of working class persuasion pushing her brood of breadwinners to the factory in a baby carriage. (They should be made to use a wheelbarrow, pile 'em in crosswise, five or six deep—that's all about those phoney barrows still stand.) All this racket about workers riding to work in Ford cars and motor vehicles is pure hooey of the most culpabull nature—I saw no motors on those baby buggies and there's no mistake; for I'm an engineer second only to Herbert Hoover himself and tight on his heels. From this it can be seen that every time one of those darling toilers learns to talk and understand English, I've got to write a thousand word article asking him to throw away his diapers and join the I. W. W.

How many times do I have to ask the working class to organize? I don't know. But this I do know: If they do not organize they will carry me along into the same prediction; and, I like myself—I'm stuck on myself—I sympathize keenly with myself and, therefore, to protect my own interest, I must request them to line up in the I. W. W. and help cook-up some soup for the boss.

Industrial Solidarity, 1 September 1931

Raising a Family

"Do they bother you on those trains?"

They do, brother, but what's bother to a life already full—each additional bother, must make room for itself by displacing another bother, thus maintaining the fulsome life we are prone to lament. Thus it is, too, owing to the universal disquietude, it makes no difference whether or no, which way-ever, the train goes or doesn't, it will land you at the right place and in plenty of time (if it never gets there)—you can't go wrong. What of it if you do have to ketch the train on the bellyside of the curve[1] and instantly became invisible to the law's cruel, calculating eye—miracles must happen. Standing in the rain waiting for the "8:30" until 10:30 p.m. then retiring soaking wet is just an incident that makes life interesting.

The scenery is just one more eyeful of cinders. The peeling skin is nothing but a ride thru the tunnel behind an ammonia car.

*

Stretching myself out in a dirty car which I selected with great care while the train was debating with itself as to whether or no it shall turn a wheel—I reasoned I shall less likely be disturbed by other travelers if I bed myself down in a car not so clean.

Woe is me, how was I to know that car had one or more three cornered wheels—I didn't sleep long.

Just as the engine sent a sigh thru the air-brakes a "cavalcade" charges the doors of my car and boosts into my car one woman, one baby,[2] one husband and two sheiks[3]—Goodnight I says to myself, my dream of sweet dreams was destined to remain a dream only—had the presence of mind tho to heave a polite snore in their direction in hopes they would pull in their "horns of nonsense" and also to assure them of my disinterestedness. . . .

(Shut up, Slim, and let the gentleman do his own talking, and tell his own story:)

. . . "then I got a job for six days and earnt $18. After I paid the rent I had

---

[1] That is, illegally hop a freight train.

[2] The Great Depression changed the makeup of train-hoppers, with far more women and families taking to the road than had been the case in the previous decade. This change became a source of much social anxiety, as expressed in mainstream newspapers and other popular media. For example, the blues musician Charley Patton sings in his recording "34 Blues" (Vocalion 02651, 1934): "Fella, down in the country, it almost make you cry, / Fella, down in the country, it almost make you cry, / (spoken: My God, children!) / Women and children flagging freight trains for rides."

[3] Slang for single men.

just $2.50 left. This kept us for three weeks but we had to live on 'pancakes.' Then I got a job and earnt $12 . . . then I was idle again for a while and finally landed a job to 'tend' sheep, on shares. This we did for a while and when that blowed-up we had lost everything, including the bedding.

"I didn't know what to do or where to go and then I got a job and earnt $15—it was then we decided to open a hamburger joint.

"Fifteen dollars wasn't enough so I borrowed five . . . then I found out the stove would not work so I had to spend $2.50 of that five for a new, second-hand stove . . . we had just enough money to buy the buns and hamburger and sugar—we borrowed the salt and paper . . ."

"Yes," interrupted the soft-spoken young wife, (Mary, age 20) "and I went out and bought a nickel can of milk."

(She seemed to possess more intelligence than the three men put together—but I shall not quote her more.)

"Well, the joint didn't pay and at times we didn't dare to eat, ourselves. Finally I got a chance and sold it for $40.00—with this money we bought a Ford and started for Spokane . . . she had a good motor and only for that motor we'd been stuck in the hills (Continental Divide) but the 'washboard' road soon got our tires and, at one time, I had three tires on one wheel—I could tell when one was slipping off by the 'side-play' of the car. Finally the roads which are built to be forever improved, never to be finished, got our tires. I had no gas, no oil and only 35 cents to eat on. 'Twas then I sold the Ford for $5 and made for this train . . ."

Such was the young man's story and if there is such a thing as salvation this young man would have found it. He had tried almost everything but bank robbery and wound up in a bouncing box car with his six-months old baby, wife and two able comforters.

The young wife, unused to this form of transportation, was "up in the air," not only in "the sense" but physically as well—the husband was holding the baby in his hands (not arms) and his lower extremity was pounding a tattoo on the car floor, for the car persisted in its efforts to shake loose a rib or two.

His punishment was SEVERE.

All this I saw by the light of the matches the worried mother was forever striking—every minute or so she would strike one.

(Note: the car was in the far rear end of the train, placed there so that if it jumps the rail no damage is done other than the killing or maiming of the rear-end crew.) The train made a long run to coal chutes without stopping and when it did, when it DID—I got off.

"ANYTHING is better than riding this car," says I, trying to throw a little light on the darkness.

No, the bulls don't bother us much!

Industrial Worker, 26 September 1931

What Was in the Wrapper?

This article, editor, is written on the paper that was around the wieners a cat stole from me in the wilderness of Glendale, California, while I was eating them—I'd be a very poor man to trust with organization matters, I am that gullible and trustful—they'd steal the seal.

But, I wish to say, editor, that cat traveled, we both traveled, and the wieners unraveled. They were strung out a full yard behind the cat—you have the paper right in front of you, take a sniff at it, if you do not believe my words. Only one extenuation for my malepheasants of stewardship—the cat was black.

Despite the fact the cat clearly registered a guilty conscience when it said good morning to me, I trusted it too far—so I did—a man never should trust a cat as far as the wieners—never.

Had the cat been snow white moer'n likely I would have tossed it in the pot; I've got no use for hypocrites and I'm happy to say that is the attitude of all leading cannibals the world over—yes.

The way this calamity befell your great author (accent on thor) is as follows: unaccustomed as I am to "slipping in soft beds," those devilish creations wherein the mattress fairly reaches out and hugs you the whole night long, I had the misfortune to give way to weakness and surrender my precious person to one such, two nights hand running, in Los Angeles.[1]

I woke up a ruined man!—let this be a warning, editor, stretch out on the floor—lest you too shall be moved to chase a cat around the block, your mouth watering for wieners.

Further, it always was my impression a great author is supposed to sleep in gutters, under tables, in blindpigs and snake rooms,[2] where the inspiration, you know, runs heavy and where you are entertained by reptiles of all descriptions and purple alligators. And here I went and ran counter to tradition and slept in one of those damnable contrivances for the second time this year.

Hardly knowing what I was doing I wrote an article entitled Laissez Faire, it was terrible—nothing like this great masterpiece. Luckily, editor, I had a lucid spell and forthwith went into a tantrum, tore the article into a million pieces, ground my leadpencils to powder under my heels, tore the tablet to shreds and chucked it in a drawer, and "flew the country," like Cheeseborough used to say. We ain't gonna have no such stuff in our papers, are we?

You're right, editor, I agree with you.

---

1 Presumably at a hotel.

2 Both terms for establishments illegally selling cheap alcohol.

That cat just now came back and I did manage to stroke its beautiful fur and let by-gones be by-gones, so I did—cats ain't getting a fair break with the families, and hunger is a driving force . . .

But let us not lose sight of our brave author, who is going across lots just as if he had a date to outfoot seventeen devils and three beezleboobs. Night ran upon him and he ran upon a box car—the box car was lonesome. There in the sanitary atmosphere, fumigated by the aromatic fumes of sulphuric acid, fertilizers and various other sterilizers and purifiers,[3] the great man was soon in the arms of Morpheus—let him sleep. In the morning his slumbers were interrupted by the realization that his brain was back on the job. Just as if the great man had never slept in a bed in all his life—calculating, inventing, creating. This morning the burden of his brain pan is: There is no such a thing as freedom of silence. No man has a right to sulk in his tent and contain in himself the thought, the knowledge, the experience, the eloquence, the prestige that might remove injustice from our fair land; that might free Mooney and Billings, illegally convicted and illegally held in the state of California; that might be just the instrument in the hands of justice, that might re-establish the right of self-defense in the state of Washington and be the means of freeing the Centralia victims; that might arrest the so called legal murders now in the making in the state of Kentucky . . .[4]

Industrial Worker, 7 November 1931

[3] This seems to be a reference to the use of creosote to coat the insides of boxcars.

[4] In 1931, employees of the Harlan County Coal Operators' Association in Kentucky had their wages cut by 10 percent. After a strike began in response, employers evicted families from company property, mobilized strikebreakers, and deployed armed guards. Following a series of skirmishes, a shoot-out on 5 May saw three deputies and a miner killed, with several more wounded. The National Guard was then brought in to break up picket lines and disperse protesters with tear gas. Forty-four strikers were arrested and indicted for murder. Although the strike was defeated in June, conflict in the area would continue throughout the decade, leading to further deaths on both sides.

The Hybrid

Ragged Individualism:

Rugged Individualism has now taken its proud place alongside Harding's "Back To Normalcy." We are now almost normal—but it took ten years to do it.

Five years from tomorrow afternoon a rugged individual will hop up and say, "O, what a yap I was!" and explain nothing.

I'll do the explaining right here:

Over there by those two cans a rugged individual is jungling up;[1] three hundred feet away another proud mortal is cooking; sixty feet to the right still another rugged "I am" is glaring at his frying pan—I see smoke to the right, left and front of me and I smell the smoke back of me and I want the world to know I, too, am a ragged individual and a jackass for I, too, am jungling by my lonesome—how ketchy it is! How was this condition brought about?

An efficiency expert sold the idea to the powers that be. The master sent a few and crude rugged stool-pigeons among the populace. The stiffs swallowed the hook, yarn, sinker and all.

Presto, change!—the sticks are full of rugged individuals. Ha, ha, haa! Ho, ho, hoo! He, haw!! First they normalize, then they individualize and next they'll moralize "O, what a yap I was!"

The "normalcy" is now long overdue and it is expected rugged individualism will put the finishing touches to it—There, I could have said that in the first place.

Industrial Worker, 12 April 1932

---

1 Slang for setting up camp or living in a "jungle," an improvised campsite associated with hoboes, often near a railway or town.

Thumbs Down

Genius?

G. B. Shaw: "Into the void left by the annihilation of Wilde he stepped, armed with a keener wit, a tenser dialogue, a more challenging theme, a stranger construction, a deeper and more natural comprehension."—Rt. Hon. Winston Churchill.[1]

Says you:—If Oscar were still alive, Winston, you'd hear wit, dialogue, theme, construction and comprehension that would make you think the grammar exploded.—George, get up and call him a prevaricator: desecrating the ashes that survived calumny? That's my point—and WILDE it stays. G. B. S. is a great man measured to prevalent specimens; Churchill one of them. Shaw is the finished product for which the obstructive Briton now wants credit.—Wilde went down under the same "encouragement," in another day.

America claims George Bernard Shaw—put that in your pipe, Johnny.

*

When a king loses his head, it's because it's empty—generally speaking—and those that parade around with it ain't much better off: I figure, while the parade is wildest another vacancy is covered with a crown—all the marchers get is a pair of sore legs and sensitive bunions.

Moral: Cut out the march instead of the head—and tend to business.

---

1 British politician Winston Churchill had a long history of anti-union activities, as well as involvement in many blunders and atrocities. As Liberal Party home secretary in 1910, he allowed the British Army to be sent against striking Welsh miners in Tonypandy. Serving as First Lord of the Admiralty, he oversaw the Gallipoli disaster during World War I and, in 1920, ordered chemical gas bombs to be dropped on civilians in what is today Iraq, an act he referred to as "aerial policing." He later became chancellor of the exchequer for the Conservative government, editing its anti-union newspaper during the 1926 general strike. He met with Mussolini the following year and praised him for his anticommunism. He moved to the backbenches in 1931 owing to his racist opposition to any concessions being made to the Indian independence movement. His hatred of Mahatma Gandhi was such that he called for him "to be laid, bound hand and foot, at the gates of Delhi and then trampled on by an enormous elephant." Churchill remained marginalized until the failure of appeasement, his long-held opposition to which catapulted him back into the position of First Lord of the Admiralty in 1939 and the prime ministership the year after. He lost a 1945 election largely because of his opposition to the creation of the National Health Service, a socialized system that has successfully provided free health care to millions of Britons up to the present day. He returned to power in 1951, and one year later put thousands of Kenyans in concentration camps following the Mau Mau Rebellion.

Moral II. A king never should be killed while other meat is plentiful—I understand they ain't the best of eating; altho, admittedly, a pound of genuine King sirloin would fetch a pretty price in Park Avenue or Riverside Drive—just for the honor of having eaten it. (Chances are Fido gets it.) Not all Kings' heads are empty at the time of the tragedy and have as many spoonfuls of gray matter as yours and mine—unfortunately they are so hedged in they cannot, will not, dare not, act and rather than act they say "**take the knob and make it snappy.**" It's the system.

Alfonso said "give me a start of three hundred yards and you won't even know which way I went"—they didn't either—for an old man Alfonso sure scratched gravel in a wonderful manner—he showed good sense and sense indicates gray matter.

He refused to shoot down his countrymen.[2]

(That last crack is just to allay your doubts.)

A King loses his head when it is empty; generally speaking—the Kaiser's got his yet.

*

Increment and excrement are two different things despite the hooking-up of filthy-incre (Increment) and tainted-money. Money is the root of all blisters.

Industrial Worker, 3 May 1932

2 Although Alfonso XIII did leave Spain following the victory of Republicans in the 1931 elections, Slim's praise of him is misplaced. A militarist and imperialist, Alfonso oversaw a disastrous war in Morocco and the repression of Spanish workers. He presided over numerous governments until a coup d'état brought General Miguel Primo de Rivera to power in 1923. Alfonso's close involvement with the dictatorship helped bring down the monarchy when democracy was restored. Though inaccurate, Slim's representation is nevertheless a good example of his opposition to violence.

Untitled

Seattle seismograph registered what was thought to be an earthquake within the radius of 500 miles. That would bring it in the neighborhood of Sacramento and Frisco—probably the beans the Salvation Army is feeding the untouchables. Strange how they can invent machines that will record beans popping five hundred miles away—after awhile they'll get it down so fine it will throw a fit every time I take a chew of snus.

Industrial Worker, 24 May 1932

Race Hatred

(Your Leaven Is a Dud, My Lords)

America was discovered by a foreigner. American government was founded by foreigners (if King George was a citizen, I don't remember it). Many foreigners selected U. S. A. their birthplace. Revolutionary war was fought by foreigners and native sons, side by side.

Other foreigners discovered America—these include Paderewski, Jenny Lind, Steinmetz and Mikko Maki.

America was built by foreigners.

America is now kept from tumbling by foreigners?

Our very president spent much of his life between England, China and Down 'n' Under. If custom crystalizes absence into fact, he is a foreigner.

America did not produce Charlie Chaplin, Sikorski, Fokker, Faversham or Greta Garbo—now Dies-Fish[1] wants to deport the foreigners.

O.K. Fish, clean up Washington first—then start in on Park Ave. and Gold Coast.

The rest will follow.

But Fish, for the good of your children, you better put a ban on our globe-trotting future presidents. How can we get the deportation idea out of the Fish-Dies head?

That is easy. "Foreigners will hereafter trade only with their own nationality—or go without."

If the so-called foreigners (who have adopted this country for better or worse) do this, Mr. Fish and Mr. Dies (if he is a mister) will "spika da engliskaa" like a son of sunny Sicily, or dragoon from Warsaw, and May Co. will change its name to Straus.

Our statesmen "can't see eye to eye,"
Tis nough to make a person cry;

---

[1] This is a compound of the names of two politicians: Hamilton Fish III and Martin Dies Jr. Fish was a military veteran, author, and politician who, in 1930, established the Congress House Special Committee on Communist Activities in the United States. The committee investigated various organizations and individuals, and called for repressive measures against radicals, including deportation. An ardent isolationist and anti-Semite, Fish opposed both Roosevelt's New Deal and, up until the bombing of Pearl Harbor, U.S. support for the Allies during World War II. Dies was a conservative congressman who blamed the Great Depression on America's "large alien population." Later, in 1938, he would become a chairman of the Special Committee to Investigate Un-American Activities.

For if their vision is too small
I doubt if they can see at all.

Rebellion begins where the dirt is, foreign or native. Remove the dirt and you remove the cause. If you deport anything let it be injustice.

Race-hatred is a dud in any country predominantly foreign—where all are offenders—tarred by the same duster and, more specifically, because in this hoss-race virtue is running seven to one favorite over vice. The sponsors of race-hatred, the spongers, feel their special privileges slipping and race-hatred is the last straw they grab before sinking to the lower levels. Their madness today takes the form of tomato-soup—also pea-soup—innocuous without previous condition of poisoning.

A Gentle Stranger (Not Strangler)

Charity itself is a rarity; its many substitutions range within second-handed justice, display and restitution—not that those are not praiseworthy endeavors. We cannot be sure that charity exists in view of the many injustices practiced under the eyes of "easy going" society. We only know charity is possible. The refusal of society to exterminate the victims of an unjust economic system by starvation cannot be considered either mercy or charity, but a duty.

Industrial Worker, 9 August 1932

That's That!

Being in full possession of all my faculties I wish to announce to the amazed public I am not a candidate for the nomination for Vice-President; it's President or nothing with me and, if it's nothing, I won't accept it.—T-bone Slim.

(That ought to fetch me at least a job as Minister—plenti Potential to Araby or Messo-Ptomainea.)

Industrial Worker, 30 August 1932

Side Door Pullman Philosopher

Grand Island, Neb., Sept 28—To the Editor of *The World-Herald*:

"I see by the papers," remarks my pardner, Bacon Butts MacDuffy, as in the opposite corner of our box car boudoir he tosses aside the paper that he used for a blanket, and proceeds to gather up the bunch of comic sections which constitutes his bedroll, "that the economic weather sharks are predicting an immediate lifting of the Depression."

"Nor wouldn't it be great," he continues, "if one of these mornings we were to slide back our side door and behold the splendorous rays of prosperity's golden sun chasing the fogs of Depression in 17 different directions?"

My friend is something of a philosopher. He contends that the Depression is a good thing for the people and the nation. Because, he avers, aside from its weeding of the misfits, and when the fog lifts, compelling them to seek a niche that shapes with their talents, it has clearly demonstrated the need of an economic readjustment by which capital must accept a curtailment of its dollar's earning power through a more equitable distribution of the rewards of scientific management and labor-saving machinery.

For, continues my friend, when an industrially invested dollar is permitted to multiply itself by five hundred in one year, as industrial dollars have often done in the past, it should be clear to the most case hardened that the human element in the deal, the factor that gives the dollar all its earning power, wasn't dealt fairly with.

Letter to the *Omaha World,* 3 October 1932[1]

---

1 This letter was discovered by John Westmoreland. It is unclear whether Slim wrote many letters to editors of mainstream newspapers. This could be a fruitful avenue for future research.

1933–1936

T-Bone Economics

Read This The Second Time: (I'm getting swelled)—To see a barber making all those skillful moves over a man's face one could not guess he is raising a family. That's precisely what he is doing, stropping gruel for Annie and Anthony—and that ain't saying a word about "Relief buying him fuel" for his workshop. Naturally one passing by would gather the impression he is administering a well-deserved shave to the guy squirming in the chair. Nothing could be farther from the truth. If you step in, in a little while, he will tell you "I just made a pair of mitts for Antonio"—and here, all along, we thought he was shaving a guy. Aren't looks deceptive!—we'd have bet money on it. A fisherman goes out on the lake and sets a mile of nets, right away we jump to the conclusion he's going to catch fish. Nothing of the kind. He set those nets to catch his wife a new coat and an oilskin for himself—our mouths watering for pickerel and perch . . .

A beggar goes out on the stem. People conclude he's out there trying to get a few nickels for himself. Ha, ha, haw, that's rich!—The bum protests: "you get me all wrong, I'm gathering these pennies and dimes for the landlord so he doesn't have to go to a poorhouse." Noble man! but who shall believe him? or me for that matter?

So it is in this capitalist country of ours—you have to do the strangest things.

If you want to eat a piece of pie you take a coal scoop and swing it eighty-eight times over your shoulder full of coal and the pie is yours. By looking at you, not a living creature could guess you were ordering a piece of pie. They'll swear up and down you were shoveling coal and stick to it. You could show them the piecrusts and they'd still insist you were shoveling coal—I'd hate to have them on a jury.

In the factories, watching the swift moves of the workers, we never would suspect they are putting together a fortune for the boss. No, we'd think they are laying away something for a rainy day. (This isn't so however, 85 out of every hundred die without a nickel.)

The poet said: (this is aside).

> Look! Look! oh anywhere,
> Where moves are fast, Labor's there.

I see you still think labor isn't a slave and working for the boss (I was going to say the butcher, baker, banker and bishop but will not because of such taxation little or much must come from the boss) and if the boss has not delivered said requisites to Labor, then Labor must of needs pay them from the little he gets—this dissipates the wet weather fund and old age fund. The giving of these is in the hands of labor and they have no quarrel with the boss—just so that they get theirs and, if they do, labor is just that much out.—Now it happens these dependents of Labor are in the habit of delivering advice to Labor; "do so and so; accept the cut" and Labor selects the smaller pay for himself. . . .

To illustrate: they told the farmers "Diversify your crops" and then went busted themselves because they had never learned to sharpen skates. Unreliable in toto! is their advice—for one thing they are impersonal and impertinent.

You just listen to me—I'm going to ask you to do a strange thing in a strange world. You saw how the barber knit a pair of mitts with a razor. You saw the fisherman pull an overcoat and an oil-skin from the net.

You was right there when the bum's eloquence saved the landlord from the poorhouse.

You, yourself, ordered a piece of pie with a coal scoop.

You saw the workers build a billionaire all the while making it look as if it were for the wife and kiddies.

I'm going to ask you to join the I. W. W.—everything else is so crazy you might hit.

Industrial Worker, 28 February 1933

Untitled Article

After Herbert Spencer[1] (He ain't too big)—(Follows the 400 words Arthur Brisbane[2] has been hollering for):—

"Evolution is union of parts and unification of their motion, during which process parts change from indefinite function to that of definite service, and during which process the parts and motion function as one."

A One Big Union, by heck!

Shortage of pork chops is what killed the Communist movement in America—that's what they get for trying to liquidate the I. W. W., the only true porkchop breeder in the world.

They was going to revolute with an empty belly and clear head. But the boss kept piling soup into the heads, and the belly never got empty enough (I don't know about the head)—they're now in the hands of providence for the next three sorry years.

Cornflakes killed socialism.

I. W. W. is struggling along on the strength of a few vagrant bullheads and terrapin and refuses to die either naturally or by accident. But it must be admitted the good old foot has slowed down.

Therefore, fellow countrymen and workers, ladies fair and we of the meeker sex: Porkchops is the issue and that takes money.

Political recovery deals in elements of uncertainty, and leaves the final operation to chance.

I. W. W. program is definite and certain—no part of it hinges on man's "antics."

Where man gets less than the full value of his production his progress is retarded in proportion to the values he doesn't get. Where he gets only a fraction

---

1 Born in 1820, English philosopher and sociologist Herbert Spencer synthesized principles of biology, psychology, ethics, and sociology to develop the doctrine of Social Darwinism. He coined the phrase "survival of the fittest."

2 A socialist turned conservative, Arthur Brisbane was one of the most famous and well-paid editors of the late nineteenth and early twentieth centuries. He worked for various newspapers in the Pulitzer and Hearst chains, and was associated with the popularization of "yellow journalism": the fabrication and distortion of facts to achieve hype and increase sales. His syndicated columns, often appearing on front pages, were among the most popular of the time, reaching a peak audience of twenty million. Brisbane was a frequent target of Slim's humor. While Slim assumed capability in his audience, Brisbane is on record as having advised journalism students "not to overestimate the intelligence of their readers." See Art Shields, *My Shaping-Up Years: The Early Life of Labor's Great Reporter* (New York: International, 1983), 166.

of the values he produces his progress is arrested in toto—in such latter case he becomes a full-fledged slave and if he has a wife he must sub-let some of his slavery to his wife. He is directly a slave and she indirectly—she has "married" slavery as well as the idol of her happiness. Where they have children the children are sacrificed on the altar of slavery at a tender age; which all causes youth to doubt the advisability of having parents. Where man and wife both are employed (in the industries) is self-evident proof that both get only a fraction of what they produce and woman in that case is directly a slave and equal to her lord and master. But it isn't anything to brag about. (—I believe men started shaving so as to soften the blow when the schoolgirl complexion hikes to the boiler works.) Remedy: Use the razor for can-opener; let the whiskers fall where they may. Make the women grow whiskers if they are to take part in supplying free board to a top-heavy society. After you have a full beard make a rule "a slave shall be known only by his whiskers." (That does away with work-ladies and babies in the industries.) That is, if you want to keep slavery for yourself. Of course, if you want to shed yourself of whiskers as well as of slavery, open the can with a cleaver and join the I. W. W. There is no other time like NOW. Today is too late. Tomorrow is never. Yesterday never was. NOW is forever. It is precisely the right time to join a One Big Union and find out if those 37 storekeepers are going to sit around waiting for customers. (It is proved beyond contravention the girls are unable to support us in the style to which we are accustomed—they might do better by joining the I. W. W.)

Industrial Worker, 15 August 1933

Untitled Manuscript Notes

Wherever you find injustice, the proper form of politeness is attack.[1]

Tis easier to sit down when you have *la grippe*[2]—you go down—kerplunk!—all in a bunch. This morning when I glanced at the mirror I decided I better not go to heaven right now looking as I do. We can't all die looking young and beautiful and I'm afraid if they don't have a rejuvenating process over there I would look like a holy fright even with a clean shave.

A new suit of clothes wouldn't help me out much and even a set of wings would still leave me looking like John Farmer's gargoyle scarecrow in his Sunday best.[3]

But we are living in realities and the unemployed army of 10 million plus is growing—and the gallon and half of stew the Pearl Street restaurant dumped in the swill-barrel didn't last five minutes . . .

No wonder the pigs are plowed-under and the dogs have a faraway look in their eyes—even the police-dogs neglect to grab us by the shanks—won't even get up to sniff our pants to verify the high emprise of our social standing.

They don't seem to give a damn who we are—or possibly they have lost confidence in us and fear they will wind-up in a stew-pot. Stranger things have happened.

You wouldn't call that fantasy or imaginings of a cracked writer! Two meals a day seems to be the rule (breakfast is composed of several groanings in bed) and, if I do say so myself, the bed and the meals doesn't look any better than the man himself.

---

1 Collected by Franklin Rosemont, this material is sourced from the T-Bone Slim Research Collection, Newberry Library, Chicago. The majority of these notes appear to date from a period of two and a half years (October 1933 to April 1936) during which Slim did not publish in the IWW's by-then primary English-language paper, the *Industrial Worker.* Evidence suggests Slim had a personal and political break with the then-editor, the legendary Wobbly poet Ralph Chaplin, who did not appreciate Slim's irreverent writing style and who was also pushing for his contributors to promote a version of technocracy developed by engineer Howard Scott, about which Slim was skeptical. A small number of Slim's manuscript notes were later published in the IWW press under the editorship of Fred Thompson. The manuscript found its way into the possession of Franklin and Penelope Rosemont in the 1960s. Following Franklin's death the notes were put up for sale and, following advocacy by Owen Clayton, purchased in 2017 by the Newberry Library and then digitized and made freely available online at CARLI Digital Collections, Modern Manuscript Digital Collection (Newberry Library), accessed 9 September 2024, https://collections.carli.illinois.edu/digital/collection/nby_mms/id/53675/rec/1.

2 That is, influenza.

3 John Farmer was a stock name for a farm owner.

Four hundred years of peace in China until the noble white man came, first with his opium containers and missionaries and then with his oil-can—since then peace has been conspicuous by its absence.

In the early days, not so long ago, before the influence of white man's refreshments took hold, the noble Red Man in our own land lived to a grand old age—Chief John Smith, the last time I saw him in Bena or Ball Club, Minn., was 134 years old.[4] I suppose he has gone to the happy hunting ground by now for that was 25 years ago.

For ten-thousand years we've been waiting for George to do it for us—but George never came.

What little is done was done by us and if we look real hard we'll find George hiding out in the WPA[5] pretending to be a communist or Alexander The Great. George is a myth even so as glamor and oomph—a mushy spot in our mentality. The only real thing is YOU—so what are you going to do about it?

Wait for the Statue of Liberty to step down and hand you bacon and eggs?

How Slowly Time Travels!

T-Bone Slim Research Collection, Newberry Library, Chicago

---

[4] Chief John Smith was a Native American of Chippewa descent who lived near Cass Lake in Minnesota and died in 1922. He had a very wrinkled appearance, and it was claimed that he had been born as early as the 1780s, although based on his recollections of his early life it was more likely the 1820s. He gained fame through being regularly photographed for postcards, touring the United States, and being featured in a film.

[5] The Works Progress Administration was set up in 1935 as part of Roosevelt-era New Deal reforms to stimulate the U.S. economy and ameliorate poverty. Over an eight-year period it provided 8.5 million people with various forms of government-funded work in projects ranging from mass infrastructure construction to cultural programs.

Resurrection

(Song)

Man that once drank at a bar[1]
Hard by a church yard gray.
When evening shadows fell bizarre
He staggered on his way . . .

Right thru the graveyard's ghostly air
His soul moved on in waves
Among the dim gray headstones there
He weaved among the graves.

Grave-diggers there had sunk a hole
For those that can't behave
And when our hero onward stole
He stepped into the grave

And there he slept in peace profound
Till after break of day
And crumbling sand did there abound
Upon his mortal clay.

In stark surprise he rubbed his eyes
And said, in mournful tone,
Don't other corpses deign to rise
But mine alone, alone?

The barkeep thought it was a joke
Straight from the churchyard-bed,
And failed to understand the soak
Was risen from the dead.

Franklin Rosemont–T-Bone Slim Research Collection,
Newberry Library, Chicago

1 The lyrics to this song do not seem to have been published in the Little Red Songbook, but they do, with an original melody, form the title track of a recent music album by John Westmoreland.

Untitled Manuscript Notes

20th 34., 7.45 AM.? Hinckley, Minn.

You think all those stories about the little bootblack that got to be a millionaire is for the purpose of encouraging your little bootblacks.[1]

Your nickel is in the wrong slot.

Those stories are for to convince you it is proper to have a million dollars.

Brevity after all is not the soul of wit. It is but the limit of coherent utterance.

Finlayson, Minn., seems to be nearer civilization (this fine, fresh, "late" May morning) than any place I know. Birds are registering their satisfaction in full-throated paeans of praise.

(I must look for hair in the butter.)

Clean-up week here (as on Wall St.) occurs 52 times per year. Nothing is allowed to mold but Graham bread.[2]

written 20 May 1934
Franklin Rosemont–T-Bone Slim Research Collection,
Newberry Library, Chicago

---

1 This is a reference to the popular series of *Ragged Dick* novels by Horatio Alger, famous for advocating a meritocratic vision in which hard work is always rewarded. The eponymous Dick is a bootblack who "pulls himself up by his bootstraps" into middle-class prosperity through "pluck and luck." Mark Twain parodied Alger in his own short stories "The Story of the Good Little Boy Who Did Not Prosper" and "The Story of the Bad Little Boy Who Did Not Come to Grief."

2 A type of whole wheat bread named after nineteenth-century health advocate Sylvester Graham. It was free of additives such as alum, which Slim criticizes in "The Lumberjack's Prayer."

Chinese Wisecracks

The greatest mountain does not regret the smallest dust.

(Hobo crack: "What's the use of ethics to a guy with mitts (hands) like these.")

A dragon floundering in shallow water incurs the ridicule of shrimps.

Mischief all comes of too much opening of mouth.

A word once spoken the fleetest horse cannot overtake it.

Fish see the bait, but not the hook; men see the profit; but not the peril.

A dead man is terrible as a tiger, a dead tiger harmless as a lamb.

The good are short lived, the evil last a
thousand years
(I'll soon be forgotten, heh, heh, heh.)

Westmoreland Archive[1]

[1] This piece, which here appears in extract form, comes from the second main archive of T-Bone Slim's work, which is in the possession of the Westmoreland family. Cherie and John Westmoreland in particular have been instrumental not only in preserving this archive but also in supporting recent advances in T-Bone Slim research. Cherie is an illustrator and artist whose lithograph of Slim appears in this volume, while John is a musician who has produced an album of his great-granduncle's music, titled *Resurrection*. Our sincere thanks to the Westmorelands for allowing us to reproduce items from their archive, which contains materials that appear to date from approximately 1935 to 1942.

Extemporaneous Bath

When Edith[1] went swimming the morning in May
Her spirits were brimming and so was the bay.
The weather was Springlike, so good for the corn,
But Edith felt more like a September Morn.

Her world seemed so narrow it evened her bloom
She felt in her marrow she needed more room;
So joyous and elfish, her caution remote,
Her thoughts far from shellfish—she stept in a boat.

The weight of her Presence upset the canoe
And Edith for once was a lady in blue (water)—
And all this I surveyed—it gave me great peace,
For O what a mermaid I have for a niece!

Now heavens may shatter and gates ajar slam
For how can that matter, our waternymph swam.
And Trudy's outswankered this morning in May
For Edith hath conquered the Presque Isle Bay.

Matt Houghton[2]

written on Mother's Day, Sunday, 10 May 1936
Westmoreland Archive

---

1 One of Slim's nieces. This poem, along with other items in the Westmoreland Archive, shows he did occasionally visit family members, in contrast to earlier assumptions by Franklin Rosemont.

2 It is notable that Slim uses this surname, which he had employed in his youth and which was used by other family members as an Anglicized version of Huhta, in this personal poem written to and about his family. There appears to be a significant difference between the literary productions of Matt Huhta/Houghton and T-Bone Slim, highlighting the way in which the latter was a literary construct. It is difficult to imagine T-Bone Slim writing an idealized, sentimental poem such as this one, as it would not have fit his wisecracking, stoic persona.

Extra! T. B. Slim's Golden Discovery Cures Everything!

Did you see where the girls of Rockwood, Tenn., returned the tear-bombs to the chivalrous cops and had the cops weeping like a lawyer over a grocery bill?[1] Girls have changed. Years ago they returned nothing but kisses . . .

Thinking of this, and having to do my own patching—both sleeves—I took to wondering, mind you I'm not in favor of sterilization (a fellow can wonder, can't he?) I took to wondering if sterilization of politicians would help the country in the long run. Understand me, I'm not trying to undermine the rights of crazy people. Under no circumstances would I endorse such a ticket—I consider a man off his base is entitled to every protection the same as us sensible people—and not have other maniacs using a pair of scissors on him, snipping a chunk off here and there. (Or do they use a stump-puller or a barbed-wire stretcher? They're crazy enough for that.)

But every little while some politician feels the asinine urge to save the working class. No other class ever gets a look in. It's always the working class. The working class has now been saved so many times in the last 4000 years that I lost count. Almost every minute up jumps a lunatic and says: "Keep your eye on me, I'm going to save the working class. Stand still, toilers," he squeals, "I'm going to emancipate you. Watch me closely. I've got nothing in my sleeves, hand or head—not even callouses. I'm going to take this nothing I'm holding in my right hand, and I'm going to put it in my left hand—thank you—and now if you will go home and examine your dinner bucket you will find an ostrich in it."

So I took to wondering—you see we once had a dog that wouldn't stay home, and, conversely visited the neighbors far and near. Now, it happened that the dog's visits were not altogether friendly visits, or good will gestures, and the neighbors began to miss chunks of meat from the most out of the way places. So one day several of the youngsters took to petting the dog, and when the dog wasn't looking one of them made a swift pass behind the dog's back, and, do you know that dog came right home, downcastlike, and crawled under the porch and stayed there. Never again did it go around wagging its tail in the next ward. . . . It turned out to be a good watch-dog.

*

1 On 6 April 1936, a strike of two hundred workers began at a hosiery mill in Rockwood, Tennessee, after employers froze pay and increased the working week by ten hours. Police and deputized security guards regularly attacked the strikers, with the result that the campaign collapsed in June.

So I set to figuring on a remedy for our maladies myself.

The trouble with the workers is: They get too much nothing, and not enough something. (Whatever that something is I leave to proletarian imagination.)

"Sarcastic again?" Who? Me? I'm not sarcastic . . . just a little blunt.

All right, since too much nothing and not enough something won't do it, it occurred to me to reverse them. I placed them in front of my plate glass mirror, in my laboratories, put on my two-bit spectacles, and sure enough, there she was, a remedy for the workers' ills—T-Bone Slim's Golden Discovery! I could hardly believe my spectacles.

In the mirror the worker is getting too much something and not enough nothing—could anything be more miraculous? He swells up in the middle and a pair of chins start sprouting on his chest. I shook hands with myself. My mirror is one of those motion mirrors—you throw a dead cat in front of it and it shows the cat tearing up a live buzzard. Says I to myself: "Slim, your discovery transcends all human imagination . . . you have today not only rescued the human race, but you have prevented the destruction of the world!"

"Well and good—there's the remedy—but how do you apply it to the malady?"

"By joining the I. W. W."

Me sarcastic? . . . pooh, pooh . . . just a little blunt!

Industrial Worker, 23 May 1936[2]

---

[2] Slim returned to writing for the *Industrial Worker* a mere three issues after Ralph Chaplin's acrimonious resignation as editor. His first article after he came back, with the suggestive title "T-Bone Slim Asks: Can Leaders Save Us Workingmen?," was published on 11 April 1936.

Untitled Manuscript Notes

Woke up stiff all over (lumpy bed). I had inadvertently spread two sheets of newspaper in one spot.

Sometimes I think the people are worse off than I am myself and I have a mind to tell the FW editor: if you want these writings, come and get 'em.

Or shall I bring them?

Il Duce,[1] direct descendant of Paul Bunyan, says: "cutting the Mediterranean in two" is farthest from his thoughts and least of his worries—no blue ox.

All down the ages it has been that some made haste to grab the best piece—that's how I won my name T-bone Slim; I use to beat the strawboss[2] to the T-bones—but I did it in spirit of mischief.

Now it comes out, "a single bomb hit an apartment house in Barcelona killing seven hundred."[3]—

That bomb was something special, if not devilish—but was the apartment a military objective?

Vain dream, for soldiers, half-berserk in the field, are incapable of compassion for victims of remote destruction—even so as are the bombers.

Franklin Rosemont–T-Bone Slim Research Collection,
Newberry Library, Chicago[4]

---

1 Il Duce is Italian for "the leader" and refers here to the title commonly associated with fascist dictator Benito Mussolini.

2 Slang for a foreperson or supervisor.

3 As part of a failed military coup against the election of the leftist Popular Front government, pro-fascist Spanish military units attempted to take over Barcelona on 19 July 1936. Resistance from community members, largely affiliated with the anarchist Confederación Nacional del Trabajo (CNT) and loyalist troops, defeated the uprising within a day. Out of this situation grew the Spanish Revolution and a civil war in which Barcelona was subject to shelling and aerial bombardment, primarily armed, led, and carried out by German and Italian forces.

4 Given the references to Spain, these particular notes seem to date from July 1936 or slightly later.

It Should Be Labor Day

Hitler visited a fortune-teller. She read his palm and shook her head.

"Bad news. You are going to die on a Jewish holiday."

"Me? On a Jewish holiday? How's that?"

"Any day you die will be a Jewish holiday."

Industrial Worker, 8 August 1936

1937–1939

T-Bone Slim Takes a Look at the Show

I was snoring so loud that they kicked me out of the movie house. It never occurs to them to put on a show to keep the patrons awake. But no, after the damage is done, after the man is dead to the world, snoring his mightiest, they kick him out.

*

Dear me, I forget, whenever there is nothing doing, labor falls asleep and begins to snore.

Therefore it is up to the unions to put on a show that the bosses will tell their grandchildren about.

*

That highest paid journalist, Arthur Brisbane, is dead.

My head is kind of sluggish this morning, and I can remember only one thing he ever said: "Real Estate is a good buy."

He was a real estate operator.

Oh yes, Arthur's last message to the world was: "Peace on earth and good will among men will surely come."

It will not.

It must be brought.

It must be carried.

Let's go after it.

Industrial Worker, 2 January 1937

Why Ask the Boss for Recognition

T-Bone Slim Has Better Plan

Seamen sent a petition, a long list of names, to Washington, and left it there.

Hm. If ever the M. T. W.[1] is dumb enough to do that I will forget them in my will.

Victory flies only on the wings of audacity. The heights of audacity have never been explored. Therefore victory, so-called, is fragmentary and incomplete. Those that courted glory and fame were riding only an apology. The wing broke and there was a crash. Hush! The pall-bearers approach.

Machine: A mechanical device used by engineers to create wealth and by financiers to create poverty.

*

Profit: The price ignorance pays greed for the privilege of starving in a world of plenty.

*

Law of Supply and Demand: The capitalist dictum that makes a commodity in the hands of a robber more deadly than a gun.

*

Tear Gas: The most effective agent used by employers to persuade their employees that the interests of capital and labor are identical.[2]

Industrial Worker, 6 March 1937

---

1 The Maritime Transport Workers union, a section of the IWW.

2 A U.S. Senate report found that from 1933 through 1937, more than $1.25 million (equivalent to nearly $27 million today) had been spent on tear gas "chiefly during or in anticipation of strikes."

Sit-Down Strikes Too Good to Stop

Sit-down strikes have given the courts plenty of rope to hang themselves—a couple of judges obliged, but the confounded sheriffs wouldn't pull the string.[1]

(This sit-down has no reference to the steel companies' sit-down against navy order.)

Note: Steal Companies' sit-down was based upon presumption they could not produce steel economically in a 40-hour week. Labor's sit-down was based upon the fact that they could not oscillate muscle economically for pennies from heaven.

Walter Lippmann recently sought truth and held his job.[2] Here it is: Employers create an army of from three to thirteen million unemployed with malice aforethought, and deviltry afoot, for the purpose of using them as strike breakers in the event the current slaves revolt. To combat that damnable conspiracy the slaves invented a sit-down strike, recognizing how difficult it is to introduce scabs into a plant where the boys are playing marbles. No self-respecting scab would think of entering such a place, no matter how hungry.

So it is plain as mud that if we can outsit our parasite lords and masters, it is our duty to do so. This nation has ever respected squatter rights—only the farmers of Hershey, Pa., hadn't heard about it.[3]

Note: The sit-down (in general) is new, so the farmers pulled a new form of

---

1 During sit-down strikes, workers halted production and occupied their workplaces to keep strikebreakers out and stop employers from removing goods and equipment. The tactic had been used previously, including by the IWW, but became more widespread from 1935 onward, with a series of occupations taking place in rubber, automobile, steel, and other industries. Although some union leaders disliked the method, its application won a number of disputes and did much to build the CIO during this period.

2 Walter Lippmann was an author, editor, and journalist who won two Pulitzer Prizes and coined terms such as "stereotype" and "the Great Society." He was a founding coeditor of the *New Republic* in 1913 and a popular columnist whose work was syndicated to more than 250 newspapers. He encouraged critical thinking, and a recurring concern in his work was the role of the media and public opinion in political decision making.

3 Following months of organization by CIO members, workers at the Hershey chocolate factory in the eponymous company town occupied their workplace on 2 April 1937. This was one of hundreds of sit-down strikes held in the United States that year. With Hershey dominating the local economy, dairy farmers and company loyalists rallied outside the factory five days later. The strikers agreed to leave the premises, but were then set upon and beaten. In subsequent union elections, an AFL-affiliated body won coverage of the site, securing improvements in pay and conditions in 1939.

strikebreaking. Such a strike-breaking is ineffective and already carries reactions; all told a gain for the workers, and next time the farmers try it I hope the horses don't run away with the widow.

What this country needs is a constitutional amendment to the effect that after a man has been robbed of everything he possesses he shall have the right to squat whenever he damn well pleases instead of turning robber himself, or committing suicide, and be it further resolved the words "wherever he damn pleases" be incorporated in that amendment.

*

It is with heavy heart I offer this reminder:

A Race Does Not Prosper Who Sell Only Within Its Charmed Circle: It is then inadvisable to stir up animosities in neighboring races. Trade when ingrown is worse than an inbred toe-nail. Be the race Bulgarian, Hungarian, or a goulash of Malarians, if they deal only with themselves they soon become impoverished—business is not production.

By the same token, it is idle for an I.W.W. to talk industrial unionism to an I.W.W.—he's already heard it. A pox on these stirrer-uppers that would destroy their own race to satisfy the spleen of their frustrations more imagined than true! Organize the workers. Forget race, creed and color. You're not going to hell—nor is there a promised land. You make your conditions right in this world by organizing industrially and it may be that the fragrance of your performance will precede you into the next. The only promised lands are those that we can take or make or forsake with our organized might. Start your heaven right in this world, not by tearing down but by building up. (Natural selection will do the tearing down: if it's good, it stands.) Hell? can't you see we're living in it? (As a jokesmith I would suggest it needs air-conditioning more so than asbestos . . .)

Verily, must I say, unorganized peace is war, and unorganized aspirations hell. Whatever you want, organize, and it shall be. Nothing is impossible to organization. The wildest of schemes is entirely possible to an organized people—so wild that ninety-nine out of a hundred would scream "impossible" and even as they scream the thing is done.

We haven't seen anything yet.

*

Supreme Court Judges are not ruined "after" they go on the bench, but before.

Immediately before they go, they lead a cloistered life (no name in telephone book) and consequently they suffer an increasingly ingrown viewpoint. The age of Supreme Court Justice should be between 16 and 46. We might lose an occasional good one, but the country could stand it. And the frustrated prospect can always go selling bonds or halibut.

The parasite press in New York City hints strongly on sending Supreme Court to reform school—on account of second childhood, I s'pose? See how those darn things hook up? And I s'pose it's because of the frailties of the British language? Darn the luck, "reform," "reform," "reform" screams the press half bereft of balanced brain pan.

(Note: This should not be construed as indicating press priorly had balanced brain-pan—each morning that I relinquish two cents for their wares, I feel gipped a penny's worth.)

*

S'meller Drama:

It's an outrage the way these shops on the Bowery hang up only one shoe, outside. Sometimes it takes a couple of weeks before you can get the other one. In the meantime every one-legged man is arrested and his residence searched. The one shoe (left) is no good to the dealer, so he puts it up for display. It disappears. Again the police swoop down on the portside cripples and haul them off to dungeons vile.

"Grig. Gen. J. P. Hill Sued for Divorce." War's hell!

"Mrs. Delafield, Social Leader, Shoots Herself." What a noble example. If this fashion "takes," the social problem is all but settled—hours and wages can be set or abolished afterwards.

Some one needed to handle workers? Well, why not at the same time handle a few parasites? "Handle 'em gently," exhorts Sullivan, "but handle 'em."

New York City is making a drive against subway spitters. The city fathers have seen the havoc caused by the overturning of a spittoon so they passed a law endeavoring to save the subway from floods. (Note: I never spit between Battery and Spuyten Duyvil—yes, I have no saliva to spare the subway.) Next case.

Albany Assembly passed a no hitchhiking law. Walk or ride the milktrain, hey? That's the same bunch that killed the Child Labor Law. And to think they get paid for it!

Industrial Worker, 24 April 1937

The Movie Stars—and a Picket Line

By Our Dramatic Editor

Hollybush stars "sashayed" through the picket lines just as if their limbs were chafed hardly none at all.[1] True it is though, they did look as if they had one foot in the poor house and one in the grave, vacant look, guilty look—so we cannot expect them to know anything about unionism, class consciousness or solidarity.

Skip that—but the stars should consider the day of reckoning when Time shall ask: Did you walk through the picket line?

People are still talking about the baseball player who failed to touch second base twenty-five years ago, so I would advise you stars: When you cross the picket line, take your shoes off, for you are walking on holy ground.

We learn the last moment of our lives; but toward the last "the flashes" grow increasingly farther apart (get that?), the mirror grows increasingly dim (from conditions) and it is then the **artistry is gone with the wind.** The farewell tour is on, and the public, fickle public, gargles no note of approval. Where is glamor then, the tinsel of "make believe," when Time shall inquire: "Did you cross the picket line?"

When workers have gone to the trouble of establishing a picket line, it ill befits any man or woman to set his judgment and will as superior to that of the offended parties. One lone star can challenge the plea of 30,000, but the thirty thousand are still right.

wIw

Emotionalism, whether it takes the form of sob action or running amuck is of the same substance—only difference is sob action, like broth, is greatly diluted.

Job action? Hm? That can be done nearer home and save Washington much heartfelt sympathy.

Sympathy? Did you ever try to smear sympathy on your bread? No, of course not.

---

1 The Federation of Motion Picture Crafts (FMPC) was formed in 1937 to represent a variety of workers in the industry, including makeup artists, hairdressers, set builders, and draftspeople. After major studios refused to recognize the union, six thousand members struck on 30 April for improved wages and conditions. They were initially joined by other tradespeople and employees, but their picket lines were regularly attacked by police and hired security. With support peeling off, the strikers agreed to an offer from employers in July and the FMPC was dissolved.

Did you ever trade in a measure of justice for a pair of Rockford sox?

I'm betting the other way—it can't be done. A man would stand a better chance of swapping the sox for justice . . . try it some time! Try to pass off an armload of justice to a bartender for a glass of McSorley's ale.

No, we want markers—markers that will pass at face value in the marts of men.

Sympathy and justice make a poor windbreak.

A shorter workday is our right and heritage, but right and heritage won't make the shorter workday hit the bull's eye.

No need to work long hours. We don't work the year 'round . . . and one quarter of the working class have no work at all. All shall live . . . even if we have to fish 365 days a year.

Shorten the hours, and wages will take care of themselves.

How? How do they shorten the wool on sheep? Shear 'em off.

Build your industrial union, and the One Big Union is built.

That last crack is important—the bridle always goes to the forward end of dobbin.

The workers don't build a One Big Union—the working class builds it.

Industrial Worker, 29 May 1937

Charity Covers a Multitude of Transgressions!

Philanthropy pays good dividends—remember this, my son, when you step out to garner your millions: Be sure to gather enough of them, five hundred million, thousand million—yea bo, two thousand million.

If you decide to select two thousand million for yourself, you can well afford to pass out five hundred million as a matter of philanthropy—for sweeet charity's sake—and you'll still have one thousand and five hundred million left over for a rainy day.

Don't get it all in one place; it will be noticed. Get, say, a thousand million from the workers and get the other thousand million from the consumers—the consumers can be depended on to refinance themselves from the proceeds of the workers' production, or pay.

Now you're all set. Your philanthropies have brought you a clear profit of a billion and a half—which same you'd never been able to get away with did you not open your heart to the gentle urging of blessed philanthropy. And when you come to die the people will say: "He had a heart like an ox"; they're that dumb.

It will make no difference how many workers you shoot down at the factory gate getting it—"industrial misunderstanding," you know, and the law is with you.

Industrial Worker, 3 July 1937

Put the Boss in Overalls, Says T-Bone Slim

On one of the planets there lived a race of giants who were ruled over by a select tribe of dwarfs. These dwarfs were so fat that they seemed low and flat, like a bedbug, and that is why, I suppose, those of that tribe were hailed parasites; the giants they ruled were known as proletarians.

But the land we speak of was not named Proletaria—I disrecall the name but it was a poetical name that made for much flag-waving and swelling of the chest, even among those of the giants. . . . Don't get that last word twisted with a famous ball club in our own unhappy land.

Now it happened that those giants had a terrific appetite, as they say in Hollywood, for they did much heavy lifting and lots of hard work laboring early and late—long hours.

That appetite was a source of great worriment to the rulers of the land—they were afraid the giants might founder themselves or rupture their belly-button. So they had a meeting and decided to slow down their eating by giving them only the toughest pieces of meat and shortening the noon-hour by half. Historians of the day refer to it as the "Age of Belly Robbing" and, you know, historians hardly ever lie.

Soon the country was overstocked with rotting T-bone steaks and pork tenderloins, for the plutes did not dare to give the giants enough money to buy them. Dogs would sniff at them and turn to hide their tears. Doctors screeched, "Drink lots of water!"

Soon it got so the farmers could not raise enough hoofs and horns and neckbones and shanks and sowbosoms and pig knuckles and the giants had to go on vegetarian diet, eat grass like horses, and root like boars.

Some of the beef was embalmed in tins but there was no market for 'em, for the giants had no money and China had gone on a rice diet long before them. **The dwarfs never did find a way to rule giants without feeding them.**

Just before the show-down everything was lovely. Strapping young giants, blue in the face from starvation, were milling around in the streets, singing Sweet Adeline, Isle of Capri, and Hinky Dinky Parley Voo. The dwarfs thought they had the world by the tail and despite the fact that Professor Phoenix Hamburger, the great axe-grinder, had told them, "their racket was built on thin ice," they kept on conniving on how to get the shirts off the backs of the giants.

Standard of living fell so low that the parasites had to start soup lines for the giants to save them from starvation and also to save wear and tear on their back doors. That was the main reason, you see: Their women folk were afraid of these overgrown yeomen.

These parasites were all kings, each ruling in his maudlin manner, more ludicrous than ridiculous. The giants were one, bound by the ties of slavery; each longing to one day be a king. Such a thing as making king the "servant of the populace" never occurred to them; a minor reform.

"They wouldn't organize even!" exclaimed the great Scandinavian poet-historian, Mr. Axel Neilsenson in disgust—the giants he meant, of course, for the pluto-parasites were already organized in a loose-fitting One Big Union of their own and were running an air-tight closed-shop for themselves.

There was some unionism among the giants, as O'Haloran, the great Irish emancipator admitted when cornered. "The percentage was," he wrote, "about one union man for every parasite and inasmuch as there were about five million employing parasites, that also was the number of organized union men. Weight for weight, like the buying of meat for the relief kitchens, **a pound of meat to each pound of eaters,** and then," he added sarcastically, "tons of eaters get all the meat below the animal's knees." He did not explain what became of the heavy part of the animals.

This was prior to the time that things got so bad that the "president" had to jump in there with a pair of bum legs (as they say in Hollywood) and demand: "What the hell's going on here, the boys are losing flesh?" And suiting action to words he turned to the cash register and hit the NO SALE key a resounding crack. "Come on, boys," sez he, "let's eat."

Well, for a while the giants were kinda gooey around the gills from eating high-pressure soups and wrestling with cows' wings. (This last crack I cannot decipher but I imagine it is the historian's sourcastic reference to the half of a boiled egg which the unemployed giants got in January and another half in February, 1937. I wish to gosh the historians would keep better track of things and skip the sourchasm.)

But before all this, education of the workers had kind of got out of the bosses' control a little through the inefficiency of their school system and there were those of the slaves that grabbed off more education "than their just share," as the parasites avered and purred.

Now education is a peculiar thing, when it sinks in, it stays sunk and there is no way to pump it out. Naturally the result was that the country blossomed with agitators—men who wanted to free the giants and toss a harness upon the parasites for a change.

Almost a similar incident prevailed in our own days and in our own land, which resulted in the organizing of the Industrial Workers of the World. The boys came out hollering for a One Big Union of the workers and threatened to put overalls on the boss.

But it seems the giants of the olden days were kind of slow in catching the joint and the sole result was, so far as recorded history affirms, "the stripteasers jumped into barrels to hide their nakedness but the parasites remained barren of overalls as ever. It is our duty now to dress them up; our duty is clear: High, low, jack and the game."

One of the chief arguments put up by the I.W.W. was this:

A wage increase lets us stay out later nights; we don't have to go sneaking back home quarter past nine, hoping the boarding house missis has had another stroke or that the landlady has fallen down stairs and broke her back.

"Low pay, low mentality," they used to say. In other words, they wanted some stepping-out money along with their watery prunes and horse feeds.

Industrial Worker, 14 August 1937

The Purest Ray Serene

Nothing I can do or say to sooth our common grief
Life is such a passing ray, evanescent and brief—
Shadows creep upon our mind, foreboding, dark and grim;
Clouds enshroud the twinkling star, the moonbeam, sun and him

Gladly would have I withstood the sorrow that he bore;
Gazed upon his pallid face and gently closed the door—
Even so, no voice can word the sorrow that I feel;
Sorrow, that now overflows and only Time can heal.

Are we men of iron then? that we can stand the woe;
Scorn rebuffs and irony, unsullied strive and go?
Mark ye: Alfred died long years before his body felt the chill
Nevertheless: his thoughtful mind can linger with us still.

See him now, in pantaloons, so wistful, coy and grave;
Born to die?—to suffer life, and just for others slave.
Heroism such as this no mind can weigh, compute!
Even so—his flashing wit, remains—and will not mute.

Distant stars may twinkle in the azure that endomes,
Shouts of joy may mingle with the squalor in our homes,
But if I—could choose surcease, upon a raft of shrouds
Certainly I'd choose the ray that breaks out thru the clouds

Mathias V Huhta

P.S. Have Helen or Ester[1] put this in ink for they may be here when I am gone

written circa August 1937[2]
Westmoreland Archive

---

1 Two of Slim's nieces, daughters of his sister Sophie.

2 Slim wrote this poem and sent it to his family following the death of his brother, Alfred Andrew Houghton (Huhta), in July 1937. The title is a quotation from Thomas Gray's "Elegy Written in a Country Churchyard" (1751), a poem that Slim also cites elsewhere.

T-Bone Slim Calls for a Housecleaning

Heaven has not two suns, nor the people two kings.
—Chinese epigram.

When the great T-Bone Slim lifted his eyes over the rims of his spectacles, he beheld a world of workers enslaved. "What ho," sez he, "they're in again!"

"Bouncer!" he roars, "c'mere this instant, for I would have speech with thee."

"What's the big idea of all those parasites prancing around on the center of the floor?"

"Master," sobbed the bouncer, "I was out last night and got ahold of some sweet wine—they must have slipped past when I wasn't looking."

"Wasn't looking? Are you still not looking? What the hell kind of a joint do you think we're running here? Don't you know this is an exclusive joint for those who work; and those that will not work, neither shall they strut?"

"Well, shall I turn them out?"

An impressive silence permeated the place. The dance had ceased. The musicians were reaching for their beers (seven deep-sea sailors fainted on the spot)—when all of a sudden, as coming from a long distance, from the dim past, came a powerful chorus:

"Arise ye prisoners of starvation!
Fight for your own emancipation:
Arise ye slaves of every nation,
In one union grand."[1]

What a beautiful tribute to Joe Hill whose ashes were blown to the four quarters of the world by the state of Utah.

"Our little ones for bread are crying,
And millions are from hunger dying;
The end the means is justifying,
'Tis the final stand."

"The Wobblies! The Wobblies are coming!" was the great cry that rose and all was excitement.

When T-Bone Slim again lifted his eyes, the parasites had disappeared. A great peace possessed his noble soul. His limped eyes shone with great Christian charity. His face was radiant with joy. The world was free. He forgave the bouncer. He forgave the parasites and went out to bum the public.

---

1 These lyrics, and those that follow below, are from Joe Hill's song "Workers of the World, Awaken."

"He painted a tiger but it turned out a cur."

"Right makes one bold."

"Cowards make the best generals," roars T-Bone Slim as he skidded around the corner, "and courage is the virtue of privates," he added.

He took another slant at the handiwork of minds as different as faces and he saw a rollicking proletariat approaching, a resilient double chin doubling from shoulder to shoulder as they walked.

A great pride filled his heart. "The boys musta been eating," he ruminated shrewdly.

And the potatoes were not all of the same size or same shape, but they were all potatoes; neither were the big ones on top. Storekeepers had dutifully removed the onions from the potato bin.

The world was all Wobblies, big and small, male and female.

"A speech," they roared. So T-Bone took a shot at the spittoon and said:

"Keep your honey and vinegar in separate bottles."

Came the end of a perfect day.

Industrial Worker, 26 February 1938

The Best of a Bad Bargain Is Plenty Tough

Why are those cinnamon buns so small?—

They have to pay for four new trucks.

Today when I had succeeded in getting patches spotted properly in my overalls, I gazed upon them with great pride—a feeling that comes to a great many who must perforce swing the needle—and, when I stepped out upon the boulevard, my many neighbors and admiring friends stood spell-bound.

"Doesn't he look natural?" they exclaimed, "just like a working man!"

I'll say I do—grocery string stitches sticking out like the golden fleece in stories of old. I'd pass for an emblem of wage slavery; no changes whatsoever.

*

The alphabet is now exhausted—catechism and prayer book comes next; cuss words are inadequate—the English language is sterile that way. Even now I have to skip "satan" and "devil" which sound like a kiss in the dark, and rasp "Portola" or "California," words that have body and spirit.

*

Roosevelt did save the small business man from insanity, suicide or untimely grave by banging away at the public till and also by putting him in office work (his vacant store is for rent), but that is all he did do.

As far as my own case is concerned, I did not get him for better or worse—I have experienced no change whatsoever. I still have the eighteen cents I had seven years ago when he came in, my clothes are just as raggety, and I'm looking for black thread, free of cost, so I can sew the knee chaps back into the pant leg.

Industrial Worker, 2 April 1938

Supplying Arms and a Matter of Business Ethics

I think I have natural talent for business. Even in early youth I was not much good at fighting but I was real good at carrying sticks and stones and other ammunition for the other boys. Isn't that just like a business man?

Business men never get into the trenches but when it comes to carrying ammunition they can't be beat. Not satisfied with carrying ammunition to their own soldiers, they help the enemy also. For a price, of course.

That's where we differ. When I carried ammunition for the other boys I did it as a work of love, patriotism. Solidarity without price. That's point No. 1. Now point No. 2: I would not carry ammunition for the other side at all, for love or money.

Either my business talents were undeveloped or business ethics are degenerated. For, can we concede that business men are internationalists and that they love the whole world so much that they are willing to carry arms to all nations so that they, in turn, can exterminate their neighbors and by them be exterminated?

Industrial Worker, 9 April 1938

Street Beggars

This is the end, the depth of all despair, the man for whom the planets toil and sing, inheritor of earth, sea and air.
Should come to be this starved forsaken thing, whose soft obsequious voice and pleading eye invokes the heedless masses "on" the street, hoping that in the crowd that pass him by, some fat-faced god may deign to let him eat.

This is the darkest deed, the deepest wrong, that man must answer in some distant dawn,
That in this focused earth, there should be need for such as these.
Beggars that pass on down dim lit streets and byways of the night—
Asking of man, what should be man's by right.

Matt V. Huhta

unpublished prose poem written between 1935 and 1942
Westmoreland Archive

Private Letter

Tears are streaming down both sides of my nose, but I never knew before that ale affected me this way.

My case is coming up next Friday; so pull for me hard. Of course I win—now or later.[1]

Joe Hilger
2036 Fifth Ave
N.Y.C.[2]

letter from Slim to his family, date unknown
Westmoreland Archive

---

1 It is unclear to which court case Slim is referring. He was arrested for "disorderly conduct" on 24 February 1939, while living in New York City. He gave his name as Joe Hilger, as he does in this letter, an obvious (though presumably not to the authorities) reference to Joe Hill. However, the disorderly conduct case was resolved in a day, and so it seems that this undated letter refers to something else. See Docket 1115, 24 February 1939, Manhattan District 1 (Tombs), New York City Municipal Archives.

2 This was the location of the Finnish IWW-affiliated Tarmo Club, based in Harlem. That Slim gives this address suggests that he still did not have a permanent address of his own. In a sign of how times have changed with gentrification, this same house and neighborhood are now considered highly desirable by the rich of New York. In 2013, the building was bought by the actor Neil Patrick Harris, who then sold it in 2022 for $6.99 million.

When Privates Fight War by Telephone

In the beginning there was war.

Oracles got up on their hind legs and shouted: "Lookit 'em! Lookit 'em! Those Phoenicians are eating all our ostrich eggs in the deserts and pulling up our mushrooms in the caves!"

So out they went, all God's children, hell-bent for election, and when they got through with the Phoenicians there were less mouths to forage for on both sides, and plenty of crowbait lying around.

Then, as now, it was maldistribution—want. A condition of HAVES and HAVE-NOTS. After the war the HAVES still had and the HAVE-NOTS were dead—on both sides.

"Half nuts," did you say? Shame on you!

Safety for War Makers

In recent days war-mongers have perfected the instruments of destruction: TNT, GAS, GERMS, etc. Civilization died young and war-mongers are crying bitterly against indiscriminate air-bombing of civilians—"the children," they scream. They want to go out and play with the children while the working classes are popping-off one another. Isn't humanity grand?

Great big pot-bellied child of 50 or better prancing around the maypole to the delight of the coming generation when along comes a prowler-plane and drops a pineapple in his coat pocket.

Privates Take Note

Exploiters of labor never come into personal contact with war; neither class war or wars between nations. They flee the war zones. Their commercial carcasses are too valuable, indeed, (to them) to risk in such unseemly proceedings. I have in mind several generations of financial glamor boys that never wore a uniform.

In this later and more enlightened day even generals are not obligated to enter dangerous zones—they can get their information over wires or by wireless and dispatch their orders in the same way; devoid of information, they can "fly it blind" according to prearranged plans and blueprints.

When the privates learn to do all their fighting over phones and wireless, the millennium will have been reached.

Industrial Worker, 23 September 1939

One Man Show Would Please Our Parasites

Ten-Day Notice

Human Rights Invaded—Human rights are those of labor.

In Minnesota they have a law. (Hear! Hear! they're getting civilized!) The law says labor must give ten days' notice of a strike—labor must see that far into the future.[1]

Bad news, labor? They must be prophets in addition to their other brilliant accomplishments.

The "invasion" is not quite apparent unless the law be put to a test.

In order for labor to abide by this law and retain its right of strike whenever the spirit moves, it must put in a notice of strike each day—365 days a year—that way he can run no "unnoticed" strike. A standing notice will not do because it leaves too many legal technicalities.

I wonder who will do the work while the boys are in conference taking their daily strike vote.

The law doesn't say labor must go through with a strike once ordered, if you have guessed wrong or changed your mind. But there might be legal repercussions and you might be tossed in the can for trying to intimidate the boss. (Good for 180 days free board.)

All told, it is best to go through with a strike and put in notice of the next one—you can't miss and the law has been observed, obeyed, and its merit proved.

Since Lindbergh flew the Atlantic we have been unable to do anything with those Minnesotans and the violence of a recent WPA strike there most probably is a parcel of violence within this law.[2]

Industrial Worker, 29 September 1939

---

1 Laws of this type are now standard in most Western capitalist countries.

2 During July 1939, WPA workers took action across the United States to protest funding cuts, the reduction of government-funded jobs, and adverse changes in wages, hours, and eligibility. Some struck for short periods, but 123,000 took action for one to five days, and thousands were dismissed for staying out for longer. In Minnesota on 14 July, one person was killed and twenty-four were wounded when police opened fire on a crowd of three thousand demonstrators. Despite the settlement of the dispute a week later, more than one hundred Minnesota workers were later charged and convicted under antistrike laws.

We Don't Want Dictatorship of Any Color

I was trying to tell our Jewish brethren about the inavailability of the promised land a couple of years ago, but it seems they took the word of Jehovah of a few thousand years ago.[1]

Recently reports from Palestine are to the effect that Jews and Arabs are entirely compatible. Jeeze, I hope Jehovah was right!

Many Americans who were born Jews for reasons beyond their control now take the position that since there is no apparent difference between bolshevism and naziism they may as well cease flirting with mirages and get right down to industrial unionism and industrial democracy—cease betting on a dead horse and recognize the fact that no matter where they go they are a minority, intelligent or otherwise.

Under democracy they have "voice and vote!" Under dictatorship they have to "put up or shut up!" Politics is not the way out.

I am happy that some of the smartest Jews have been and are today members of the Industrial Workers of the World.

Minorities from all over the world look to the IWW for a fair break—they'll get it. And the oppressed minorities in time will see the futility of seeking redress in extraneous channels.

Won't that be a happy day when every "bum" has a bathtub and rolls out a "nature's nobleman"; when both justice and injustice are in a dog house with their many implications? Fairness is inherent.

Industrial Worker, 2 December 1939

---

1 A reference to the growing Zionist movement, which would lead to the establishment of the state of Israel in 1948 and the subsequent ethnic cleansing of millions of Palestinians.

1940–1942

Nobody Is Shooting at the Rulers

Only ten years now the cracker sandwich economists have been solving unemployment. First hundred years are worst.

In a gale of wind shorten sail, or slow the ship; in a doldrum of hot air, shorten hours and let nature take its course.

Organize industrially and acknowledge your corn.

wIw

Verily, I say unto you that a cube of butter spreads kind of thin on the orphan slice, and secures nothing but our appetite.

Machine-cut ham reaches a greater number of the sandwich buying masticators. However, the bread is not cut thicker, it only seems so. Law of compensation determines that any deficiency in ham emphasizes the potentialities of bread. (See Einstein's Theory of Relativity.)

wIw

Heywood Broun is dead!

There are some people that could not fully appreciate him. It is one of the seriousities of my life that I have not found him wanting. Whenever there was a question, we found there an answer.

Words fail me . . . He was a union man.

So do we mourn Heywood Broun. That he disagreed with his all-powerful bosses repeatedly is not the least of his accomplishments.

Industrial Worker, 6 January 1940

Should Indians Have Registered the Foreigners?

Nothing uncertain about Europe's fate except uncertainty. Minorities are still being pushed off the deep end. Right here in Pennsylvania, of all states, the courts had to step in to prevent half-baked legislators from registering aliens—they wanted to create a raft of untouchables here and subdivide the USA and call it Disunited States of America.[1]

Luckily the judges were sober.

But you do not have to be a part of the (intelligent) minority and get hexed up that way; you can join the working class and be a part of the Big Majority, the One Big Union.

Yes, they were going to get the "John Hancock" of the stranger in a strange land and further disrupt the nation by creating a raft of voluntary spies—same as the purple gods do in Yurrop.

Seems to me I didn't see any Indians meeting our illustrious Puritans, and the *Mayflower*, with a registration sheet in their hands. All they said was, "How, How"—and offered to chop codfish bait for our forefathers.

It is argued now, however, with the vast registration schemes and regimentation, that the Indians made a mistake when they did not clap our illustrious forefathers in irons.

All that will be a bad dream, a vanished nightmare, when the good people get hep to themselves and join the Big Majority—the working class—and recognize the fact.

There's a vast difference between commonsense and common nonsense: one puts butter on the bread.

wIw

Barometric "millibars," that's what we're going to have now. How everything changes! Instead of "bull," we will have ebullience; instead of "sassy," we will brace ourselves and say insouciance; instead of "stinko," we say binge—damme if we ain't getting polite in our old age!

Industrial Worker, 27 January 1940

---

[1] The Alien Registration Act, which by this time had passed the U.S. House of Representatives but not yet the Senate, established criminal penalties for promoting the overthrow of the U.S. government through force or violence and required all noncitizen adult inhabitants to register with the federal government. It would be signed into law on 28 June 1940. Slim is likely also referring to earlier state-level laws that were intended to accomplish the same goals.

How Slim Brought Peace to Frazee

Despite the fact that USA is strictly snootral on the matter of the Finn-Russian war,[1] the great preponderance believe the war ended too soon—the newspapers were just getting so they could talk Finn better than I can myself. Radio, too, was getting so that it could spiel **äidin kieltä**[2] like thoroughbreds.

wIw

Now on coal barges, they load you one day, the tug tows that night; next day they unload you and the tug tows you that night.[3] Next day they load you and the considerate tug again tows you under cover of darkness. Tugs tow only in the night time and many of them would be ashamed to show themselves in broad daylight.

This goes on indefinitely and the captain is supposed to get his sleep—in the grave; and remain cheerful in the meantime.

After the captain is thoroughly exhausted and staggers a little on his off-hoof, the offices at both ends of the "run" conclude "the captain has bent a knee to the powerful John Barleycorn[4] in hope of gaining enforced wakefulness." What an outrageous calumny! Who ever heard of a barge captain "bending a knee" to say nothing about bending an elbow. And they pull down the telephones and notify the poor captain's boss: "Your captain on the coal barge *Paradise* is—drunk." Not satisfied with that they spell it right out D-R-U-N-K. And the poor man was only T-I-R-E-D.

A married captain once hadn't seen his home and family for 37 days. When he showed up at the house his dear wife failed to recognize him and his children crawled under the bed.

And still the boatowners have the guts to deny these workers even simple, fair, single-time for double-time work and they stalk them night and day trying to place a wolf upon their doorstep.

---

1 The Soviet Union invaded Finland on 30 November 1939, beginning the so-called Winter War. The Soviets met unexpected resistance from Finnish armed forces and signed a peace treaty on 13 March 1940. Slim was outraged by the invasion and makes repeated reference to it in his work. The invasion seems to have hardened his anti-communism and made him relate more closely to his Finnish heritage.

2 Finnish for "mother tongue."

3 Slim is describing his work as a deck scow captain, which was not a captain in the popular sense but rather a cross between a night watchman and a maintenance man. Deck scows, typically manned by a single worker, did not have engines and so had to be pulled by tugboats. Slim seems to have slept aboard the scow, which was not unusual. Our thanks to Saku Pinta for his excellent research in this area.

4 A slang term for alcohol.

A little organization just about now would be of great benefit to the boatmen of the gilded harbor.

wIw

The nerve of those Finns, trying to lick half of Asia and the big half of Europe reminds me of the time I tried to bring law and order to Frazee, Minn. Elmer Buddinger, strapping lad of 5 ft. 1, wrote me afterwards: "You ought to know better than to try to lick a town the size of Frazee without my assistance." And him 48 miles away!

It was thought that peace could best be preserved by having a deputy walk guard in front of my cell.

Industrial Worker, 30 March 1940

Masters Start War but Won't Stay to Fight

For some we loved, the loveliest and best
That from this vintage rolling Time
has prest,
Have drunk their cup a round or two
before.
And one by one crept silently to rest.

—Omar[1]

We who have attended the funeral of the IWW so often feel that a good word might be said for its birth, the birth of a working class—the working class is now 35 years young—same age as the IWW.

Be it noted the two shared the same cradle when they were bouncing babies, and even today no threat of death to their hope or ideal hath risen to disturb the serene equanimity of these two "Siamese Twins." No accoutrement of undertakers, flowers, mourners, graves or headstones hath harassed this great body—in fact, it is just beginning to feel its oats, and kicking the bucket physically or spiritually is farthest from its thoughts. (Learning to live is the present peccadillo.) Just like that, mysterious and mischievous as a lad trying out each new-found muscle or power.

Three hundred twenty-five years ago Cervantes hauls off in his *Don Quixote* and says (in effect) "Industry is the mother of success." Just 300 years later the IWW says, "Cerv, you've got something there" and, determining to have the name as well as the game, they organized the Industrial Workers of the World. That was 35 years ago and it seems like only the other day.

So why should we that took 300 years to discover the truth in Cervantes' crack, "industry is the thing" despair of the handful of wobblie years?[2]

Must we wait another 300 years to be showered with the accolade, "IWW was right"?

Industrial Worker, 29 June 1940

---

1 From *The Rubáiyát of Omar Khayyám.*

2 A reference to the IWW's relative weakness at this point, compared to its earlier years.

Don't Stop to Rest on Dead Center

Alas and wurra wurra, the alarm clock manufacturers got caught with their pants slightly down!

So many of the workers were dispossessed of their jobs[1] and put on relief that the sale of alarm clocks fell off tragically. Manufacturers discovered alarm clock production terrifically over-expanded—and there they stood, fingers, hearts and legs crossed. But they hope to recoup the price of brass by high-pressure advertising.

They now offer a first class dollar alarm clock for 54 cents. That would seem to indicate that about half of the early risers are idle or on the government payroll. And, they swear by all that's pure and holy that these alarm clocks will actually coax you out of bed and find your shoes for you, even if you left them on the porch last night.

That's what I call service, and if I had the 54 cents I would buy me one of them; if for no other reason than as a memento of the days when I too had a job, so long ago. As it is, I get up too early, for I cannot sleep, thinking about where's the breakfast coming from.

Industrial Worker, 17 August 1940

---

[1] That is, fired.

Politicians Will Squirm after the War

Owing to the collection of bundles for foreign sufferers, the great American hobo is denied his customary finery and is far from being the fashionplate of the happier years.[1] I would therefore suggest the government proclaim a national year-around summer so that my compatriots may pull a strip-tease and join a nudist colony. They haven't much to take off.

We have a shortage of paper and a surplus of cotton but we do not know how to make paper from surplus cotton. Yeah, our tears are genuine. Maybe some schoolboy can tell us.

*

"Coordination of collective action," is the big word Harvard boys hung onto the neck of the One Big Union. You've got to be almost a contortionist to say it. However, it means the same as "Scat, capitalism," or "Scram, privilege," as Victor Hugo would say it.

*

I started out to be an editor when I was young and foolish and I might still be in the toils were it not for a slight error.

I was supposed to headline that "Rev. Bonso Celebrates His Fiftieth Year as St. Alban's Pastor." I ran it, "Rev. Bonso Celebrates His Filthiest Year," etc.

I didn't notice it myself, or I would have said my prayers. But finally, after a couple of weeks, somebody accidentally glanced at a back number of the sheet I'm editing and the headline that I'd labored over so lovingly almost knocked his eye out. The words had too many vitamins.

After that it was the talk of the town (Pueblo or Dobeyville) but I got 723 new subscribers before the can was tied to my tail.

All my friends still insist, "Slim, you were positively correct in that headline and since you left that paper—that (cuss word) disgraceful sheet has lost all sense of civic hygiene and plenty subscribers."[2]

*

"Canadian priests that first prayed for peace (that they didn't get) now are praying for victory."—Quebec.

---

1 This article appeared after another long publication break for Slim, for which there is currently no clear explanation. Of the forty-five issues of *Industrial Worker* published from July 1941 through May 1942, only six featured writings by Slim.

2 This story seems fanciful. As noted in the Introduction, in his youth Slim had been a "literary agent," most likely meaning that he handled correspondence, including writing to newspapers, for a temperance society.

I suppose if that fails they'll pray for mercy.

German people were promised "peace"; they got war. They were promised a short war; they got a long war. They were promised "victory"; they got . . . ?

Industrial Worker, 5 April 1941

Warning of Cannon Fodder Shortage for War of 1960

Official spokesmen close to hind-quarters intimate that if the folks don't get busy right now and produce boy-children, the politicians won't be able to rig up a war in 1960–65—unless they adopt foreign children.[1]

Adopting foreign children is out, because foreigners expect to sacrifice their children in the present fracas. (Thanks, professors, for the info.)

Scientists have already prepared a formula whereby parents can determine the sex of prospective offspring as much as a year and a half in advance. Now isn't that nice?

Doting parents can bend the column-gossip's ear and whisper at the top of their lungs, "I've got a soldier on the way." Or a Red Cross nurse, as the case may be.

The beauty of this arrangement is that if the birthrate of nurse-maids out-strips that of armor-bearers, the doctors can switch signs on the bottles.

Is that goose-stepping or mere duck-waddle?

Industrial Worker, 3 May 1941

[1] This is prescient, given the United States' official entry into the Vietnam War in 1965 (and the presence of U.S. military "advisers" in the years before that).

Produce for Use and Peace Will Come at Last

"Let's stop thinking that all business leaders are Satans."

Second the motion; we ain't a bit superstitious. Business leaders are very gullible chaps that have allowed themselves to be snared into foreign entanglements—the whole world was to be dished them on a platter. Yea bo, and they'll be lucky if they get a few comebacks from the larder that is the world's swillbarrel. Satan would blush! Let us for cripes sake quit kidding ourselves that our belligerency is merely an act to kid Britain out of a few war orders.[1] (The accusations will come later, much later, and we shall be hailed as low-down, double-crossing hypocrites.)

*

Unionism is as disunited as the nation, but the "wob" is not to blame. Some characters mourn the fact that the IWW is allergic to political action; that it doesn't make of the House of Labor a variety show; that it stands uncompromisingly on industrial action at the point of production, uninfluenced, unafraid, refusing to hash the detail.

Political action has put many a promising nation on the rocks; job action never yet wrecked a nation.

*

It has been said that the great T-Bone Slim is slipping—and don't I know it, that his present day catarrhal outbursts are as nothing compared to the time he had rheumatism? I subscribe to that viewpoint and can only mourn the fact that the IWW trusted the care of my head to a wrong guy. Plenty of fellow workers in the movement could take better care of it than I can.—Mourn no more, what's one head among so many?

Industrial Worker, 14 June 1941

[1] The United States would declare war on Japan and Germany on 11 December 1941.

I Didn't Know It Was Loaded

An entirely wrongful impression has gone forth about army training. People gird themselves to the belief it consists of scrubbing deck, smoothing the bed, peeling the spud and rushing a swamp or tangle of barbwire. All those come later.

The paramount maneuver is to train the stomach to accept of food after all these years of depressive fasting. Indeed, the army had to take the stress off of beans in favor of foods that lie lighter on the stomach. Now, however, our valiant sojers are fairly well stuffed up and we are practically prepared to take on any second rate power that gives us a dirty look with more than one eye.

*

My ace correspondent takes the spotlight away from me by saying "seems to me as if all god's chillun would be better off if they started some wholesale thinking instead of wholesale slaughter among themselves; just because they hear the howl of werewolves is no reason they should run with them."[1]

*

How we used to laugh when we read historical documents to the purport that ancient lowbrows used to sacrifice to their deities made of wood and plaster of Paris; and now, when we sacrifice millions of soldiers to the war gods and to brainlessness, we cannot even crack a smile. . . .

About the only man that's getting a laugh out of it is our own good T-Bone Slim—

You drink some rock and rye,
Then take the crock and cry . . .

There's possibilities in poesy, but out of consideration for Covami I am persuaded to hold my peace.[2]

*

---

1 This is another reference to calls for the United States to enter the war, something that Slim strongly opposed.

2 Covami, who also wrote under the names Covington Ami and Covington Hall, was born William Covington Hall. He was an IWW newspaper editor, columnist, and prolific poet whose work was often featured in Wobbly newspapers. Born into a white plantation-owning Southern family that lost its wealth when he was twenty years old, he was also a member of the Sons of Confederate Veterans, but lost his position within that organization for arguing against racial segregation. Covami surely deserves his own collected edition one day.

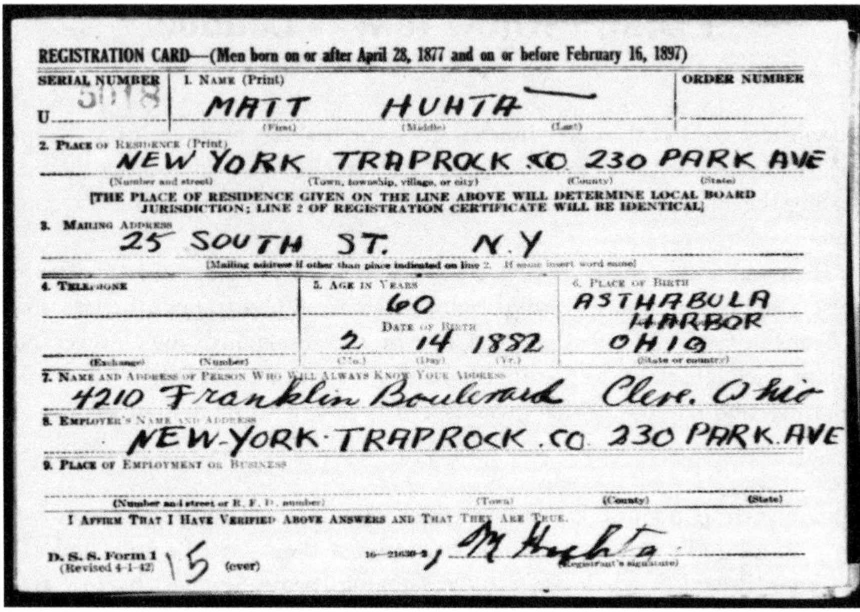
REGISTRATION CARD—(Men born on or after April 28, 1877 and on or before February 16, 1897)

SERIAL NUMBER U 5018 | 1. NAME (Print) MATT HUHTA (First) (Middle) (Last) | ORDER NUMBER

2. PLACE OF RESIDENCE (Print) NEW YORK TRAPROCK CO 230 PARK AVE (Number and street) (Town, township, village, or city) (County) (State)

[THE PLACE OF RESIDENCE GIVEN ON THE LINE ABOVE WILL DETERMINE LOCAL BOARD JURISDICTION; LINE 2 OF REGISTRATION CERTIFICATE WILL BE IDENTICAL]

3. MAILING ADDRESS 25 SOUTH ST. N.Y

[Mailing address if other than place indicated on line 2. If same insert word same]

4. TELEPHONE (Exchange) (Number) | 5. AGE IN YEARS 60 DATE OF BIRTH 2 14 1882 (Mo.) (Day) (Yr.) | 6. PLACE OF BIRTH ASTHABULA HARBOR OHIO (State or country)

7. NAME AND ADDRESS OF PERSON WHO WILL ALWAYS KNOW YOUR ADDRESS 4210 Franklin Boulevard Cleve. Ohio

8. EMPLOYER'S NAME AND ADDRESS NEW-YORK TRAPROCK .CO 230 PARK AVE

9. PLACE OF EMPLOYMENT OR BUSINESS

(Number and street or R. F. D. number) (Town) (County) (State)

I AFFIRM THAT I HAVE VERIFIED ABOVE ANSWERS AND THAT THEY ARE TRUE.

D. S. S. Form 1 (Revised 4-1-42) 15 (over) 16—21630-2 M Huhta (Registrant's signature)

Slim's World War II draft card. 25 South Street was the address of the Seaman's Church Institute, which provided dormitory-style accommodation for sailors and other maritime workers. The SCI also housed a doctors' clinic, dental and eye clinic, employment bureau, bank, library, and restaurant.

Doctor ordered me to eat no meat, so in all the lunchowonetts I visit, I always order meat balls, knowing there is no meat in them. Just sprinkle them with a little salt and pepper, and you can imagine you are eating venison and bear steak.

I feel stronger already.

*

Fellow Worker "Nick"[3] startled me out of my death rattles this very day and I am half tempted to leave the metropolis flat, and hie myself to the beauteous Los Angeles and do some viewing with pride, and stroll the dry river bottoms for the sake of my morals. . . .

Industrial Worker, 27 September 1941

[3] A writer named "Old Nick" had filled in for Slim during his most recent publication absence, producing articles purporting to be letters to Slim, as well as some fake replies from him.

Yes, Labor Is Partly to Blame

We know how much rubber we have but we do not know how many unemployed rubbernecks grace our thoroughfares.

We know a matter of nine million men face the draft this semester but we do not know how many of them will be culled.

Therefore: It is good policy for the draftees not to brag about their possible induction because, if they fail, they may frighten their boss and be thereafter professional culls so long as they live. How much nicer it is to remark nonchalantly, "They're not sending their best men to the front lines first."

That builds morale!

*

Ordinarily in peacetime I would say it is well for Uncle Sam to cancel all of his foreign shipping, but now in wartime I must observe: Uncle Sam should not cancel any of his shipping, because to do so will draw bombers to his cities and hamlets.

A pretty good tip right there. We may as well be aggressive and keep score.

When New York City is bombed, say May 10–20, you may be sure I will not run. Not that I'm brave or bullheaded, but I've been reading in the press reports that the only ones that get hit by bombs are a few children, women, a nurse or two and a blind newsboy. I'd be an awful donkey, were I to skedaddle, good as my insteps are. No, I would give them the Bronx cheer and stand my ground. (Note: I'd get pinched for this, because the goodly Mayor LaGuardia has said "DON'T SHOUT.")

*

Last night we had a test blackout and, as is customary with me in an emergency, I went to bed and covered up my head with a Navajo blanket so as to keep the darkness out.

To say the least, blackout is a promise, a prophecy, foreboding eternal darkness.

*

Seamen, however, cannot cover up with blankets when the ship is at sea, dark and lumbering through the dark—for they know they are in a terrible jeopardy. They may be blown-up, shot or sunk.

It might happen off Sandy Hook, 900 miles out, off the east coast of Norway, New Zealand, etc.; or in the Caribbean, half-way point, where the axis submarines get them coming and going in the lukewarm southern seas.

*

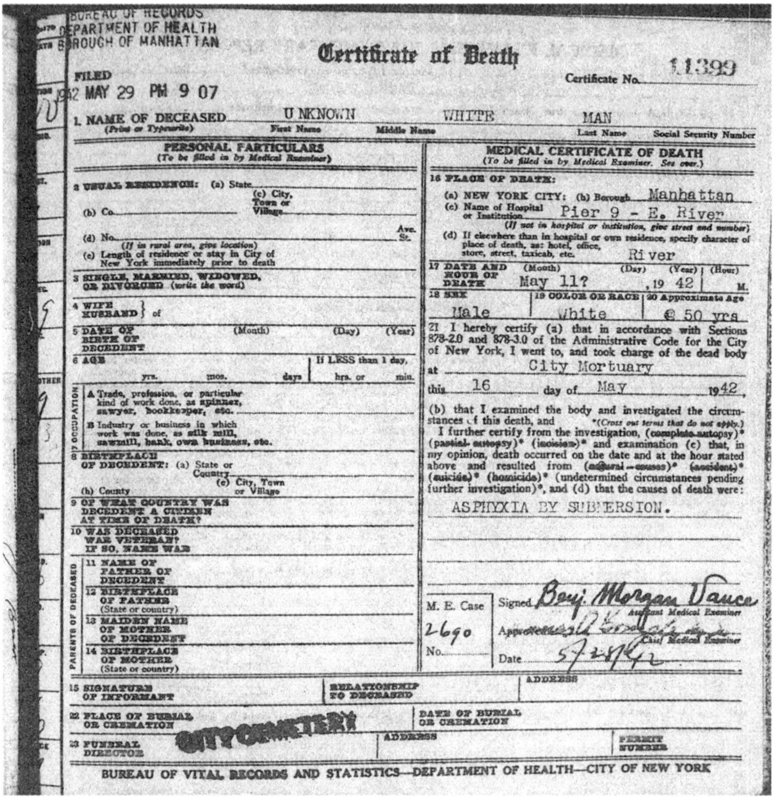

BUREAU OF RECORDS
DEPARTMENT OF HEALTH
BOROUGH OF MANHATTAN

Certificate of Death

Certificate No. 11399

FILED
1942 MAY 29 PM 9 07

1. NAME OF DECEASED UNKNOWN WHITE MAN

PERSONAL PARTICULARS (To be filled in by Medical Examiner)

MEDICAL CERTIFICATE OF DEATH (To be filled in by Medical Examiner. See over.)

16 PLACE OF DEATH: (a) NEW YORK CITY: (b) Borough Manhattan
(c) Name of Hospital or Institution Pier 9 - E. River
(d) If elsewhere than in hospital or own residence, specify character of place of death, as: hotel, office, store, street, taxicab, etc. River

17 DATE AND HOUR OF DEATH May 11? , 1942

18 SEX Male 19 COLOR OR RACE White 20 Approximate Age @ 50 yrs

21 I hereby certify (a) that in accordance with Sections 878-2.0 and 878-3.0 of the Administrative Code for the City of New York, I went to, and took charge of the dead body at City Mortuary this 16 day of May 1942,

(b) that I examined the body and investigated the circumstances of this death, and I further certify from the investigation, (partial autopsy) (inquiry) and examination (c) that, in my opinion, death occurred on the date and at the hour stated above and resulted from (undetermined circumstances pending further investigation), and (d) that the causes of death were:

ASPHYXIA BY SUBMERSION.

M. E. Case No. 2690

Signed Benj. Morgan Vance, Assistant Medical Examiner

Date 5/28/42

22 PLACE OF BURIAL OR CREMATION CITY CEMETERY

BUREAU OF VITAL RECORDS AND STATISTICS—DEPARTMENT OF HEALTH—CITY OF NEW YORK

Slim's death certificate. His body was never formally identified, as that would have required the presence of a family member.

To a certain extent, we are experiencing a compulsory isolation, much to our sorrow.

Unemployment still graces our land as a result of half-way measures and equally half-baked gestures to mollify the gullible.

Half-way measures, however, are dear to a trusting soul and even today we ration sugar mostly at the expense of John Workox.

Why not eliminate sugar entirely from our diet, instead of nursing us with a teaspoon?

How many labor hours are lost in the hasher questioning a sweet-tooth "how many dabs of sugar do you want?"

Hasher stands poised, the sweet-tooth squirms and tries to analyze his cravings—both superpatriots, plus.

Industrial Worker, 4 April 1942[1]

---

1 This was Slim's final article before his death in mid-May 1942.

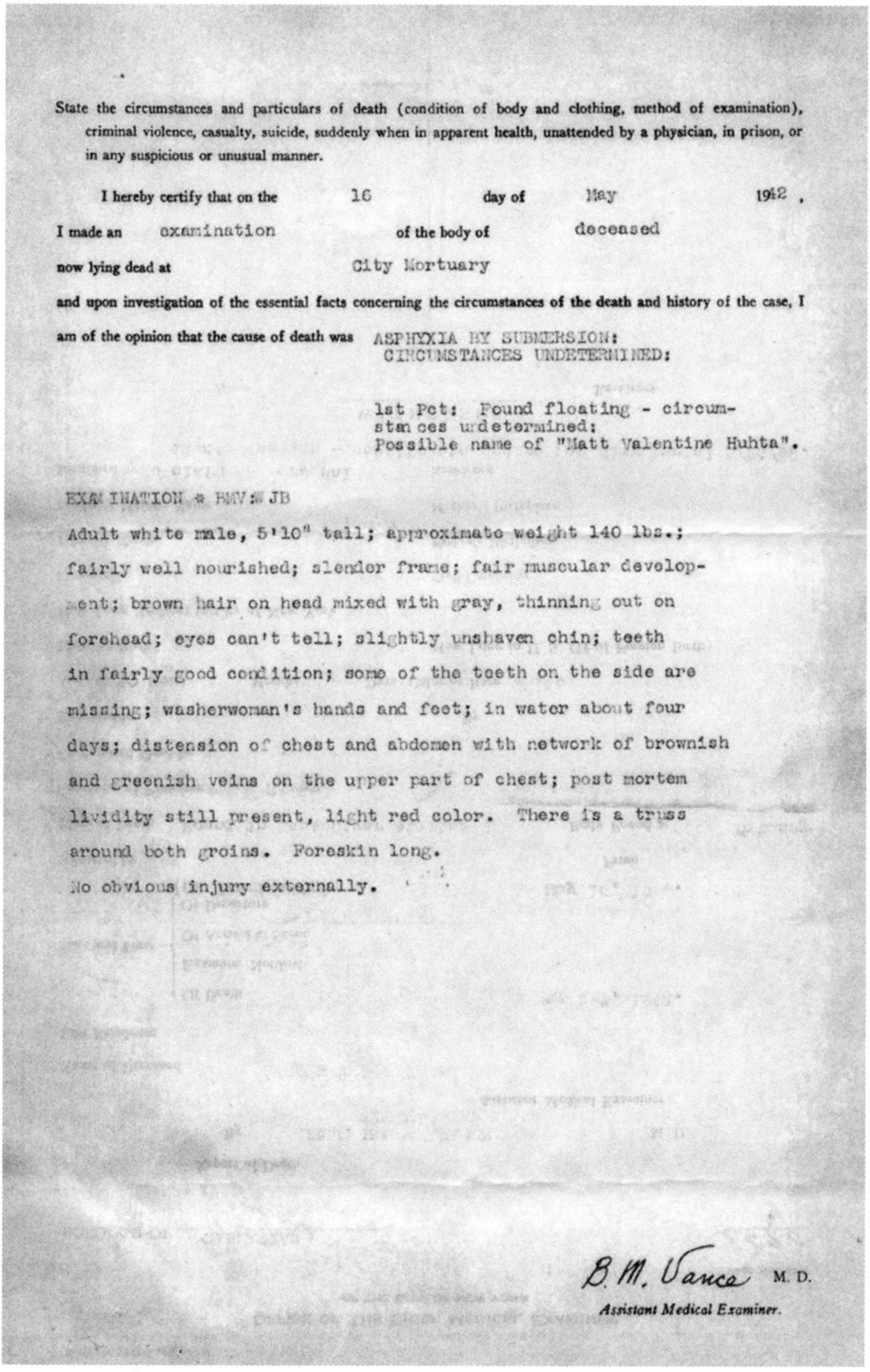

State the circumstances and particulars of death (condition of body and clothing, method of examination), criminal violence, casualty, suicide, suddenly when in apparent health, unattended by a physician, in prison, or in any suspicious or unusual manner.

I hereby certify that on the 16 day of May 1942,

I made an examination of the body of deceased

now lying dead at City Mortuary

and upon investigation of the essential facts concerning the circumstances of the death and history of the case, I am of the opinion that the cause of death was ASPHYXIA BY SUBMERSION: CIRCUMSTANCES UNDETERMINED:

1st Pct: Found floating - circumstances undetermined: Possible name of "Matt Valentine Huhta".

EXAMINATION - BMV:W JB

Adult white male, 5'10" tall; approximate weight 140 lbs.; fairly well nourished; slender frame; fair muscular development; brown hair on head mixed with gray, thinning out on forehead; eyes can't tell; slightly unshaven chin; teeth in fairly good condition; some of the teeth on the side are missing; washerwoman's hands and feet; in water about four days; distension of chest and abdomen with network of brownish and greenish veins on the upper part of chest; post mortem lividity still present, light red color. There is a truss around both groins. Foreskin long.
No obvious injury externally.

B. M. Vance M. D.
Assistant Medical Examiner.

The coroner's report on Slim's death.

Responses to T-Bone Slim

To T-Bone Slim

George Baker

There's a man in our organization
Who's acquired a fine education.
Most of the members envy him—
Known to us all as T-Bone Slim.

This man whom we envy has sure
made a hit
With men who are doing their bit
To rid this world of greedy shirkers
And make it safe for us common
workers.

The stories he writes are so clear and
plain,
When you've read them once you'll
read them again.
They're so interesting and crammed
with jest—
He believes in giving the workers his
best.

This intelligent person oft works in
the woods,
And has proved himself able in pro-
ducing the goods.
He can take any job, be it swamper
or skinner,
And as well blow the horn that calls
them to dinner.

In the harvest fields he can also be
seen
In back of a binder or driving a team;
Or on a threshing machine, all covered
with dust,
He can feed her so fast you'd think
she would bust.

When this man comes to town, it's so
sad to state,
Never thinks of retiring, till it's al-
most too late.
He's surrounded with books and pam-
phlets galore,
You'd think he was running a news-
paper store.

You'll find him sitting with pencil and
book,
And on his face a most dignified look:
He's remodeling a clipping from out
of the press,
And you can bet your life it will be
a success.

When he comes in the hall he is given
the floor,
'Cause the members are ready and
anxious for more
Of his enthralling talks, they are al-
ways so thrilling.
And to enlighten the members he's
always so willing.

So here's to the man who has proved
himself true
To the Industrial Workers, as all
members should do;
So let's get together and take exam-
ple from him—
Let us keep up the good work of
T-BONE SLIM.

Industrial Solidarity, 18 March 1925

T-Bone Slim Ill

"Editor Worker"

We recently had a letter from Fellow Worker T-bone Slim in which he stated that he is sick and will be unable to write for the *Worker* again for some time. Luckily we have a few of his inimitable articles which will be printed from time to time, but we sincerely hope he will soon recover his health.

Of all the writers for the I. W. W. press, there is not one who has laid bare the rotten sores of capitalism so unerringly as has this fellow worker, whose very name is unknown to nine-tenths of his readers. Perhaps his great power of expression has been gained through the third of his three great ambitions, as expressed in the *Worker* of April 18:

"To be a party to all current heartaches, want and oppression—we desire no special privilege."

Here's to you, Slim;
  You're one of our own!
We wish you long life,
  Fellow Worker T-Bone.

Industrial Worker, 22 April 1925

Why No News from Our "T-Bone Slim"?

Sam Murray

Some time ago the *Worker* announced that T-bone Slim had gone to the hospital and that he would be unable to write for some time.[1] I have no doubt that most of our members are anxious to hear of him and there must be someone who is visiting him wherever he is and could furnish the news for the papers. It is seldom that an organization has a member with the genius of our gifted columnist and it is natural that the membership should be concerned about his condition and prospects of returning to health.

Who is Slim anyhow?

Some time ago a discussion was brought out by someone who thought he knew the mysterious character who furnishes the laughs for our press. As to the possibility of his having been a herring choker,[2] I have no opinion, but having just read my May Day number of *Sol* I am inclined to think that I have learned something about the previous condition of servitude of our humorist. Look at this:

"Flettners 'rotor sails' would be more 'efficient' still if they were modeled after a lady's corset: It would have a tendency of creating a regular 'pocket' of suction that would stay by the ship till the last sailor had starved to death munching seabiscuit and salt horse—or choked to death over vacuum created by plum duff once a week—on Thursdays."—From May Day *Sol.*

Now I want to ask any old salt, who has managed to live through into this age of marine janitors, if this does not bear prima facia evidence of having been written by someone who has bucked a head wind around the Horn or crossed the western ocean in the dead of winter without seaboots—or both. You can study literature but you can only learn seamanship by practice and the article in question is seamanship.

I claim that nothing but numerous trips in the good old ships that were propelled by canvas and pea soup could have inspired that article.

The final test of good humor!

This also reminds me that, inasmuch as we see too much of the tragic and too little good humor in our press that our membership should try to cultivate

1 While working at a lumber camp in January 1925, Slim suffered an accident that injured his ankle. One month later he wrote of being affected by an illness that made him feverish and possibly bronchial, which put him in bed for weeks and may have led to his becoming hard of hearing in one ear. In August 1925, he reported that he was "still in bad shape."

2 In the United States, this term referred to a person from Scandinavia.

their talents along that line. We can all get off the solemn stuff—the boss has taken care of that—and it is not the fault of the I. W. W. that our members are somewhat lacking in the gift of humor but our press is in need of stuff that will even make a slave of laugher if it is to be built up. If you think you can do the trick, write up something and try it on the editor. If it gets by him you still want to be sure so show it to the next "Emergency"[3] guy you meet and if he laughs you know damn well it is good.—

Industrial Worker, 9 May 1925

[3] A reference to the section of the IWW that broke away from the union in 1924 to set up a separate organization of the same name. At that year's convention it had offered up an "Emergency Program" that involved major decentralization and abolishment of the General Executive Board. This rival IWW lasted until 1931.

A Reader Appreciates Our T-Bone Slim

T-Bone Slim's writing re: the cherry-pie-fly is surely a classic.[1] It is universal, appeals to fundamental human feelings, and does so with keenest wit and comprehension.

T-Bone does not waste any tears, yelps, or growls about things. He is consistently superior to circumstances. The appeal of his writing is nevertheless very great. You can't forget what he says. You are carried on in reading his stuff by his kaleidoscopic humor.

Of course his articles would not look so good in a book[2] (for example, the references to the editor mean most right in the paper), but they are truly classic, representative of our times, with universal appeal. I trust they will be filed and preserved for posterity.

Industrial Solidarity, 23 September 1925

---

1 See, in this volume, the article "T-Bone Slim Discusses: Chop Suey," *Industrial Solidarity,* 26 August 1925.

2 We would respectfully disagree!

THE INDUSTRIAL WORKER, wobbly organ of the imminent revolution of the proletariat, has for its columnist one **T-Bone Slim,** a gentleman I strongly suspect of originating many of the newer wobbly words and phrases. In a recent number he wrote:

"A working stiff often gets it into what he thinks is his head that by merely saving what money he can spare from his $3.50 per day, and investing it in **Just Some Good, Safe Stocks,** he will some day surely become a **Ford** or a **Rockefeller.** Such a working stiff, gentlemen, should be treated at once. He is suffering from the first stages of **hydro-forbesia.**"

A great Hearst publicist comes in for much razzing at the hand of Slim, and **brisbanalities** is now official in the wobbly thesaurus.—Stewart H. Holbrook, in **The American Mercury.**

T-BONE SLIM

Has An Article Every Week In

SOLIDARITY

There is a lot more in Industrial Solidarity and Industrial Worker than T-Bone Slim's column. These two papers are the I. W. W. weekly publications, packed full of news about the labor movement; and about the workers' correct form of organization.

Industrial Solidarity is the official organ of the I. W. W., published at General Headquarters, 3333 Belmont Ave., Chicago. Sells for $2 a year; single copies five cents; bundle orders of five or more, three cents a copy.

Industrial Worker is the newspaper of the Northwest Branches of the I. W. W., same price as Industrial Solidarity, published at Seattle, Wash., Address P. O. Box 1857.

You are missing a lot if you don't get each of these papers. You can't say you know the labor movement of America unless you read the journals of its most militant section. Written by workers, and written for workers.

Write for sample of Solidarity to

3333 Belmont Avenue, Chicago, Illinois

Advertisement from *Industrial Pioneer,* February 1926. Newberry Library, Rosemont–T-Bone Slim Research Collection.

Interviewing T-Bone Slim

In Which the "Brisbanalities" of Brisbane Are Traced to Moronistic Origins

Covami

Coming across T-Bone Slim, the great Wobblie Filosofer, in Dreamlandville the other night, I says to him: "T-Bone, how did you come to invent that word 'Brisbanalities'?[1] It's the most expressive term incorporated into the American language for decades," I says.

"I thank you for the compliment, Covami," he says, "but I really don't deserve the credit. The word really created itself. It slips out of Arthur's name as naturally as a duck slides into water, once a fellow realizes how slickily Arthur slips over things that ain't so with an air of uttering unquestionable facts and eternal verities. The guy that invented half-truth-lying ain't in it with Arthur. Arthur can make the truth itself lie, and do it so plausibly and pleasantly that only those who are used to doing their own thinking—and blamed few are guilty of that—would ever suspicion there was even a modicum of propaganda in the education he was handing out. What makes it easier for him is that Arthur is in complete atone-ment with the moron mind and so he does not have to reason with his fellow patriots. All he has to say is: 'Boys, there's no limit to the price we can put on California climate, Florida sunshine and Wall Street water. Buy while the buying is going up, and the more you buy the better off you'll be. Remember, He who hesitates is lost! But, don't gamble, boys, don't gamble.' Well, they buy and, when the crash comes and they get stung, does that faze Arthur? Not on your life it don't. All Arthur has to say then is: 'Well, brother morons, I told you not to gamble. So I'm not to blame. My conscience is clear and easy.' And I'm derned if they don't beg him for some more investment advice."

"T-Bone," I says, "you are too hard on him. Arthur is a master of moronic psychology. He and Cal Coolidge were pals, two hearts that beat as one, two servants of the people with but a single thought."

"Yes, to do the aforesaid people," says T-B. buttin' in.

"Shame on you!" I shrieks.

"All right," says Slim, "shame on you; but listen to this recent blurb from Arthur's colyums."

"A report published by Mr. Frederick H. Ecker, president of the Metropolitan Life

---

1 Widely credited to Slim, this neologism is a play on the name and work of Arthur Brisbane. It entered public consciousness to a degree and was picked up by H. L. Mencken in the fourth edition of his book *The American Language* (1937).

Insurance company, concerning 19,000,000 industrial policy-holders in the United States and Canada, shows that workers are living longer than they used to.

"Thanks to science and prosperity, the death rate among wage-earners has diminished. Mr. Ecker's statistical bureau shows a new low death rate of 9.4 per 1,000 during March.

"More adults that live, fewer babies that die, is a good program.'

"Now Arthur knows better than that, or ort to. He knows, first, that no insurance company president, especially one working the 'Industrial insurance' graft on poor folks, could tell the truth about his business and continue to lap up the profit from the 'lapses.' Arthur knows that and, second, he knows he is straining the facts beyond the breaking point when he states that, due to 'science and prosperity' (?), 'the death rate among wage-earners has diminished.' Arthur knows that according to all medical authorities that his assertion ain't so; knows that all that has happened is that 'fewer babies die' and so live to be 'adults'; which may be, as he 'says,' 'a good program,' but nobody is 'living longer than they used to.' All that has happened is that the 'average age' has been lengthened but there's a heluvalot of difference between our 'average age' and our actual individual share of earthly existence, as will become clear to any jobhunter who compares the 'average wage' we freeborn Americans are supposed to get with the wage we actually annex on payday. That is something else again, as the Dutchman correctly observed."

"I guess you are right, as usual, T-B," I says.

"Sure, I am," he rejoinds. "And that ain't all. Don' it make you just too happy for anything to learn that 'Mr. Ecker's[2] statistical bureau shows a new low death rate of 9.4 per 1,000 during March'? Jeewhillikins! the Met sure must either be picking out perfect specimens of homo sapiens or the old uns must be 'lapsing' like lightning to make a record as far below the National average as that! Their motto ort to be: 'Insure in the Metropolitan and outlive Methuselah'!"

"Maybe so," I says; "but as for me, right now I'd rather gulp some of the bevo that made Milwaukee famous and"—

"Covami," he says, with a mournful look in his luminous eyes, "I got a damgood notion to knock your block off for that and"—

Well, right there I woke up and, unless I badly miss my guess, just in time to save my psyche from a sock on the snout. Anyhow, just as I complimented him, there has been no finer word added to the American language than "Brisbanalities."

Industrial Worker, 31 May 1930

---

2 Frederick Ecker served as the president of the New York–based Metropolitan Life Insurance Company, better known as MetLife, from 1929 to 1936. During this period the company came to insure roughly 20 percent of the American and Canadian population and diversified into real estate, financing the Empire State Building as well as racially segregated housing developments.

Foes Recognize Power of Our Inimitable Columnist, T-Bone Slim

Denver, Colo.—Writing in his column "By Way of Observations" in *The Rocky Mountain News* of July 23, Lee Taylor speaks of revolutionary publications coming to his desk, for which he subscribes and which are given him. He says:

"They include organs of the I. W. W., the communists, the socialist labor party and other proponents of an industrial revolution. Many of them are exceptionally well written; the column signed by 'T-bone Slim' in *Industrial Solidarity* has the force of Hemingway plus the sting of Swift: although his audience is necessarily limited, he is one of the most vigorous publicists in the nation."

Industrial Solidarity, 5 August 1930

Hobo Poet

Anonymous

He's just one of the wobbly gang
    For better or for worse;
And yet the thought is dynamite
    That pulses in his verse.
Why wait until he's in his grave
    And then acknowledge him?
Come, fellow workers, give a hand—
    Hats off to T-Bone Slim!

With nothing in his pockets
    Save a scrap of scribbling song
Or a bit of tempered irony
    To prick the core of Wrong.
Out on the curving roads that cut
    The far horizon's rim,
In shack or jungles, camp or field,—
    Persistent T-Bone Slim!

When boxcars are forgotten
    As things men live without,
And even Grand-dads can't recall
    The "pesky Go-About";
In that fair world he fought for
    Which seemed so far and dim,
Men yet may pause amidst their joy
    To think of T-Bone Slim.

Industrial Worker, 14 June 1932

Work People's College Youngsters Study and Frolic

O.K.L.

Duluth, Minn.:

Does the studious atmosphere at Work People's College give the students headaches? We'll say not. The class in labor drama takes the sad story of Mr. Peel in the famous 33rd chapter of *Capital* Volume I and dramatizes it. You know the story:

"Capital is not a thing, but a social relation between persons, established by the instrumentality of things. Mr. Peel, he moans, took with him from England to Swan River, West Australia, means of subsistence and of production to the amount of £50,000. Mr. Peel had the foresight to bring with him, besides, 300 persons of the working class, men, women, and children. Once arrived at his destination, 'Mr. Peel was left without a servant to make his bed or fetch him water from the river.' Unhappy Mr. Peel who provided for everything except the export of English modes of production to Swan River!"[1]

The drama class is also busy with T-Bone Slim's new masterpiece "The Uplifters," a comedy on the charity racket.[2] They are putting their heads together to scheme appropriate action for the lines that portray the T-Bone Marxian analysis of capitalism.

Another student persists in trying to sing the opening lines of the 32nd chapter about the historical tendency of accumulation to the tune of "The Irish Washerwoman";[3] another tries to reduce it all to rhyme as well as reason[4]—but

---

1 Karl Marx, *Capital: A Critique of Political Economy* (originally published in German, 1867; New York: Modern Library, 1906), 839–40.

2 An editor's note accompanying a December 1932 Slim column had stated: "T-bone Slim has gone out of circulation—he is retired to a convent to write a play for the working class—one of those pathetic plays, drama, where you laugh and promptly wish you hadn't—its name is 'Uplifters' and among these following are the leftovers therefrom. The play should be on the boards at an early date—start saving ticket money." See Slim, "T-Bone Slim," *Industrial Worker*, 13 December 1932. Despite the statement that "among these following are the leftovers therefrom," the article that followed was neither a play nor about charity. Though there is evidence that "The Uplifters" was rehearsed, it does not seem to have been performed when WPC's drama students went on a brief tour. It seems that the play itself has not survived, though a future discovery might change that assessment.

3 A traditional jig dating from the late eighteenth century.

4 That is, to put this chapter from *Das Kapital* into verse.

the less said about these aspects of the case, the better. Anyway we actually do study, even though at times we do find outlets for extra energy. Should we let enthusiasm drag, all we need to do is look out the window at the empty silent steel mill to start us anew.

Industrial Worker, 14 February 1933

A Torch for T-Bone Slim

Floyd Hoke-Miller

Words with a touching of fire
Vitriolic in the humorous vein
Crushing the plain or subtle liar
Plying his ever fertile brain:

Defending the true and truthful
Flagrant with vigor and vim;
Defending the old and youthful,
That's our faithful T-Bone Slim.

Industrial Worker, 30 August 1941[1]

[1] The author of this poem is not the Floyd Miller who would later write *The Savage Streets,* but rather an IWW and CIO activist who at this time was working at the Chevrolet factory in Flint, Michigan. He wrote many poems and articles for the CIO's *Auto Worker* and Local 659's *Search-Light,* as well as for the *Industrial Worker.*

Yours for the IWW

From Slim

"Old Nick"

I am doing pretty well on my rocket.[1] In the regions where I travel men look after their T-Bone steaks instead of building battleships for the military, swimming pools for the rich, and tightening their own belts. Neither do they travel to far off jungles to protect Bauxite mines for their exploiters. . . .

All the working class has to do is to take possession of the machinery of production and henceforth produce for workers.

Fake letter in *Industrial Worker,* 29 November 1941[2]

[1] That is, spaceship.

[2] During the publication gap at the end of Slim's life, "Old Nick" wrote "letters" to Slim that appeared in the *Industrial Worker,* and he also wrote replies, such as this one, purporting to be from Slim. Old Nick did not intend for readers to believe the replies were really written by Slim, as is clear from the conceit in this letter that Slim has not been not writing for the paper because he has been traveling in space! Given friendly references to "Fellow Worker Nick" in Slim's actual columns, it is likely that Nick wrote these pieces with Slim's permission, perhaps during a time when Slim was unable to write for health or other reasons. Future research may uncover the reason for Slim's drop-off in writing during 1941 and early 1942.

Slim's Obituary

T-Bone Slim, IWW Humorist, Passes Away

T-Bone Slim is no more: That incomparable working class humorist, poet and traveler, took his last leave of absence both from industry and his literary work on May 15, 1942, and made it permanent. On that day, official records show, Valentine Huhta, Captain of the Hudson river barge Casey was drowned while on duty for the New York Trap Rock Corp.

Though few people knew it, Matt Valentine Huhta was the one and only T-Bone Slim, author of the "Lumberjack's Prayer," of "Starving Amidst Too Much," and of uncounted columns of critical but always humorous comment which he contributed over a period of many years to the IWW press.

While there have been few working class writers in our time better known than T-Bone Slim, little was known about the man himself, even to those with whom he worked or who crossed his trail and stopped for a chat with him in his frequent tours of observation about the country. He is said to have two children somewhere in Ohio. Beyond this, even rumor says little or nothing about his personal relations.

At the time of his death, Slim was a member of the IWW and of Barge Captain's Local No. 933-4 of the AFL. Relatives or others who desire further information about his passing may write to State Fund, New York City, N. Y.

Having lived almost a full lifetime in anonymity, Fellow Worker Huhta died that way, and was buried that way. We have an idea that's the way he wanted it to be.

Industrial Worker, 24 October 1942

Homage to T-Bone Slim

Franklin Rosemont

Think of the snow that could once have fallen on your grave
even before you died
Think of the highways laughing in and out of the empty eyes
asleep in New York
the bottles of words which you hurled through the silent glass
of solitude
the water too deep to touch
the calendar too far away to mean anything
the door that kept swinging open
the dog that kept howling
the roads that kept leading nowhere
the world had no beginning for you
but it ended all the time
If I were you I'd have laughed at them
set their horses free
made them walk
the white clown dead in the moonlit street
a horse trampling a glass accordion
midnight is something more than a razor slicing an owl in two
something more than a blind man eating an orange
You knew this you tried to tell us
The helpless arson of your eyes
sets fire to the past
every word you wrote makes mirrors useless
You lived on what you grew in your black garden of tomorrows
The sleepwalker dies in the middle of the street
The streetcar covers its lips with blood
and says hello
A passing girl
her eyes closed
throws away a glove
without a word she speaks of tigers
of darkness
of a folding fan and a strawberry made of stone
and she too dies
In the violet rain that falls on the beckoning hands of shadows
In lithographs of flame and canaries
In the medieval wind that settles in cracked mirrors

In the scarlet leaf of gold that nails laughter to a wooden fence
You redefined the parts of speech
in terms of cutlery and heat
To be free
You fled everything you could have been
preferring to be free
In jail the crocodiles slept in unopened envelopes
You wandered across the verbal sand
tying red ribbons to oblivion
Balancing rocks in the black velvet wind
every word every promise shipwrecked on the shores of a dream
too far away to reach without going mad
You knew this too it is the risk one takes
the closed gate the stupid smile the blue hair
There are no wings on the enameled laughter
of dead trees
But in the quiet blood of deserted streets
blind falcons close their speechless eyes
wave their immovable hands
surrender like paper pigeons die like iron fleas
The rebel wheat of stone burns like a violin
in the white and voiceless sea
It is the night rocking to sleep its terrors
with songs themselves too terrible to sing alone
You rewrote the script of darkness to throw at the dismal light of day
The red wreath of your laughter
the black flowers of your scorn

Chicago, Fall 1965
Morning of a Machine Gun (Chicago: Surrealist Editions, 1968)[1]

1 Our thanks to Penelope Rosemont for permission to reproduce this poem.

Image of Slim by Mike Konopacki, originally drawn for the publication of *Juice Is Stranger Than Friction* (1992) but redrawn especially for this volume. Reproduced, with our thanks, by permission of the artist.

Cartoon originally drawn on a postcard by Mike Konopacki, created for the publication of *Juice Is Stranger Than Friction* (1992) but redrawn for this volume. Reproduced, with our thanks, by permission of the artist.

A Man Called America

Ville-Juhani Sutinen

Sun rises from the east and sets in the west. I stand at the edge of the map, southeast corner of Manhattan, where the waters of Hudson River, East River and Atlantic Ocean mix and merge. The whole world is here, drifting together and swirling around in broken reflections. Then it disappears again.

The water has risen and gone down countless times after an unknown drowned man was hoisted from the water in 1942. His body was found, but it seems that the man himself has stayed lost.

I have come to the dock because his life ended here. In a way, he had already ended it long before because he didn't want to leave any traces. Today it is worse than death. New York City, sprawling around me as a collage of steel, stone and glass, doesn't remember him. But somewhere in its veins, in the city's memories, there is a piece of the mosaic I'm trying to put together. Same goes for the entire country: scattered here and there are more fragments that begin to form a picture.

T-Bone Slim, aka Matt Valentine Huhta, was a Finnish-American writer, musician and radical who lived many years as a hobo. He died in the harbor and was born in the harbor. In between, he toured the United States as if he hadn't traveled on land at all, but always drifted along with the currents, sometimes well aware of the direction, sometimes driven by the wind.

He was just one of the millions of people of the turbulent times, no more, no less. Still, or precisely because of that, he can tell us a lot. His footsteps have been swept away by the tidal wave of history, but everyone who drifts along with it leaves some marks. Following them is important so that the tracks are not completely forgotten and lost.

It's not too late, I tell myself. At the same time I regret not taking on the project earlier, when there were still memories left. On the other hand, I myself have not lived long enough to have reached many of Matt Huhta's contemporaries, and I know that there are still people in different parts of the United States who have heard stories about him and met people who knew him. And knowledge that is preserved in books and archives will not disappear, even if buried in dust and rolling years.

However, I sometimes wonder why I am looking for this man in the first place. For it may be that Matt Huhta has sunk into the mud of history for a good reason and of his own free will. Be that as it may, his significance, even if it was not extensive, was and still is valuable to working-class culture, to Finnish-Americans, as well as to the general idea of a different way of life. He does not deserve to be buried in the past without some kind of celebration, whatever he himself thought about it.

Living on the flip side of America, he was America itself, its alternative and sometimes forgotten story.

In addition, Huhta, or T-Bone Slim, was an interesting musician and writer. He sought to change the world through his writings, but his art was not reduced to agitation. It had a stylistic power that outlived the social order he sought to overthrow.

But back to the harbor, to the southeast side of Manhattan. I'm having this monologue on the dock because I'm trying to get a glimpse of the past. It is sometimes difficult to find in the cities of the United States where the new has buried the old. But when you manage to imagine it, it is easier to place the character in the middle of the scene and think how he looked and what he would have done in certain contexts.

That is the method of my book. Matt Huhta is so unreal that we have to imagine him. One has to trust probabilities, possibilities, coincidences. They guide this book as they guided the road that brought Huhta here more than seventy years ago.

Flowing like water from harbor to harbor; jumping over obstacles or crashing straight into them; sometimes drawing a deep track, sometimes barely perceptibly trickling forward—this is where Matt Huhta's story begins and ends.

Extract from Ville-Juhani Sutinen, *Hobon elämän mysteerit: T-Bone Slimin jalanjäljillä* [The mysteries of a hobo's life: In the footsteps of T-Bone Slim] (Palladium Books, 2018), translated from Finnish by, and reproduced with permission from, Ville-Juhani Sutinen, with our sincere thanks.

Antti Männynväli, *The Only Real Thing Is You*, drawing, 2020. Reproduced with permission from the artist, with our thanks. The caption reads: "What little is done was done by us and if we look real hard we'll find George hiding out in the WPA pretending to be a communist or Alexander The Great. George is a myth even so as glamor and oomph—a mushy spot in our mentality. The only real thing is YOU—so what are you going to do about it? Wait for the Statue of Liberty to step down and hand you bacon and eggs? How Slowly Time Travels!"

Themes in the Writing of T-Bone Slim

For readers unfamiliar with Slim who are interested in particular issues, or who are using this book in a class (either the working class or a seminar room), we provide the following list of key articles in this collection in which he touches on six themes especially common in his work: capitalism, food and drink, his life as a transient worker/hobo, war, race and immigration, and prison and political persecution. Such a list cannot capture all of the themes in Slim's work, of course, or the many overlaps and nuances across his writings, but we hope that readers will find this guidance helpful.

Capitalism

The Power of These Two Hands, 1922
Das Kapital, 15 July 1922
Early History, 31 October 1923
T-Bone Slim Discusses: Discrimination, 1 October 1924
Roosevelt Was Right, 1 September 1931

Food and Drink

Headin' In, 17 December 1921
The Lumberjack's Prayer, 6 January 1922
Nosebags, 9 December 1922
Starving amidst Too Much, 1923
T-Bone Slim Discusses: The Off-Set, 16 February 1923
Indiana Moon, 12 April 1924
Oranges, 21 January 1925
T-Bone Slim Discusses: Chop Suey, 26 August 1925

Slim's Life as a Transient Worker/Hobo

Normalcy Has Arrived, 24 June 1922
T-Bone Slim Discusses: Sample Camps, 22 March 1923
Off Colors, 28 March 1923
Bugs and Fords, 10 September 1924
Shortcuts, 12 December 1925
Hall of Fame, 9 January 1926
"Sundownitis," 29 July 1930
It Do Seem So—, 16 August 1930
A Peach of a Story, 9 September 1930

T-Bone Slim Takes to the Air, or Saved in the Nick of Time, 13 September 1930
Elastic Transportation, 20 September 1930
On Popular Sanitation, 22 November 1930
A Mosquito's Lunch, 8 August 1931

War

War, 13 February 1923
Golf, 10 March 1923
Odds and Ends, 2 May 1923
T-Bone Slim Discusses a Peace Plan, 2 February 1924
True to Form, 13 September 1924
Supplying Arms and a Matter of Business Ethics, 9 April 1938
When Privates Fight War by Telephone, 23 September 1939
Warning of Cannon Fodder Shortage for War of 1960, 3 May 1941
Produce for Use and Peace Will Come at Last, 14 June 1941
I Didn't Know It Was Loaded, 27 September 1941
Yes, Labor Is Partly to Blame, 4 April 1942

Race and Immigration

Best People, 20 January 1923
Between These Two, 27 January 1923
An Eighty Year Boy, 13 October 1923
Three Bottles, 6 June 1931
Race Hatred, 9 August 1932
Should Indians Have Registered the Foreigners?, 27 January 1940

Prison and Political Persecution

Prepare for the Worst, 7 July 1923
Rock of Ages, 30 April 1924
Razzpectability!, 23 July 1927
Untitled, 24 December 1927
Boneyard, 15 February 1928
That "Triple Threat," 18 February 1928

Acknowledgments

Our particular thanks to Kayleigh Mansell, the transcriber of this volume, for doing such a wonderful and painstaking job.

We are extremely grateful to the Westmoreland family for allowing us to quote and reproduce material from their private archive.

Our thanks also to the Newberry Library in Chicago, the New York Municipal Archives, and the University of Michigan. The staff at these institutions deserve medals for the number of times they have helped us out over the years. We also wish to thank the State Library of New South Wales and the University of Melbourne for assistance with locating archival materials.

We thank the Kone Foundation for its support of T-Bone Slim research.

Iain McIntyre would like to acknowledge the support of the Gerda Henkel Stiftung with his research.

Finally, we thank all the individuals who contributed to this volume in one way or another, including John Beck, "Beni," Billy Bragg, Scott Brewster, Leonard Cassuto, Marcus Cederstrom, Noam Chomsky, the Claytons, Peter Cole, May Colling, Margaret Creagh, Marija Dalbello, Bruce dePyssler, Katie Dorr, Liza Enos, the Evans–McIntyre clan, Michele Fazio, Ben Fortun, Bucky Halker, Robert Jay, Mike Konopacki, Jim Leary, Lotta Leiwo, John Lennon, Marko Leppänen, Vanessa Lynn-Beazle, Antti Männynväli, Karri Miettinen (Paleface), Tom Morello, Lorcan Otway, Saku Pinta, Carl Rahkonen, Saijaleena Rantanen, Peter Riley, David Roediger, Penelope Rosemont, Kirsti Salmi-Niklander, Samira Saramo, Sean Scalmer, Ville-Juhani Sutinen, Hilary-Joy Virtanen, Cherie Westmoreland, John Westmoreland, and Steve Wright. We have definitely missed people with this list, so please accept our apologies if this is you.

Further Reading

Allsop, Kenneth. *Hard Travellin': The Hobo and His History.* New York: New American Library, 1967.

Anderson, Nels. *The Hobo: The Sociology of the Homeless Man.* Chicago: University of Chicago Press, 1923.

Bird, Stewart, Dan Georgakas, and Deborah Shaffer, eds. *Solidarity Forever: An Oral History of the IWW.* Chicago: Lake View Press, 1985.

Bodkin, Jane Little. *Frank Little and the IWW: The Blood That Stained an American Family.* Norman: University of Oklahoma Press, 2019.

Clayton, Owen. *Vagabonds, Tramps, and Hobos: The Literature and Culture of U.S. Transiency, 1890–1940.* Cambridge: Cambridge University Press, 2023.

Cresswell, Tim. *The Tramp in America.* London: Reaktion Books, 2001.

Dalbello, Marija. "Fluid Media of Proletarian Protest and Creativity in the Late 1910s and Early 1920s." Paper presented at the symposium "T-Bone Slim and the Transnational Poetics of the Migrant Left in North America," Kälviä, Finland, 18 August 2023.

Dalbello, Marija. "From My Archival 'Digs': Part I: Finding Slim!" *T-Bone Slim and the Transnational Poetics of the Migrant Left in North America* (blog), 12 December 2022. https://blogs.helsinki.fi/tboneslim.

Dalbello, Marija. "From My Archival 'Digs': Part II: Envelopes." *T-Bone Slim and the Transnational Poetics of the Migrant Left in North America* (blog), 30 January 2023. https://blogs.helsinki.fi/tboneslim.

Daniel, Bill. *Mostly True.* Portland, Ore.: Microcosm, 2008.

DePastino, Todd. *Citizen Hobo: How a Century of Homelessness Shaped America.* Chicago: University of Chicago Press, 2003.

Gold, Mike. *Mike Gold: A Literary Anthology.* Edited by Michael Folsom. New York: International, 1972.

Green, Archie, David Roediger, Franklin Rosemont, and Salvatore Salerno, eds. *The Big Red Songbook.* Oakland, Calif.: PM Press, 2016.

Higbie, Frank Tobias. *Indispensable Outcasts: Hobo Workers and Community in the American Midwest, 1880–1930.* Urbana: University of Illinois Press, 2003.

Kornbluh, Joyce, ed. *Rebel Voices: An IWW Anthology.* Oakland, Calif.: PM Press, 2011.

L'Amour, Louis. *Education of a Wandering Man.* New York: Bantam Books, 1989.

Lennon, John. *Boxcar Politics: The Hobo in U.S. Culture and Literature, 1869–1956.* Amherst: University of Massachusetts Press, 2014.

London, Jack. *The Road* [1907], in *Novels and Social Writings*. Edited by Donald Pizer. New York: Library of America, 1982.

Mayer, Heather. *Beyond the Rebel Girl: Women and the Industrial Workers of the World in the Pacific Northwest, 1905–1924*. Corvallis: Oregon State University Press, 2018.

McIntyre, Iain. *On the Fly! Hobo Literature and Songs, 1879–1941*. Oakland, Calif.: PM Press, 2018.

Milburn, George. *The Hobo's Hornbook: A Repertory for a Gutter Jongleur*. New York: Ives Washburn, 1930.

Monkkonen, Eric H. *Walking to Work: Tramps in America, 1790–1935*. Lincoln: University of Nebraska Press, 1984.

Rosemont, Franklin. *Joe Hill: The IWW and the Making of a Revolutionary Workingclass Counterculture*. Oakland, Calif.: PM Press, 2015.

Salerno, Salvatore. *Red November, Black November: Culture and Community in the Industrial Workers of the World*. Albany: State University of New York Press, 1989.

Salmi-Niklander, Kirsti, Lotta Leiwo, Owen Clayton, Iain McIntyre, John Westmoreland, Saku Pinta, Marija Dalbello, Samira Saramo, and Saijaleena Rantanen. *T-Bone Slim Corpus, Source*. 2024. Available for download in Kielipankki—The Language Bank of Finland, http://urn.fi/urn:nbn:fi:lb-2022111621.

Shields, Art. *My Shaping Up Years: The Early Life of Labor's Great Reporter*. New York: International, 1983.

Thompson, Fred. *Fellow Worker: The Life of Fred Thompson*. Chicago: Charles H. Kerr, 1993.

Index

T-Bone Slim (1882–1942) was a hobo and transient worker, a humorist, musician, and prolific writer. He went by many names, including Matt Huhta, Matt Arlund, Matt Arnold, Matt (sometimes Matthew) Houghton, and Joseph Hilger.

Owen Clayton is senior lecturer in English literature at the University of Lincoln (UK). Among his previous books are *Vagabonds, Tramps, and Hobos: The Literature and Culture of U.S. Transiency, 1890–1940*; *Roving Bill Aspinwall: Dispatches from a Hobo in Post–Civil War America*; and *Representing Homelessness.*

Iain McIntyre is an honorary fellow with the School of Historical and Philosophical Studies, University of Melbourne. He is the author and coeditor of eleven books, most recently *Knocking the Top Off: A People's History of Alcohol in Australia* and *Mr Block: The Subversive Comics and Writings of Ernest Riebe.*

David R. Roediger is Foundation Professor of American Studies at the University of Kansas. He is author of *The Sinking Middle Class: A Political History of Debt, Misery, and the Drift to the Right* and *The Wages of Whiteness: Race and the Making of the American Working Class.*